CONTENTS

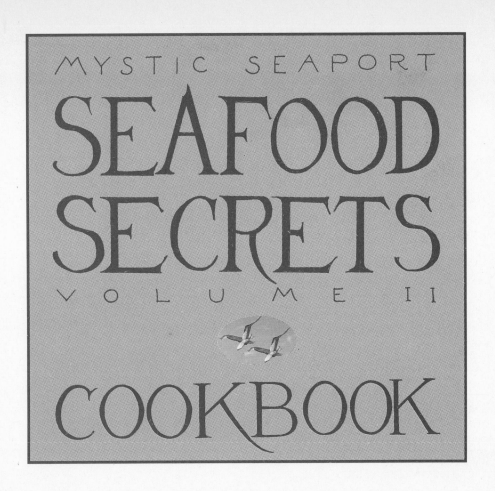

MYSTIC SEAPORT
SEAFOOD SECRETS
VOLUME II
COOKBOOK

EDITED BY AINSLIE TURNER

ILLUSTRATED BY SALLY CALDWELL FISHER

PUBLISHED BY MYSTIC SEAPORT MUSEUM STORES
MYSTIC, CT

Published by: Mystic Seaport Museum Stores
                  75 Greenmanville Avenue
                  Mystic, CT 06355

© 1998 Mystic Seaport Museum Stores

ISBN 0-939510-68-5

Printed in Hong Kong

First Printing 1998
Second Printing 2001

Additional copies of this book may be obtained by using the
order form in the back of the book, by writing to the address
listed above, or by calling 1-800/331-BOOK. To order
Seafood Secrets Volume II for re-sale purposes,
call 1-800/248-1066.

**Your purchases support the maritime preservation work of
Mystic Seaport, The Museum of America and The Sea.**

INTRODUCTION

With an enthusiasm for seafood cookery at an all-time high, we must remember that man has captured fish and food ever since he has been on Earth. From earlier times, the mummified bodies of Nile perch have been found in the tombs of the ancient Pharaohs—a symbolic sacrifice between Heaven and Earth. Also, the organs and ashes of various fish were believed to hold curing powers, from herring roe salve to the discoveries of the many virtues of that nasty old tonic, cod liver oil. As early as 1741 (as noted in "Recipts of Pastry"), cooks were passing along their best seafood recipes. An example:

CRABE LOAFE: hollow out roll, fry in deep drippings, fill with chopped crab, oyster, and eels, cover with anchovy-mushroom sauce and top with lobster claw. Toast over coals and cut into sizzling slices.

Mind you, all this preparation done by the light of a candle—no Cuisinart here!

The real reason, however, to become an ichthyophile (from the Greek word for fish) in the 90s and beyond, is for the enjoyment of such a variety of tastes as well as the health benefits derived from "the meats of the sea." Why should you include more fish in your diet? For all the right reasons. A rich source of essential nutrients referred to as "brain food", seafood studies have also linked diets high in fish products to a significant reduction in heart disease. From the Eskimos in Greenland to the fishermen in Japan, low cholesterol levels prove that increasing fish consumption on your food pyramid really works. Calorie for calorie, fish is a complete protein package on your plate.

Most people buy their seafood at supermarkets these days, and the condition of the fish counter is one of the most popular reasons they choose a store (aside from produce and bakery). Consumers are enjoying fish in their favorite restaurants all over the country in droves, but some are still hesitant to try new recipes at home. So, consider these tips when buying fish...use your senses.

First: The fish must look fresh, the skin should be bright and shiny and, if purchased whole, the eye should sparkle like a marble. Don't be shy, ask your fish department manager to turn the fish over, look at the filet to make sure the skin is moist and clean.

Second: Ask to smell the fish (most reputable markets won't object), and let your nose be your guide.

If you are pleased on both counts, take it home and be sure to refrigerate immediately until ready to cook.

Of course, the ideal fresh fish that come with a 100 percent guarantee are those you have caught yourself, just hours out of the water, cleaned on the dock and dressed for the oven. Watching my mother's neighbor surf fish from her porch in Florida, knowing that we will reap the catch later in the day, brings the cast iron skillet out from the far corner of the cupboard in anticipation.

So, whether a novice or an experienced cook, you too should grab a pan, snag the fish of the day, savor the salt breeze, and propose a toast as wise as any of old.

"Fish should swim thrice; first it should swim in the Sea, then it should swim in sweet butter, and at last, sirrah, it should swim in a fine old claret!!"

– Jonathan Swift (1700)

Ainslie Turner

RECIPE CONTRIBUTORS

A special thank you to all the members of Mystic Seaport
who made this cookbook possible.

Mrs. William Adams
Randy Adams
Trevor Ainsworth
Betty Amoroso
Barbara Anderson
Margaret Anderson
Rick Anderson
Mary Arthur
Edward Babcock
Beverly Balch
Sue Banford
Priscila Bayreuther
Barbara Bergman
John Birch
Martha Blake
Naomi Bloundin
Connie Boehm
Margaret Brady
Charles Breed
Joan Brew
Joanne Brooks
Dorothy Brubaker
Adair Burlington
Mona Cadoret
Mike Callahan
Ian Campbell
Sarah Campbell
Connie Chamberlain
Marty Chambers
Kay Chapin
Mrs. Donald A. Chiofolo
Lanie Christopher
Bill Clark
Tom Class
Betty Cleghorn

Joanne Collier-Shaw
Senator Cathy Cook
Donna Cooper
Peter Crandall
Sue Culter
Nealy Dickinson
Valentini Dole
Lori Doolittle
Mrs. James K. Duffes
Donna Duffy
David Eichblatt
Dudley Fay
Amy Fay
Nina Ford
Ann Freeman
Dorothy Garofola
Patricia Gates
Mimi George
Joseph Gernhard, Jr.
Bea Goldblatt
Ruth Goring
Howard Grant
Phylis Griffith
Ian Griffiths
Nathan D. Hale
Sally Halsey
Charles Hamm
Dot Hazlin
Scott Heilbron
Jane Hendricks
Janet Hodnett
Heather Honiss
Judi Honiss
Pam Hotch
Martha Hurtig

Connie Jacobsen
Morra Kelleher
Barbara Kerin
Nancy Knowles
Joe Knowles
Bruce Kueffner
Thomas L'Heureaux
Karen Lamb
Jim Lewis
Pat Mackay
Barbara Mahaney
Ginger Martus
Lil Maxwell
Steve Mazur
Thomas McClaine
Peter McIntyre
Betty Meehan
Lee Merritt
Scot Michaelson
Georgia Middlebrook
Jeff Milne
Myrna Mitchell
Tara Moore
Mrs. Mose
Ruth Nast
Florence O'Brien
John Osborne
Peter Pappas
Steve Parker
Martha Paul
Bonnie Pederson
Gary Peterson
Sandy Phelps
Sara Pinto
Lucinda Powers

John Rachleigh
Tina Reimers
Mike Reimers
Barbara Repko
Nancy Richartz
Lynn Rinek
George Romero
Mary Ann Root
Amanda Rutledge
David Sacerdote
Mrs. Schimmel
Peter Shakely
Charles Shane
Jim Sherman
Steven Shilowitz
Sue Shipman
Stephanie Silva

Carolyn Simons
Marilyn Sly
Dorothy Snyder
Irene Sok
Jack Spratt
Georgia Spratt
Phil Stamford
Jerome Staples
Beverly Starr
Carter Stilson, M.D.
Melinda Stuk
Bea Swedien
John Tanner
Lisa Taylor
Loretta Taylor
Maurie Tempesta
Dr. H. Gregory Thorsell
Mrs. James W. Tower

Tammy Trebra
Diane Tripp
Alexandra Tupper
Roberta Turner
Alex Turner
Brie Turner
Claudia Van Ness
Rosemary Veery
Roger Verges
Susan Wainio
Beth Walker
Liz Watson
Patricia White
Kathy Wilcox
Mary Wohlleb
Gail Woodrow
Dale Zumsande

MARTINI BAIT

Smoked Salmon Tortilla Spirals   Makes 4 dozen

A South of the Border specialty

6 flour tortillas (10 inches each)
2 8-ounce packages cream cheese, softened
6 ounces thinly sliced smoked salmon, chopped
4 tablespoons capers, drained and chopped
$^1/_4$ cup chopped fresh dill

"Dried salmon must be differently managed ... when laid on the gridiron, they should be moderately peppered."
              – "The Art of Cookery" 1765

1. In a medium bowl, combine cream cheese, salmon, capers and dill.
2. Spread evenly over tortillas and roll up tightly, jelly-roll style. Wrap each roll in plastic wrap and refrigerate 4 hours or overnight.
3. To serve, unwrap and trim ends. Cut rolls on an angle into thin slices about $^1/_2$ inch thick and arrange on a platter.

Smoked Haddock Mousse   Serves 8-10

A Ram Island Yacht Club favorite

$1^1/_4$ cups water
1 bay leaf
1 onion, chopped
1 pound smoked haddock
1 envelope (1 tablespoon) unflavored gelatin
2 eggs, separated
grated rind and juice of 1 lemon
1 tablespoon dry sherry
3 anchovies, finely chopped
2 tablespoons chopped fresh parsley
$^3/_4$ cup heavy cream, lightly whipped
sliced cucumber
green olives
lettuce leaves

1. Put the water, bay leaf and onion in a medium saucepan and bring to a boil. Add the haddock and poach gently for 10 minutes or until fish is cooked. Remove fish from pan, flake, and strain cooking liquid. Whisk in gelatin and set aside to cool.
2. Beat the egg yolks with the lemon rind, lemon juice, sherry, anchovies and parsley. Beat in the cooled aspic, then stir in flaked fish. Place in the refrigerator for $^1/_2$ hour or until mixture begins to set.
3. Beat the egg whites until they form soft peaks. Gently fold in the whipped cream and fish aspic mixture, mixing lightly until blended.
4. Pour into a lightly oiled mold or cake pan and refrigerate until set.
5. Unmold onto lettuce leaves and surround with sliced cucumber and green olives.

Soused Herrings

Serves 8-10

A Scandinavian classic

6   herrings
salt and pepper
$^3/_4$ cup vinegar
$^1/_2$ cup water
1   tablespoon mixed pickling spice
4   bay leaves
2   small onions, sliced
1   lemon, sliced

1. Scale, clean and bone the herrings. Season well with salt and pepper.
2. Roll up the fillets, skin outwards, from the tail end. Place in an oven-proof dish. Cover with the vinegar and water and sprinkle with the pickling spices, bay leaves, onion and lemon.
3. Cover loosely and cook in a slow oven, 300° for 1$^1/_2$ hours.

Serve hot or cold with dark bread, butter and sour cream.

Mini Shrimp Empanadas

Makes 48

A taste of Tijuana – olé!

1   pound shrimp (the small peeled ones are best)
2   tablespoons oil (olive or vegetable)
$^1/_2$ cup green pepper, chopped
1   cup chopped onion
1   garlic clove, minced
1   16-ounce can tomatoes, well drained and chopped
1   tablespoon parsley
1   tablespoon cilantro
1   teaspoon cumin
$^1/_2$ teaspoon dried oregano
$^1/_2$ teaspoon red pepper flakes
few dashes of Tabasco sauce
2   15-ounce packages refrigerated pie crusts (4 crusts)

1. Add oil to a large non-stick skillet and bring to medium heat. Sauté shrimp, onion, green pepper and garlic for 5 to 6 minutes until shrimp and vegetables are tender.
2. Stir in tomatoes, parsley, cilantro, cumin, oregano, pepper flakes and Tabasco sauce. Reduce heat and simmer for 10 to 15 minutes until liquid is evaporated. Remove from heat and cool.
3. Using a 3-inch round biscuit cutter, cut 12 rounds from each pie crust, combining remaining crust to make 48 rounds. Spoon a heaping teaspoon of shrimp filling on each round. Fold each pastry in half and pinch edges to seal.
4. Place empanadas on 2 10x15 inch cookie sheets which have been lightly sprayed with vegetable oil. Bake at 400° for 15 to 20 minutes until golden brown.

"Potiquet" of Stuffed Mussels   Serves 4

Serve a little pot to each guest

2   quarts mussels
$^1/_4$ cup dry white wine
$^1/_4$ cup water

Filling:
$^1/_4$ cup finely chopped parsley
1   small head of garlic, peeled and chopped
10 medium mushrooms, finely chopped
2   slices (2-ounces) boiled ham, chopped
$^1/_2$ pound butter, softened
4   slices white or French bread, crusts removed
salt and freshly ground pepper

**Some mussels have such long and brassy beards
that, in ancient times, the filaments were woven
into a cloth of "gold."**

1. Discard any mussels which are slightly open and wash remaining under cold running water. Scrub until each shell is smooth and remove "beard". Drain.
2. Place mussels in a large pot with water and white wine. Cook over high heat, shaking the pan frequently for 5 to 6 minutes or until shells open. Remove and discard the empty half shell from each mussel. Reserve 2 tablespoons of poaching liquid.
3. Mix the parsley, garlic, mushrooms, and ham with the butter and work it with a fork to blend thoroughly.
4. Divide the mussels between 4 "Potiquets" or other individual ramekins or casseroles and top with the stuffing mixture. Cover with bread slices and moisten with mussel liquid. Bake in a preheated 325° oven for 10 minutes.

Swedish Christmas Herring Salad   Serves 4

Also beautiful served in a crystal bowl.

4   pickled herrings
1   apple, cored and sliced
2   teaspoons fresh lemon juice
1   small onion, finely sliced
2   medium cooked beets, peeled and diced
     medium potatoes, cooked and diced
$^3/_4$ cup sour cream
2   tablespoons chopped celery leaves
1   tablespoon chopped fennel leaves, with
     additional sprigs for garnish
salt and pepper
lettuce cups

1. Cut each herring in half lengthwise, then cut each half into 4 strips. Put in a bowl with the apple and lemon juice and toss lightly.
2. Add the remaining ingredients and mix together. Mound salad onto lettuce cups and garnish with additional fennel sprigs.

Scandinavian Pickled Salmon   Serves 6

An exceptional change from smoked salmon.

1¹/₂ pounds salmon fillet, from the tail end
2   tablespoons sea salt or kosher salt
1   tablespoon sugar
12 black peppercorns, crushed
2   tablespoons chopped fresh dill with
    additional sprigs for garnish

Sauce:
3   tablespoons Dijon mustard
1   tablespoon sugar
1   egg yolk
6   tablespoons olive oil
2   tablespoons wine vinegar
1   tablespoon chopped fresh dill
salt and pepper

1. Cut the salmon fillet into 2 pieces on a bias, creating similar-sized triangular pieces.
2. Mix the salt, sugar, peppercorns and dill together and spread a quarter of this mixture over the bottom of a flat dish. Lay the first piece of salmon, skin side down, on top of this and spread half the remaining mixture over the cut side.
3. Place the other piece of salmon, skin side up, over the first piece and spread with the remaining mixture, making sure you rub it well into the skin. Cover with foil and a heavy weight, such as a brick . Put in refrigerator for at least 24 hours, or up to 5 days, turning occasionally.
4. Beat the mustard with the sugar and egg yolk until it is smooth and creamy. Gradually add the oil, a few drops at a time, then the vinegar and mix well. Add the dill and season with salt and pepper.
5. To serve the salmon, slice it thinly, parallel with the skin, and arrange on a serving dish. Garnish with sprigs of dill and serve the sauce on the side.

After the Race Best Stuffed Eggs   Makes 12

These disappear fast – so make extra!

6   eggs
3   tablespoons chopped parsley
2   tablespoons olive oil
2   tablespoons capers, chopped
3   tablespoons tuna, in oil, drained
paprika
chopped black olives

1. Hard boil eggs; peel and cut in half. Mix yolks with parsley, oil, capers and tuna. Stuff back into whites, sprinkle with parsley and olives. Best served at room temperature.

"Hunger finds no fault with the cook."
– William Shakespeare

Grilled Stuffed Clams Melanie   Serves 4

From a favorite Brittany port – St. Malo.

$^1/_2$ pound sweet butter
2 tablespoons minced shallots
2 tablespoons minced scallions
2 tablespoons minced parsley
$^1/_2$ teaspoon tarragon
pinch of dried mustard
freshly ground black pepper and a pinch of salt
4 dozen littleneck or cherrystone clams
1 cup bread crumbs

**"First catch your clams; along the webbing edges
on saline coves you'll find the precious wedges."
– Croffut**

1. In a mixing bowl, soften the butter by mashing it with a fork. Work in the shallots, scallions, parsley, tarragon, dried mustard, pepper and a little salt until well blended.
2. Wash the clams under cold running water. Place in a large shallow pan, add a few tablespoons of water, cover, and quickly bring to a boil. Steam to open the shells. Remove and discard empty top shells.
3. Spread about $^3/_4$ teaspoon of the prepared butter over each clam and sprinkle lightly with bread crumbs.
4. Bake in a preheated 400° oven for 5 minutes, or until the bread crumbs are toasted and butter is sizzling.

Serve at once.

Grilled Oysters for Two   Serves 2

For that special occasion dinner.

14 oysters
8 tablespoons butter, softened
2 cloves garlic, crushed
1 tablespoon fresh parsley, chopped
$^1/_2$ cup fresh white bread crumbs
$^1/_2$ cup grated Swiss cheese
paprika
1 lemon

1. Open the oysters but leave them attached to the deep halves of their shells. Arrange the shells in a flat pan.
2. Mix the softened butter with the garlic and parsley. Cover the oysters with the prepared butter. Sprinkle with bread crumbs and pinches of Swiss cheese. Dust with paprika and a few squeezes of fresh lemon juice. Bake at 325° for 8 to 10 minutes until golden brown.

Year of the Tiger Scallop Toasts

Makes 48

1 pound fresh scallops
³/₄ cup chopped scallions, including green tops
1 teaspoon peeled fresh ginger, minced
1 egg
1 tablespoon cornstarch
1 teaspoon salt
¹/₂ teaspoon sesame oil
freshly ground black pepper
12 thin slices stale white bread
peanut oil for frying

1. Finely mince scallops with remaining ingredients (except bread and oil) or process in a food processor until well mixed but not pureed. Mixture should be slightly lumpy. Spread mixture on 1 side of each bread slice.
2. Heat oil in a large frying pan. Fry slices in batches, mixture side down until golden brown. Turn and fry for a short time on other side. Drain well on paper towels. Cut each slice into 4 triangles and serve with mustard sauce.

Zippy Mustard Sauce
¹/₂ cup Dijon mustard
¹/₄ cup sesame oil
3 tablespoons rice wine vinegar
¹/₄ teaspoon sugar
pinch of salt

Mustard Sauce preparation:
Whisk all ingredients together in a small bowl and serve with scallop toasts. Best to make a double batch for later to serve with cold chicken or fish.

Any Man's Favorite
(a.k.a. Cape Cod Salmon Mousse)

Serves 12-14

2 cups cooked and flaked salmon
2 scallions, chopped
¹/₄ cup fresh dill, chopped
¹/₄ cup fresh lemon juice
2¹/₂ cups chicken stock
      (saving ¹/₂ cup for gelatin)
2 cups sour cream
2 packets unflavored gelatin
fresh greens
Melba toast rounds

1. In a medium bowl, mix salmon, scallions, dill, lemon juice and stock. In a food processor fitted with a steel blade or a blender, puree until smooth. Pour into a large bowl, fold in sour cream.
2. In a saucepan, heat remaining ¹/₂ cup chicken stock, add gelatin and stir until completely dissolved. Add to salmon mixture and blend thoroughly. Pour into a lightly oiled decorative mold and chill until set. Unmold on a bed of fresh greens and serve with Melba toast rounds.

Commodore's Crab Cakes

Serves 8

1   pound lump crab meat
$^1/_2$ cup fresh bread crumbs
2   tablespoons chopped parsley
2   tablespoons heavy cream
1   tablespoon lemon juice
1   tablespoon Tabasco sauce
1   tablespoon Dijon mustard
salt and black pepper to taste
1   egg, plus 1 egg yolk
4   tablespoons butter
1   cup dry bread crumbs
8   anchovies
shredded lettuce

1. Place all ingredients, except butter, bread crumbs, anchovies, and lettuce in a large bowl and mix well but gently, trying not to break up the crab. Refrigerate for 1 hour.
2. Shape crab mixture into 8 patties, squeezing out excess liquid. Coat both sides of each patty with bread crumbs. Heat half the butter (2 tablespoons) in a skillet. Add 4 crab cakes and cook until golden brown (4 to 6 minutes), turning once. Keep in a warm oven (250°). Add remaining 2 tablespoon butter to pan and cook other 4 patties. Serve the crab cakes on small fish plates with shredded lettuce, a spoonful of tartar sauce (recipe follows) and an anchovy fillet, cut in half and crisscrossed over the top.

Garlicky Tartar Sauce
$^3/_4$ cup mayonnaise
2   tablespoons capers, chopped
2   tablespoons gherkins, chopped
2   cloves garlic, minced
2   tablespoons fresh chopped parsley
juice of $^1/_2$ lemon
dash of Tabasco sauce

Tartar Sauce preparation:
Put all of the ingredients in a bowl and stir together well. Best if made in advance to serve with the crab cakes.

Tuscan Tuna Toasts

Serves 6

1   6-ounce can white tuna, packed in oil
$^1/_2$ cup white beans, cooked and coarsely chopped (cannelini are best)
$^1/_4$ cup butter
2   tablespoons chopped Italian flat parsley
2   tablespoons fresh lemon juice
black pepper to taste
toasted French bread

1. Drain tuna and flake. Mix in the remaining ingredients, and season to taste with pepper. Serve on toasted bread. This is even better if made the day before serving.

Beer Puffs with Curried Crab   Makes 50 puffs

Make an extra batch of puffs and freeze to stuff later.

1   cup of beer
$^1/_4$ pound butter
1   cup flour
$^1/_2$ teaspoon salt
4   eggs

Crab Meat Filling:
$^1/_2$ pound crab meat
2   tablespoons chopped scallions
4   ounces shredded Swiss cheese
$^1/_2$ cup mayonnaise
1   teaspoon lemon juice
$^1/_2$ teaspoon curry powder

Mix crab meat filling ahead by combining all ingredients.

1. Preheat oven to 450°. For the puffs, bring beer and butter to a boil in a medium, heavy saucepan. When the butter melts, add flour and salt at once. Stirring, cook over low heat until mixture leaves side of pan. Remove from heat, beat in 1 egg at a time until dough is shiny. Drop by teaspoonfuls 1 inch apart on a buttered baking sheet.
2. Bake for 10 minutes at 450°, then reduce to 350°, and bake for an additional 10 minutes until brown and crisp. Cool, split and fill with crab meat.

"Taste of it first."

– William Shakespeare

S.S.S.S. - Simple - Sage - Shrimp - Sauté   Serves 6

1   pound tiny shrimp
$^1/_4$ cup olive oil
a handful of fresh sage leaves ($^1/_2$ cup)
salt and cayenne pepper to taste
toasted pita bread or French bread slices

1. Pat the shrimp dry. In a heavy skillet, warm the olive oil over low heat. Toss in the sage leaves and sauté for 1 minute. Add the shrimp and cook for 1 more minute. Season with salt and cayenne pepper.
2. To serve, transfer shrimp onto a warm platter, tuck toasted bread slices around outside to absorb the juices, and garnish with additional fresh sage leaves.

Roasted Garlic, Anchovy and Plum Tomato Bruschetta

Serves 10

A Martha's Herbery staple.

8   plum tomatoes
1   head garlic
3   tablespoons olive oil
salt and pepper to taste
2   tablespoons chopped flat Italian parsley
pinch of oregano
1   tin flat anchovies, drained
French bread sliced and toasted
Parmesan cheese

"He doth learn to make strange sauces, to eat anchovies ...."

– Ben Johnson

1. Cut tomatoes in half and place in a small roasting pan. Cut the top off the head of garlic and remove any of the loose paper skin from the outside. Nestle beside tomatoes, drizzle with 2 tablespoons olive oil and season with salt and pepper. Bake at 375° for 1 hour. Let cool.

2. Squeeze the garlic from the bottom and the cloves will come out easily. Mash with a few drops of olive oil and spread on the toasted bread. Chop the tomatoes, add the herbs and the olive oil. Spread on the bread and top with anchovy fillet and a small slice of Parmesan cheese. Broil for 1 minute to melt cheese. Serve hot or at room temperature.

Budapest Smoked Salmon Bites   Makes 24

1   8-ounce package cream cheese, cubed
$^1/_4$ cup butter, cubed
$^1/_3$ cup minced onion
1   tablespoon capers, drained
1   tablespoon paprika
1   teaspoon Dijon mustard
1   teaspoon anchovy paste or 2 anchovies
2   teaspoons caraway seeds, optional
6   slices pumpernickel bread, crusts trimmed
6   ounces smoke salmon, thinly sliced
fresh dill sprigs
paprika

1. In a food processor fitted with a steel blade, mix cream cheese, butter, onion, capers, paprika, mustard, anchovy paste and caraway seeds until just combined. Transfer to a small bowl and refrigerate several hours.
2. To serve, spread the mixture over pumpernickel and top with a thin slice of smoked salmon. Cut into quarters and garnish with fresh dill and a dash of paprika.

Cheesy Shrimp Sizzlers   Makes 24 to 28

1   pound medium shrimp, peeled
$^1/_4$ cup grated cheddar cheese
2   tablespoons freshly grated Parmesan cheese
$^1/_4$ cup cream
1   tablespoon dry sherry
2   tablespoons minced scallions
12 to 14 slices homemade-type white bread, trimmed of crust
$^1/_4$ cup (4 tablespoons) melted butter

"Heaven defend me from the Welsh fairy lest he turn me into a piece of toasted cheese."
– William Shakespeare (Falstaff)

1. In a large saucepan of boiling salted water, cook shrimp until just cooked through, 1 to 2 minutes. Drain and rinse under cold water. Pat dry and chop fine.
2. In a bowl, mix shrimp together with cheeses, cream, sherry and scallions. With a rolling pin, flatten each bread slice. Spread 2 tablespoons shrimp mixture on each bread slice and roll up tightly. Put rolls, seam side down, on a baking sheet and brush all over with melted butter. Chill rolls, covered loosely at least 1 hour.
3. Cut shrimp rolls in half and arrange on baking sheet 2 inches apart. Bake in a 425° oven about 12 minutes until golden.

Tapenade Fish Cut-Outs

Makes 12-24 depending on size of fish cutter.

Pastry:
1$^{1}/_{2}$ cups flour
$^{1}/_{4}$ teaspoon salt
4 tablespoons butter, cubed
4 tablespoons olive oil
ice water

Tapenade:
$^{1}/_{2}$ cup Niçoise olives, pitted
2 tablespoons capers
1 teaspoon lemon juice
1 clove garlic
$^{1}/_{4}$ cup tuna, drained
olive oil
chopped pimento

1. Mix flour and salt together in a bowl. Add butter and olive oil and blend well with fingers until mixture resembles coarse meal. Add just enough water to bind dough together and form a smooth ball. Wrap and chill for 30 minutes.
2. Puree olives, capers, lemon juice, garlic and tuna with just enough oil to make mixture spreadable.
3. Roll out dough on a lightly floured surface to $^{1}/_{4}$ inch thick. Cut out 4-inch long fish shapes with a cookie cutter or use a cardboard pattern and cut around it with a knife. Prick fish cut outs with a fork and bake at 350° for 15 to 20 minutes until crisp and golden. Cool and spread tapenade on the pastry fish. Make an eye with a pimento. These are great as part of a first course with a salad or you can make them smaller and serve as an appetizer.

Brittany Stuffed Clams with Herb Butter   Serves 4

A true French clam recipe.

24 cherrystone clams
1 cup butter ($^{1}/_{2}$ pound), softened
$^{1}/_{2}$ cup chopped fresh parsley
$^{1}/_{4}$ cup minced shallots
2 teaspoons fresh lemon juice
2 teaspoons Pernod or other anise-flavored
    liqueur
salt and pepper to taste
1 cup fresh bread crumbs

1. Wash clams and open, discarding the top shells and releasing the clam from the bottom shell.
2. Mix butter, parsley, shallots, lemon juice and Pernod until well blended. Season with salt and pepper. Spread the butter mixture over the clams, top with bread crumbs and place in a shallow baking pan. Broil the clams under a preheated broiler for 5 to 6 minutes until the crumbs are golden.

Blue Ribbon Gingered Shrimp   Serves 12-14

1¹/₂ pounds shrimp, peeled and deveined
   (about 60)
¹/₄ cup soy sauce
2   tablespoons chopped fresh ginger root
¹/₄ cup vinegar
2   tablespoons sugar
2   tablespoons sherry or sweet sake
1   teaspoon salt
¹/₂ cup chopped scallions
few pinches chopped red pepper flakes

1. Cook shrimp in a pot of boiling water until water just returns to a boil, about 3 minutes. Drain well and arrange in one layer in a glass or non-metallic oblong baking dish.
2. Heat soy sauce in a small sauce pan, add ginger root. Reduce heat and simmer uncovered until liquid has reduced by half (5 minutes). Stir in the vinegar, sugar, sherry or sake, and salt, pour over shrimp. Cover and refrigerate for at least 2 hours. To serve, remove shrimp from marinade and sprinkle with scallions and red pepper flakes.

On a sailing trip to Coecle's Harbor at Shelter Harbor, Long Island, the North Cove Yacht Club held a Member's Rendezvous Party. We were all asked to participate in an appetizer contest. So to be creative, I used a ceramic row boat with holes in it for arranging flowers. I skewered the shrimp (several on a stick) and stuck them in the holes, looking like long oars. Then I filled the boat with parsley and topped it with the scallions, resembling a handful of seaweed - took home the first prize!

It's in the Bag   Serves 4

From a renowned Stonington hostess.

4   4 to 6-ounce flounder fillets (1 per person)
2   tablespoons olive oil
salt and pepper to taste
8   slices Genoa salami
fresh lemon for garnish

Choose one flounder fillet per person as an appetizer or first course. Brush each fillet on both sides in olive oil. Sprinkle with salt and pepper. Top with 2 slices of Genoa salami. Place fillet, white side up, in a small paper bag or parchment paper. Place bags on a baking sheet and cook for 15 to 18 minutes in a 350° oven. Serve on small plates and let your guests open the bags at the table. Garnish with fresh lemon slice.

Pandora's Box

Serves 6

The treasure within.

1   loaf unsliced white bread
30 shucked oysters
salt and pepper to taste
flour
2   eggs, beaten
fresh bread crumbs (from loaf)
2   tablespoons butter

White Wine Butter:
2   teaspoons garlic, minced
2   teaspoons shallots, minced
8   ounces butter
$^1/_2$ cup white wine
1   teaspoon fresh lemon juice
2   teaspoons Worcestershire sauce
2   tablespoons chopped parsley

**"Homer, less modern, if we search the books
will show us that his heroes all were cooks."
– Art of Cookery**

1. Trim crust from bread and slice loaf into 6 2-inch slices. Cut out the center of each slice half way through to make a box or "barquette". Brown in a 325° oven or toast in a toaster oven. Set aside and keep warm.
2. Drain oysters, season flour with salt and pepper. Lightly dredge oysters in flour, dip in egg and coat evenly with bread crumbs. Sauté oysters in butter, turning once, until golden brown. Place five in each barquette and pour white wine butter over all.

Butter preparation:
Lightly sauté garlic and shallots in butter. Add wine and remaining ingredients. Simmer sauce for 2 minutes and drizzle over the oyster boxes.

Island Club Caviar Spread

Serves 8

4   ounces cream cheese, softened
$1^1/_2$ tablespoons fresh lime juice
1   teaspoon Dijon mustard
few dashes Worcestershire sauce
4   tablespoons red or black caviar
parsley sprigs and lime slices for garnish
toast points or crackers

In a bowl, beat together the cream cheese, the lime juice, mustard and Worcestershire. Fold in 3 tablespoons of the caviar and transfer to a small glass bowl. Garnish the mixture with remaining 1 tablespoon of caviar, parsley and lime slices. Serve the caviar spread with the toast points or crackers.

Shrimp and Ginger Potstickers   Serves 10

Add this to your repertoire – it's easier than it appears.

1   pound small shrimp, finely chopped
$^1/_2$ cup bok choy (Chinese cabbage), finely
   chopped
2   teaspoons minced fresh ginger
2   scallions, chopped
1   tablespoon dry sherry
$^1/_2$ teaspoon white pepper
$^1/_2$ teaspoon salt
package 3-inch round won ton wrappers
peanut oil for frying

Dipping Sauce:
$^1/_2$ cup soy sauce
1   tablespoon honey
1   tablespoon rice or white vinegar
1   teaspoon chili paste or $^1/_8$ teaspoon hot
   pepper flakes
$^1/_2$ teaspoon sesame oil

1. Mix all filling ingredients well and refrigerate 3 hours. Place 1 teaspoon of stuffing in center of each won ton skin, fold over and crimp the edges to seal.
2. Drop dumplings in boiling water, stirring to prevent from sticking. Drain very well. The dumplings may be served at this point with the sauce or in a clear broth with additional chopped scallions and shredded bok choy. To serve as an appetizer, fry in small batches in a small amount of peanut oil and pass the chopsticks.

Rummy Rhumb Line Shrimp   Serves 4 to 6, depending on size of shells

Created while cruising the British Virgin Islands.

1   pound small shrimp, cooked
3   cloves garlic, minced
$^1/_4$ pound of butter
1   teaspoon tarragon
2   tablespoons chopped fresh parsley
$^1/_4$ cup dark rum
$^1/_2$ cup bread crumbs
$^1/_2$ cup grated Swiss or cheddar cheese
scallop shells or individual serving dishes

1. Cream the butter together with the garlic, tarragon and parsley. Add the rum and bread crumbs, mix well.
2. Spread a little of the mixture on the bottom of scallop shells, top with shrimp, and dot more of the mixture on top. Sprinkle with grated cheese and bake at 375° for 10 minutes until brown.

Smoked Salmon Cheesecake with Dill Toasts   Serves 20

This savory cheesecake, flecked with smoked salmon, lemon zest, and grated Parmesan cheese, makes a showstopper appetizer served on lemon leaves with a garnish of dilled toast triangles.

Nonstick vegetable cooking spray
$^1/_2$ cup dried bread crumbs
1$^1/_4$ cups grated imported Parmesan cheese, divided
3 tablespoons unsalted butter, melted
5 ounces smoked salmon
2 pounds cream cheese, at room temperature
4 large eggs
$^3/_4$ cup chopped fresh chives or parsley, divided
$^1/_2$ teaspoon salt
1 teaspoon lemon zest
freshly ground black pepper to taste
1 cup sour cream

Dill Toasts:
22 slices very thin white bread
6 tablespoons unsalted butter, melted
2 tablespoons olive oil
1 tablespoon plus 1 teaspoon dried dill
lemon sprigs, for garnish
2 cucumbers, peeled and sliced, for garnish

Dill Toast preparation:
Mix butter, olive oil, and dill in a small bowl. Brush on bread and place on a baking sheet. Brown on both sides in a 375° oven, turning once.

1. Preheat the oven to 350° and arrange rack in middle shelf of oven. Spray a 9-inch Springform pan with nonstick vegetable cooking spray.
2. Place the bread crumbs and $^1/_4$ cup of the Parmesan cheese in the springform pan and toss to mix. Add the melted butter and blend. Press the crumb mixture into the bottom of the pan. Set aside.
3. Chop the smoked salmon fine in a food processor fitted with the metal blade, or by hand. Set aside in a medium bowl.
4. In the bowl of an electric mixer, beat the cream cheese on medium speed until smooth, about 2 minutes. Beat in the remaining 1 cup Parmesan cheese and blend well. Add the eggs, one at a time, mixing well after each addition. Add $^1/_2$ cup of the chives or parsley, the lemon zest, salt, and pepper and mix well. Gently fold in the sour cream.
5. Remove 2 cups of the cheesecake batter and add to the reserved smoked salmon. Blend thoroughly. Pour the remaining batter into the prepared pan and level with a spatula. Spoon the reserved smoked salmon mixture over the batter and gently level it with the spatula.
6. Place the cheesecake on the middle rack of the oven and bake 45 minutes. Turn the oven off and set the door ajar. Leave the cheesecake in the oven for 30 minutes, then remove and let cool 15 minutes. The cheesecake can be served warm at this point or it can be cooled to room temperature, covered, and refrigerated for up to 2 days. Bring to room temperature 30 minutes before serving. Remove from pan and surround with cucumber slices, accompanied with a basket of Dill Toasts.

Mustard Glazed Tropical Scallops   Makes 20 skewers

Try these outside on a grill.

1 pound sea scallops, cut in half
10 slices bacon
1 mango, peeled, cut into 1 inch pieces
6 scallions, cut into 1^1/$_2$ inch pieces
^{3}/$_4$ cup heavy cream
1 tablespoon Dijon mustard
1 tablespoon chopped fresh parsley
20 6-inch bamboo skewers, soaked in water

1. Partially cook bacon in broiler or frying pan, do not crisp. Drain and cut in half.
2. Thread 1 piece each of scallion, mango, and scallop on skewer, intertwining with the bacon. Arrange in a single layer on rack of a broiler pan or a foil lined baking sheet (for easier cleaning).
3. Combine cream and mustard in a saucepan. Heat gently until slightly thickened, about 5 minutes. Add parsley, and brush mixture on skewers. Broil scallops 6 inches from heat 4 to 5 minutes, turn and brush with sauce. Cook for 2 more minutes until firm, depending on the size of the scallops.

Quarterdeck Smoked Bluefish Pâté   Makes 2 cups

From a Cove Street kitchen.

^{1}/$_2$ pound smoked bluefish
4 ounces cream cheese, softened
8 tablespoons (1 stick) unsalted butter, softened
1 tablespoon minced onion
1 teaspoon cognac or brandy
1 teaspoon Worcestershire sauce
2 tablespoons fresh lemon juice
1 tablespoon chopped fresh parsley

In a food processor, puree the bluefish, cream cheese, butter, onion, cognac or brandy and Worcestershire sauce, scraping down the side of the bowl several times. Add the lemon juice. Mix well and transfer to a small bowl. Sprinkle with chopped parsley and serve it with crackers. The pâté keeps chilled for up to 3 days.

"The devil is in you if you cannot dine."
– Alexander Pope

Seared Oysters with Cracked Pepper Vinaigrette   Serves 2

Little medallions of salmon can be done the same way and served on mixed greens as an appetizer.

1   dozen fresh oysters
1¹/₂ tablespoons cracked black peppercorns
¹/₄ cup plus 1 tablespoon olive oil
1   tablespoon red wine vinegar
¹/₂ teaspoon sugar
1   tablespoon fresh chopped parsley
1   tablespoon chopped shallots
salt to taste

"Take your oysters boiling hot, and fill rolls full. Set them near the fire on a chafing dish of coals, and let them be hot through. So, serve them up with a pudding."
– The Complete Housewife, 1750

1. In a small mixing bowl whisk together cracked pepper, ¹/₄ cup olive oil, vinegar, sugar, parsley and shallots. Season with a little salt.
2. Shuck oysters, remove from the shells, rinse and pat dry with paper towels. Brush with remaining tablespoon of olive oil.
3. Preheat a cast iron or other heavy skillet over medium-high heat. Cook oysters on each side for one minute. Remove oysters from pan and place each on a dried oyster shell. Spoon vinaigrette over each oyster and serve.

Miami Orange Lime Scallop Seviche   Serves 6

A tangy citrus combination.

1   pound sea scallops, cut in quarters
6   scallions, chopped
1   cup fresh orange juice
¹/₂ cup fresh lime juice
6   tablespoons onion, chopped fine
4   tablespoons parsley, chopped fine
2   tablespoons green pepper, chopped fine
¹/₂ cup olive oil
¹/₂ teaspoon oregano
¹/₂ teaspoon salt
ground black pepper
crushed red pepper to taste
dash of Tabasco sauce
lettuce cups

1. Marinate scallops and scallions in orange and lime juice at least 6 hours, or best overnight. Drain well and discard marinade.
2. Add remaining ingredients, mix well and serve in lettuce cups.

Fresh Salmon Carpaccio with Chablis

Serves 6

1 pound fresh salmon fillet, skinned and boned
$1/4$ cup coarse sea salt
$1/4$ cup shallots, chopped
2 tablespoons fresh chopped herbs (chives, parsley, and chervel for example).
juice of 2 lemons
$1/2$ cup chablis
freshly ground black pepper
$1/2$ teaspoon coriander seeds, crushed
olive oil

1. The day before serving, place the salmon in a long deep dish. Coat with the salt and chill for 3 hours. Wipe salt off the fish and return to a clean dish. Sprinkle with the shallots, herbs, lemon juice, chablis, pepper and coriander seeds. Refrigerate overnight.
2. To serve, cut the salmon into very thin slices and place on individual serving plates. Drizzle with a little olive oil, garnish with some greens and serve with lemon, toasted dark bread and butter.

Captain Jack's Conch Fritters

Makes $1^1/2$ dozen

A Point Judith standby.

$1/2$ pound conch, ground, or you may substitute clams
1 large onion
1 red pepper
$1/2$ teaspoon salt
$1/8$ teaspoon black pepper
$1/2$ teaspoon garlic powder
1 teaspoon baking powder
few dashes of Tabasco sauce
$1/2$ cup flour
1 egg, slightly beaten

1. Coarsely grind conch in a food processor or a meat grinder and place in a medium bowl. Repeat for onions and peppers.
2. In a separate bowl, combine salt, pepper, garlic powder, flour and baking powder, mix well. Add conch and pepper mixture to flour, stir in the beaten egg. You may have to add a little more flour to bind the mixture if the conch meat is particularly juicy. Season with Tabasco sauce.
3. Form mixture into balls, about 1 inch in diameter. Heat oil in a frying pan to 350°. Deep fry fritters, a few at a time, until deep golden in color.

Drop-In Tuna Mushroom Canapés   Makes 24

For unexpected guests – right off the shelf.

1   6$^1/_2$ ounce can tuna, drained and flaked
$^1/_2$ cup canned cream of mushroom soup
1   tablespoon chopped pimento
2   teaspoons chopped green pepper
dash of Tabasco sauce
$^1/_2$ cup grated cheese (cheddar, Swiss, or
   Monterey Jack)
6   slices pumpernickel or rye bread
paprika

Flake tuna in a small bowl, add mushroom soup, pimento, pepper and Tabasco sauce. Spread on bread, sprinkle with cheese and Tabasco sauce. Cut into quarters and place on a baking sheet. Broil 3 inches from heat for 5 minutes until cheese browns.

Crab Puffs with Chives   Makes 40 toasts

8   ounces cooked lump crab meat, fresh,
   canned or frozen
$^1/_2$ cup chopped scallions
$^3/_4$ cup mayonnaise
$^3/_4$ cup Parmesan cheese
1   tablespoon chopped fresh chives
dash cayenne pepper
paprika
10 slices white bread, crusts trimmed

1. Drain the crab meat well and pick out any cartilage. Combine with scallions, mayonnaise, cheese, chives and cayenne pepper.
2. Spread on bread slices, dust with paprika and cut into triangles. Bake in a 350° oven for 8 to 10 minutes until crisp and puffy.

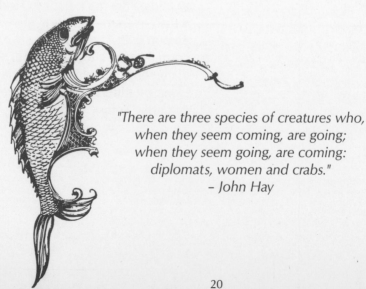

"There are three species of creatures who, when they seem coming, are going; when they seem going, are coming: diplomats, women and crabs."
– John Hay

Peppercorn Salmon Crue

Serves 8

1   1-pound fresh fillet of salmon
2   tablespoons green peppercorns, drained
    and rinsed
$^1/_2$ cup freshly squeezed lemon juice
2   tablespoons white wine
pinch of salt
pinch of sugar
4   tablespoons fresh chives, chopped
$^1/_4$ cup olive oil
toast (rye or wheat)

**"A solid man of Boston, a comfortable man with
    dividends,
And the first salmon and the first green peas."
    – Henry Wadsworth Longfellow**

1. Make sure there are no little bones in the salmon. Starting at the small end, skin the fillet if it has not already been done. Starting at the large end, slice it very thinly on the diagonal from head to tail. Arrange the slices on a chilled dinner platter so they cover the bottom of the plate, touching each other.

2. In a small bowl, crush the peppercorns and mix together with the lemon juice, wine, salt and sugar.

3. Pour a little olive oil over the salmon slices and with your finger, spread the oil to coat all of the fish. Cover the salmon with the green peppercorn sauce and sprinkle with freshly chopped chives. Wrap tightly and refrigerate for at least 4 hours. Serve very cold with toast points.

Seared Sea Scallops with Crème Fraîche and Caviar   Makes 24

A simple and sensational starter

1   teaspoon vegetable oil
12 large sea scallops, cut horizontally in half
salt and pepper
$^1/_4$ cup crème fraîche or sour cream
2   tablespoons chopped chives
$^1/_2$ ounce caviar, black or red

1. Heat oil in a large nonstick skillet over medium-high heat. Season scallops with salt and pepper. Cook scallops for 2 minutes until golden, turn and cook for 1 more minute. Drain on paper towels.

2. Mix crème fraîche and chives in a small bowl. Top each scallop with $^1/_2$ teaspoon of the mixture and then a small amount of caviar. Garnish with chive sprigs and serve at room temperature.

Bahama Scallop Seviche

Serves 10-12

This recipe is often prepared in the islands using the meat of a conch. The same marinade can be used for fresh fish, as is done in Mexico.

$1^1/_2$ pounds fresh sea scallops
juice of 2 lemons
juice of 2 limes
4 tablespoons olive oil
dash of Tabasco sauce
salt and freshly ground white pepper
2 ripe tomatoes, peeled, seeded, and finely diced
2 stalks celery, finely diced
2 small red onions, finely diced
1 bunch cilantro, finely diced
6 oranges

1. If the scallops are large, cut into quarters. In a shallow, non-aluminum dish, combine the scallops with the citrus juices, olive oil, Tabasco sauce, salt, and pepper. Cover and marinate overnight in the refrigerator.
2. To prepare the seviche, combine tomatoes, celery, onions, and cilantro with the scallops. Cut the "cap", the top $^1/_2$ inch, off each orange and hollow out the inside with a spoon, taking care not to pierce the skin. Correct the seasoning of the scallop mixture and spoon it into the hollow oranges. Serve very cold on chilled salad plates lined with doilies or fresh green leaves. Garnish with slice or wedges of lemon.

Tuckie Road Crab Canapés

Makes 3 dozen

When you need something quick and easy.

1 tube refrigerated Crescent rolls
1 6$^1/_2$-ounce can crab meat, drained and flaked
$^1/_4$ cup chili sauce
few dashes Worcestershire sauce
$^1/_3$ cup sour cream

Separate dough into 8 triangles, cut each into 4 small triangles. Combine crab, chili sauce, and Worcestershire in a small bowl. Spread 1 teaspoon of mixture on each triangle. Place on an ungreased cookie sheet, top with a dollop of sour cream and bake in a 375° oven for 10 to 12 minutes until puffed and golden.

Make Ahead Thanksgiving Shrimp   Serves 10

No last minute fuss.

2   pounds medium shrimp, frozen, peeled and deveined (21 to 25 to a pound)
$^1/_2$ cup freshly squeezed lemon juice
3   tablespoons white wine vinegar
2   tablespoons Dijon mustard
2   cloves garlic, minced
1   4-ounce jar pimentos, chopped
1   4-ounce can sliced ripe olives, drained
1   small red onion, thinly sliced
$^1/_2$ cup fresh dill, minced
salt and freshly ground black pepper

1. Prepare marinade. Whisk together lemon juice, vinegar, mustard and garlic. Add pimentos, olives, red onion and dill, season to taste with salt and a good amount of black pepper. Set aside while cooking shrimp.

2. Bring a large pot of water to a boil over high heat. Add frozen shrimp and cook, stirring a few times for 2 to 3 minutes until just cooked through and pink. Drain.

3. Add the hot shrimp to the marinade, stir to coat well. Let cool to room temperature, cover and refrigerate for at least 1 or up to 3 days. Stir mixture several times. Serve shrimp piled on a nice platter, with cocktail forks.

Ocean Drive Anchovy Puffs   Makes 40 to 45 puffs

Islandia II – back again.

$^1/_2$ cup butter
1   3-ounce package cream cheese
1   cup flour plus 1 tablespoon
1   2-ounce tube anchovy paste
$^1/_2$ cup chopped pecans

1. In a medium bowl, cream butter and cream cheese until well blended. Add 1 cup of flour and mix well. Chill for at least 1 hour. Lightly dust a cutting board or work surface with remaining tablespoon of flour. Roll dough very thin and cut into 2-inch circles with a biscuit cutter or small glass.

2. Spread each round with $^1/_2$ teaspoon anchovy paste and add a few pecans. Fold in half and crimp edges with your fingers or a fork to seal edges. Bake in a preheated 400° oven for 10 minutes until hot and puffy.

Southwestern Shrimp Quesadillas   Makes 18

6   8-inch flour tortillas
1   cup small shrimp, cooked and coarsely
    chopped
1   cup grated Monterey Jack cheese
    (4 ounces)
2   tablespoons chopped scallions
2   tablespoons chopped mild green chilies
1/3 cup mayonnaise
1/3 cup sour cream
few dashes of Tabasco sauce
salt
1   tablespoon butter, melted
red pepper flakes (optional)
salsa, your favorite
lime wedges

1. Mix shrimp, cheese, scallions, chilies, mayonnaise and sour cream in a medium bowl. Season to taste with a little salt and a few dashes of Tabasco sauce.
2. Lay tortillas out on counter and spread about 1/3 cup of the shrimp-cheese mixture on one half of each tortilla. Fold other half over to form a half circle. Brush both sides of tortilla with butter and sprinkle with a few hot pepper flakes as you wish. Place on a large baking sheet and bake in a 375° oven for 10 to 12 minutes until heated through. Cut each quesadilla into 3 wedges and serve with lime wedges and salsa.

Swiss Scallop Puffs   Makes 6 dozen

1/2 pound scallops, coarsely chopped
2   tablespoons butter
1   teaspoon grated lemon rind
2   cloves garlic, minced
1/2 teaspoon dill weed
1   cup shredded Swiss cheese
1   cup mayonnaise
1/8 teaspoon black pepper
6   dozen bread rounds or 2-inch triangles,
    crusts trimmed
paprika to taste

1. Melt butter in a saucepan. Add scallops, lemon rind and garlic. Sauté 2 to 3 minutes and stir in the dill. Cook for another minute, transfer to a mixing bowl and cool.
2. Add Swiss cheese, mayonnaise and black pepper. Mix well and spread by the teaspoonful on each bread round. Sprinkle with paprika and place under a preheated broiler for 2 to 3 minutes until puffed and golden brown.

Tycoon Scalloped Oysters *   Serves 2

A succulent Thanksgiving tradition.

12 oysters in shells
$^1/_2$ cup soft bread crumbs
1 tablespoon melted butter
1 tablespoon chopped fresh parsley
$^1/_8$ teaspoon salt
$^1/_8$ teaspoon white pepper

Tycoon Sauce:
2 cloves garlic, minced
1 tablespoon butter or margarine
2 tablespoons dry white wine
1 cup whipping cream
1 teaspoon Dijon mustard
$^1/_4$ teaspoon dried thyme, crushed
$^1/_8$ teaspoon pepper

"Sometimes with oysters, we combine."
– John Gay

1. Thoroughly wash oysters. Open shells with an oyster knife or blunt-tipped knife. Remove oysters, pat dry with paper towels and discard flat top shells. Set oysters on drained bottom shell and arrange on a baking sheet. Use crumpled foil or rock salt to steady the shells.
2. In a small bowl, mix bread crumbs, melted butter, parsley and salt and pepper; set aside.
3. In a saucepan, sauté garlic in butter for 1 minute. Add remaining ingredients and bring to a low boil, scraping sides and bottom of pan. Reduce heat and simmer 10 minutes or until liquid is reduced to $^3/_4$ cup. Cool.
4. Spoon 1 teaspoon of the sauce on top of each oyster and sprinkle the bread crumbs on top, pressing the crumbs down lightly. Bake in a 425° oven for 10 to 12 minutes or until the oyster edges begin to curl.

Seafood Velvet   Makes 2 dozen

Always a hit at the Stonington Antique Show.

$^1/_2$ pound cooked shrimp
$^1/_2$ pound butter, softened
2 tablespoons freshly chopped parsley
$^1/_4$ teaspoon curry powder
salt and pepper to taste
Melba toast rounds
$^1/_4$ cup mango chutney

Mince the shrimp. Cream the butter with the parsley, season with salt, pepper and curry, add shrimp to the butter mixture. Spread on Melba toasts and top with a dollop of chutney.

Chilled Mussels Billi-Bi

Serves 12

A Watch Hill house tour show stopper

4   dozen mussels, washed well and beards
    removed
1   cup white wine
4   shallots, minced
$^1/_2$ teaspoon black peppercorns
1   bay leaf
$^1/_2$ teaspoon salt
$1^1/_2$ cups heavy cream
1   envelope (1 tablespoon) unflavored gelatin
dash of white pepper
chopped fresh parsley
small pimento strips

1. Place mussels in a large sauce pot with wine, shallots, peppercorns, bay leaf and salt. Cover and steam for 5 minutes until all shells are open. Drain mussel broth into a bowl. Remove mussel meats and place one mussel on each half shell.
2. Soften gelatin in $^1/_2$ cup cream, stirring well. Add remaining cream and white pepper; whisk into the warm mussel broth. Simmer for 3 minutes and cool over a bowl of ice or place in the refrigerator for 1 hour, stirring until slightly set.
3. Nap the billi-bi cream over each mussel, sprinkle with parsley and top each with a small piece of pimento. Chill well before serving.

Barbara's Sardine Bait

Makes 16

Jensen Beach at its best.

2   4-ounce cans sardines, chopped
3   tablespoons fresh lemon juice
1   tablespoon tarragon or white wine vinegar
$^1/_2$ teaspoon Worcestershire sauce
2   tablespoons melted butter
2   tablespoons chopped fresh parsley
salt and pepper to taste
4   slices white bread, crusts trimmed, toasted
    and buttered
finely chopped hard boiled egg whites
    (2 eggs)
sliced olives

Mix all topping ingredients and spread on toast fingers. Garnish with a border of chopped egg white and top with olive slices.

"By the way, we had half a dozen sardines while the dinner was getting ready."
– William Makepeace Thackeray

New Potatoes Stuffed with Smoked Salmon   Makes 24

Chilled champagne or dry martinis are perfect with these appetizers.

12 baby red-skinned potatoes
1 tablespoon olive oil
3$^1/_2$ ounces smoked salmon, finely chopped
2 tablespoons sour cream
2 teaspoons minced red onion
1 teaspoon drained capers plus additional
    drained capers for garnish
$^1/_2$ teaspoon horseradish
black pepper
$^1/_2$ ounce thinly-sliced smoked salmon, cut into
    24 squares

1. Preheat oven to 400°. Cut potatoes in half crosswise. Mix with oil in bowl. Place cut side down on large baking sheet and bake until just tender, about 25 minutes. Cool.
2. Mix 3$^1/_2$ ounces salmon, sour cream, onion, capers and horseradish in a small bowl. Season with black pepper, cover and refrigerate. Potatoes and salmon mixture may be prepared a day ahead.
3. Cut a thin slice off rounded end of each potato so that potatoes will stand upright. Turn potatoes over and scoop out some of the center to make a little bowl. Spoon 1 teaspoon filling into each, garnish with a slice of smoked salmon and a caper.

A Chilled Oyster and Clam Martini   Serves 2

From the Nantucket Quaker House.

6 oysters, shucked
6 clams, shucked
1 tablespoon chopped cilantro
1 tablespoon diced red pepper
1 tablespoon diced green pepper
1 teaspoon olive oil
1 teaspoon chopped shallots
1 teaspoon chopped chili or poblano pepper
    (medium-hot)
salt and freshly ground pepper
chopped lettuce
2 lime wedges
2 cooked shrimp
pearl onions

1. Shuck clams and oysters in a small bowl, discard juice. Add cilantro, peppers, oil, shallots and chili or poblano. Toss gently and season with salt and freshly ground black pepper.
2. Put a little chopped lettuce in the bottom of 2 chilled martini glasses. Top with the clams and oysters and garnish, using a toothpick with the lime wedge, shrimp, and pearl onion.

Mandarin Shrimp and Orange Potstickers   Makes 40 dumplings

A Kon-Tiki Ports adaptation.

1   ounce dried mushrooms, preferably Chinese black mushrooms
1½ tablespoons minced fresh ginger
4   scallions, trimmed and minced
1   small carrot, peeled and minced
½ cup canned whole water chestnuts, drained and minced
1   tablespoon grated orange zest
2   tablespoons minced cilantro (fresh coriander)
1   large egg white
1   pound raw shrimp, peeled and deveined
1½ tablespoons soy sauce
2   tablespoons dry sherry
1   teaspoon sugar
1   teaspoon Oriental sesame oil
dash of hot chili oil
cornstarch
40 prepared wonton skins
3   tablespoons vegetable oil

Dipping sauce:
1   cup fresh orange juice
2   tablespoons dry sherry
2   tablespoons soy sauce
1   tablespoon chopped fresh ginger
2   tablespoons toasted sesame seeds
1   tablespoon chopped orange zest
1   teaspoon Oriental sesame oil
1   tablespoon light brown sugar
1   tablespoon hoisin sauce
several drops hot chili oil

1. Soak the mushrooms in hot water to cover until softened, about 30 minutes. Drain and finely mince.
2. Combine the mushrooms, ginger, scallions, carrot, water chestnuts, orange zest, and cilantro in a large mixing bowl. Set aside.

3. Beat the egg white in a small bowl just until foamy. Place the shrimp in a food processor, add the egg white, and process until the shrimp is very finely minced. Add the mushroom mixture and process to combine. Add the soy sauce, sherry, sugar, sesame oil, and chili oil; process just to combine. Transfer the mixture to a mixing bowl and set aside.
4. Line a couple of baking sheets with waxed paper and sift cornstarch lightly over the paper. Place a scant tablespoon of the shrimp filling on the center of each wonton skin. With your finger, moisten the edges of the skin with water, fold the skin in half into a triangle, and pinch the edges together to seal. Moisten the 2 opposite points of the triangle with another drop of water and pinch the points together. Place the dumplings on the prepared trays as you work. (The dumplings can be prepared ahead up to this point; cover with a clean, dry kitchen towel and refrigerate up to 4 hours).
5. Prepare the sauce by combining all the ingredients in a small bowl.
6. Coat 2 heavy 12-inch skillets each with 1½ tablespoons vegetable oil. Heat the skillets over high heat. When sizzling, add half the dumplings to each pan. Brown the bottoms evenly, lifting carefully every now and again with a spatula to prevent burning. The dumplings will brown in 5 to 7 minutes. Divide the sauce equally between the skillets and continue cooking until the dumplings are cooked through and translucent and the sauce is reduced to a glaze, about 5 minutes more.
7. Transfer the dumplings to a serving platter and pass with either toothpicks or, more authentically, chopsticks.

Vero Beach Conch Fritters

Serves 10-12

Just like you get at those great seaside stands.

1¹/₂ pounds conch, cooked and finely ground
    or chopped
1 egg, beaten
2 tablespoons water
¹/₄ cup chopped onion
2 small hot peppers, red or jalapeño, seeded
    and chopped
¹/₂ teaspoon freshly ground black pepper
1 teaspoon salt
¹/₂ teaspoon thyme
1 cup flour
1 teaspoon baking powder
vegetable oil

1. Beat egg and water together. Add conch, onion, hot peppers, black pepper, salt and thyme. Stir in flour and baking powder, blending well. The batter should be able to hold its body in a teaspoon. You may need to add a small amount of flour, depending on how juicy the conch is.
2. Heat vegetable oil in a skillet (375°) and drop by teaspoonfuls and cook, turning, until golden brown. Do not crowd pan. Drain on paper towels and serve with Heather's sauce.

Heather's hot sauce:
¹/₂ cup catsup
¹/₂ cup chili sauce
1 tablespoon lemon juice
1 tablespoon horseradish
1 teaspoon Worcestershire sauce
2 tablespoons capers, drained

Hot sauce preparation:
Mix all ingredients and chill for at least 1 hour before serving.

Mermaid's Delight

Makes 1¹/₂ cups

¹/₂ pound cooked shrimp
1 3-ounce package cream cheese
2 tablespoons mayonnaise
¹/₂ cup chopped stuffed green olives,
    about 24
2 teaspoons fresh lemon juice
1 teaspoon grated onion
¹/₂ teaspoon salt
Tabasco sauce
crackers or Melba toast rounds

Coarsely chop shrimp. In a separate bowl, blend cream cheese with mayonnaise until smooth. Add shrimp, chopped olives, lemon juice, grated onion, salt and a few dashes of Tabasco sauce. Mix well, cover and refrigerate. Serve with crisp crackers or Melba toast rounds.

Super-Spiced Spicey Shrimp   Serves 8-10

An easy to make but messy to eat starter.

$^1/_2$ cup prepared horseradish
$^1/_3$ cup olive oil
$^1/_4$ cup Worcestershire sauce
1$^1/_2$ teaspoons Tabasco sauce
2 quarts water
1 12-ounce bottle amber beer
10 small dried chilies (such as jalapeños)
8 large garlic cloves, peeled
1 tablespoon yellow mustard seeds
4 bay leaves
2 pounds uncooked medium shrimp, peeled and deveined
1 large lemon, thinly sliced
1 tablespoon salt

1. Whisk first 4 ingredients to blend in bowl. (Can be prepared 8 hours ahead. Cover and let stand at room temperature).
2. Bring water, beer, chilies, garlic, mustard seeds and bay leaves to boil in heavy large saucepan over high heat. Reduce heat to medium and simmer 10 minutes. Add shrimp, lemon and salt to beer mixture. Simmer until shrimp are just cooked through, about 3 minutes.
3. Pour shrimp mixture through large strainer, discarding liquids. Transfer contents of strainer to large bowl. Add horseradish mixture and stir to blend. Cool to room temperature, about 30 minutes.
4. Put a big bowl of shrimp in the middle of the table and give everyone an ice-cold beer, plates for discarded shells and hot, damp towels to clean up afterward.

Swiss Crab Bites   Makes 36

A Bake Off winner.

1 7$^1/_2$-ounce can crabmeat, drained and flaked
1 scallion, minced
4 ounces grated Swiss cheese
$^1/_2$ cup mayonnaise
1 teaspoon fresh lemon juice
$^1/_4$ teaspoon curry powder
1 package flaky refrigerator rolls (12 rolls)
1 5-ounce can sliced water chestnuts

1. Combine crabmeat, scallion, cheese, mayonnaise, lemon juice and curry powder, mix well.
2. Remove rolls from package and separate each roll into 3 layers. Place on a baking sheet and top each with a teaspoon of the crab mixture. Finish off with a few slices of water chestnut and bake in a 400° oven for 10 to 12 minutes until puffed and brown.

Mustard Ginger Shrimp Pitas   Makes about 50

From a local caterer – always requested.

1   cup cider vinegar
³/₄ cup vegetable oil
2   tablespoons sugar
1   tablespoon Worcestershire sauce
1   teaspoon Tabasco sauce
2   teaspoons English-style dry mustard
4¹/₂ teaspoons minced peeled fresh ginger root
2   pounds medium shrimp (about 50), shelled
     and, if desired, deveined
1   cup julienne strips of assorted red, yellow,
     and green bell peppers
¹/₄ cup finely chopped fresh coriander plus
     sprigs for garnish
dried hot red pepper flakes to taste
pita pockets, cut into about 50 wedges and
     toasted lightly

1. In a saucepan, whisk together vinegar, oil, sugar, Worcestershire sauce, Tabasco sauce, mustard, ginger root, and salt and black pepper to taste; bring the mixture to a boil and simmer it, stirring occasionally, for 5 minutes.

2. Add the shrimp and simmer, stirring occasionally, for 3 to 5 minutes, or until cooked through. Transfer the mixture to a heat proof bowl, add bell peppers, tossing the mixture well, and chill, covered, for 2 hours.

3. Drain the mixture, discarding the liquid, and stir in chopped coriander, red pepper flakes, and salt and black pepper to taste. Arrange a shrimp and several pepper strips on each pita wedge and garnish the canapés with the coriander sprigs.

"The gentleman who dines the latest
    Is in our street esteemed the greatest;
But surely greatest of them all
    Is he who never dines at all."
                                    – A. Lyman Phillips

Stuffed Quahogs Wainio

Makes 20 to 30

Make no substitutions, your family will swoon.

10 to 15 medium quahogs
1/2 pound hot pork sausage (Jimmy Dean brand is best)
2 medium onions
1 green pepper
1 tablespoon butter or margarine
1 teaspoon crushed red pepper
1 6-ounce package chicken stuffing mix, Stove Top variety
1 egg, beaten

1. Rinse quahogs under cold water and place in a saucepan with 3 cups of water; cover and cook over medium-high heat until shells open, about 8 minutes. Shuck clams, set aside and reserve broth in a mixing bowl.
2. In a food processor fitted with a steel blade or a grinder, grind clams, onions, pepper, and sausage meat. Melt butter or margarine in a skillet and sauté for 15 minutes until vegetables are done and sausage has lightly browned.
3. Substitute and measure broth for liquid called for in the stuffing mix preparation. Add hot pepper and egg, mix well with the mixture in pan. Simmer for 10 minutes, stirring frequently. Pack stuffing mixture into reserved shells and bake in a 350° oven for 25 minutes. These may be cooked frozen, increasing time to 45 minutes.

The Breakers Salmon Mousse

Serves 8-10

With Palm Beach style.

1 pound fillet of salmon, poached, cooled and flaked
2 tablespoons tomato paste
2 tablespoons lemon juice, freshly squeezed
1 tablespoon horseradish
1/3 pint of heavy cream
freshly ground black pepper
pinch of salt
1/8 teaspoon Tabasco sauce
2 tablespoons chopped fresh parsley
1 envelope of unflavored gelatin

1. Place cream in a food processor and whip until it is the consistency of mayonnaise. Mix the gelatin with 1 tablespoon of water and set aside.
2. Add remaining ingredients to processor and blend for 30 seconds. Add the gelatin and blend until smooth. Place mixture in a lightly-oiled 3 cup mold or individual ramekins. Refrigerate for at least 6 hours before serving with squares of pumpernickel bread or homemade buttered toast points.

Hot Creamy Crab Dip

Makes about 4 cups

This dip always disappears fast, so make plenty.

1 6$^1/_2$-ounce can crabmeat, drained and flaked
2 8-ounce packages cream cheese at room temperature
$^1/_2$ cup sour cream
$^1/_4$ cup mayonnaise
2 tablespoons sherry or white wine
2 tablespoons grated onion
1 tablespoon Dijon mustard
1 teaspoon minced fresh garlic
4 dashes Tabasco sauce
$^1/_2$ cup minced fresh parsley
$^1/_2$ cup slivered almonds
paprika
assorted crackers

1. Mix cream cheese, sour cream, mayonnaise, sherry, onion, mustard, garlic and Tabasco sauce in a medium-size saucepan. Fold in crabmeat and $^1/_4$ cup parsley.
2. Over medium heat, warm, stirring gently, just until hot, do not boil. Spoon into a warm serving dish or chafing dish; sprinkle with remaining parsley, the almonds and paprika. Serve with crackers.

Southborough Stuffed Clams

Makes 18 to 24 clams depending on size

18 large hardshell clams (quahogs are best)
$^1/_2$ cup clam juice
    or
2 6-ounce cans chopped clams with juice
40 saltine crackers (1 sleeve), crushed
4 tablespoons melted butter
3 tablespoons Parmesan cheese
1 teaspoon Worcestershire sauce
Tabasco sauce
1 tablespoon fresh lemon juice
1 small onion, minced
$^1/_2$ green pepper, minced
2 tablespoons fresh chopped parsley
paprika

1. Shuck clams over a bowl, reserving juice if using fresh clams. Coarsely chop. Mix clams with remaining ingredients except paprika; the mixture will be moist. Refrigerate for 2 hours.
2. Stuff clam shells and sprinkle with paprika. Save remaining clam shells for another time when you might not have fresh clams or would prefer to use canned clams. Bake at 350° for 20 minutes until brown. These may be frozen, individually wrapped; defrost before cooking.

China Pavilion Steamed Clams   Serves 4

An Oriental twist for your next picnic.

24 littleneck clams
3 tablespoons soy sauce
2 teaspoons sesame oil
2 cloves garlic, minced
2 scallions, finely chopped
2 tablespoons chopped fresh parsley
1 tablespoon sesame seeds
1 teaspoon sugar
1 jalapeño pepper, seeded and finely
   chopped

1. Scrub clams, discarding any that do not close when you give them a sharp tap. In a pot large enough to hold clams in a single layer, heat 1 cup of water to boiling, then drop in the clams. Cover and steam until they open, 5 to 7 minutes. Remove clams with a slotted spoon. When cool enough to handle, remove the upper shell from each clam and discard. Place the clams in their half shells on a serving platter. With a small, sharp knife, loosen each clam in its shell.

2. In a small bowl, mix the remaining ingredients together and pour a little of this sauce into each shell. (The clams can be steamed up to 8 hours ahead, doused with sauce and then refrigerated. Either serve cold or steam briefly to eat hot.)

Carol's Curried Mussels o' Calcutta   Serves 6

4 dozen mussels
1¹/₂ cups water

Curry sauce:
3 tablespoons chopped scallions
2 tablespoons fresh parsley
2 teaspoons curry powder
¹/₈ teaspoon salt
¹/₈ teaspoon pepper
2 teaspoons lemon juice
2 tablespoons chili sauce
1 cup mayonnaise
paprika

1. Prepare sauce ahead of time by combining all ingredients and refrigerating for several hours.

2. Scrub mussels under cold water and remove the beards. Steam in 1¹/₂ cups water, covered, for 6 to 8 minutes or until shells open; discard any that do not open. Discard top shells and loosen meat from the bottoms, place on a large platter. Spoon sauce on top of each shell and sprinkle each with paprika. Chill for several hours before serving.

Little Rock Shrimp Pots

Serves 8

Mary's quick and easy party make-ahead.

2   7¹/₂ ounce cans of small shrimp, drained
     and rinsed
¹/₄ pound butter, softened
dash of Worcestershire sauce
2   teaspoons fresh lemon juice
2   teaspoons fresh tarragon, chopped or
     1 teaspoon dried, crumbled
salt and pepper to taste
lemon wedges
minced lettuce
Melba toast

Empty one can of shrimp into food processor and add remaining ingredients, except lemon wedges, minced lettuce and melba toast. Process until smooth. Transfer into a bowl and add the second can of shrimp. Mix well and pack into 8 demmitasse cups or small pot-de-crêmes. Serve to each guest surrounded by lemon wedges, minced lettuce and melba toast. Top each with a sprig of tarragon if available.

Odin's Temptation

Serves 10-12

From a family in Sweden - serve at home or onboard

6 to 8 large potatoes, peeled and cut into sticks
     like French fries
1-ounce tin anchovy fillets
2   onions, thinly sliced
1¹/₂ cups cream or half-and-half
freshly ground black pepper
2   tablespoons butter

"Where love has entered as the seasoning of food, I believe it will please anyone."
                                        – Platus

1. Layer potatoes, onions and anchovies in 2 to 3 layers in a buttered baking dish, giving it a few grinds of pepper as you go. The first and last layers must be potatoes.
2. Dot with butter and pour half of the cream into dish. Bake in a 375° oven for ¹/₂ hour. Add the remaining cream and bake for another 30 minutes or until potatoes are tender. Recommend serving with Jarlsberg cheese, Rye Crisp Crackers and lots of good beer.

Brazilian Crab and Onion Bites   Makes 32 bites

One is never enough.

1   small onion, finely chopped
6   ounces crab meat (if canned, drain and rinse)
8   tablespoons mayonnaise
4   dashes Tabasco sauce
salt
8   slices white bread, crusts removed
4   tablespoons fresh grated Parmesan cheese

1. Mix onion, crab meat, 6 tablespoons of mayonnaise, Tabasco sauce and salt to taste.
2. Spread 4 slices of bread on one side with the remaining mayonnaise. Cut these into 4 quarters or triangles.
3. Cut the remaining 4 slices of bread into quarters and spread each evenly with the crab onion mixture.
4. Top with the reserved bread squares, mayonnaise side up. Place on a baking sheet and sprinkle tops generously with the Parmesan cheese. Bake at 350° for 15 minutes until golden and puffy. Serve immediately.

Block Island Oyster Bites

Best at anchor.

Per person, plan on at least 6 oysters, shucked and left on the half shell
Top each with:
1. 1 drop Worcestershire sauce
2. 1 drop Tabasco sauce, sprinkle of salt
3. 1 teaspoon chili sauce
4. 1 square of bacon
5. $1/2$ teaspoon Parmesan cheese

Bake in a 400° oven for 8 minutes until brown and bubbly.

"The first Roman to great Egypt sends his treasure of an oyster."

**– William Shakespeare:
Antony and Cleopatra**

PUT ON THE POT

Seafood Stew in a Basket

Serves 6

1 pound of fish fillets, at least 2 varieties of firm fish, such as cod, haddock, halibut or tuna. You can often purchase some "ends" from your fish market

$1/2$ pound of squid, cleaned and cut into $1/2$ inch rings or pieces

1 pound mussels or clams, rinsed

$1/2$ cup olive oil

4 medium onions, sliced

4 cloves garlic, crushed

1 green pepper, chopped

5 medium tomatoes, peeled, seeded, and chopped

2 tablespoons chopped parsley

1 tablespoon chopped basil

2 bay leaves

salt and freshly ground black pepper to taste

$1/2$ cup dry wine, red or white

2 tablespoons butter

6 thick slices French or Italian bread

1. Heat oil in a large saucepan. Add onions, garlic and pepper, sauté until onions are translucent. Add tomatoes, parsley, basil, bay leaves and simmer for 20 minutes. Add wine and butter, remove from heat and season with salt and pepper.

2. Spoon a little of the sauce on the bottom of a heavy oven-proof casserole. Arrange layers of the fish, squid, and clams or mussels, alternating with the tomato sauce. Place bread slices on top, cover casserole, and either bring to a boil, lower heat and simmer for 10 to 15 minutes until fish is tender and the mussels open, OR bake <u>uncovered</u> in a 350° oven for 25 minutes until bubbly and bread is golden brown.

Serve in individual bowls dotted with butter and sprinkled with paprika. Serve oyster crackers alongside if desired.

"A genial savor of certain stews."
– Lord Byron

Baltimore Sherried Crab Stew

Serves 4

Best when in season – early spring.

1 pound crabmeat (Maryland crab is best)

3 tablespoons butter

$1/2$ teaspoon salt

$1/2$ teaspoon Tabasco sauce

1 teaspoon Worcestershire sauce

2 cups milk

2 cups half-and-half

6 tablespoons sherry

lemon slices

parsley sprigs

paprika

1. Melt butter in a medium saucepan. Add crab, salt, Tabasco sauce, Worcestershire sauce and milk. Simmer very gently for 10 minutes.

2. Stir in cream and simmer for 5 more minutes, being careful not to break up the crab. Remove from heat and add sherry. Serve in warm soup bowls, top with lemon slice, parsley and a sprinkle of paprika.

All Wrapped Up Wonton Soup   Serves 4 to 6

Shrimp and pork filling:

6 ounces shrimp, peeled, cooked and chopped
$1/2$ cup pork, cooked and chopped
$1/2$ cup mushrooms, finely chopped
$1/2$ cup sliced scallions
2 tablespoons finely chopped pimento
2 tablespoons cilantro, chopped
2 tablespoons soy sauce
1 teaspoon sesame oil
$1/8$ teaspoon red pepper flakes

Combine above ingredients in a small bowl and mix well. This can also be done in a food processor fitted with a steel blade. Proceed as shown below.

How to wrap a Wonton

FIG. 1   Put $1/2$ teaspoonful of the filling in the center of the wonton skin. Support the skin on the fingers of both hands with your two thumbs in the top center.

FIG. 2   Now fold the outside edge even with the inner edge by using your thumbs and two index fingers.

FIG. 3   Using both thumbs, press the wonton skin firmly around the filling.

FIG. 4   Now make a fold with the filling at the center, using the two thumbs to hold the fold and to keep the skin firmly pressed around the filling.

FIG. 5   The fold you have just made will form two wings on either side of the filling. Now fold these two wings together backwards.

FIG. 6   Wet the corners of these two wings with water or egg whites, overlap, and press them firmly together between your right thumb and index finger (left thumb and index finger if you are left-handed).

Homemade Wonton Soup   Serves 4-6

20 filled wontons
4 cups chicken broth
$1/2$ cup thinly bias-cut carrots
6 scallions, thinly sliced
10 water chestnuts, thinly sliced
1-inch piece fresh ginger
sesame oil
cilantro leaves

1. In a medium saucepan, combine chicken stock, carrot, scallions, water chestnuts and ginger. Bring to a boil and add wontons, one at a time. Reduce heat and simmer for 4 to 5 minutes until wontons are plump. Remove ginger and discard.
2. Stir in sesame oil and divide wontons among bowls and ladle broth on top. Sprinkle with cilantro.

Block Island Steamer Stew

Serves 10-12

A true stew – you may add potato if you desire.

2 quarts fresh steamer clams
1 2-inch piece salt pork, cubed
$^1/_2$ medium onion, chopped
few celery leaves, chopped
8 cups half-and-half or 4 cups whipping cream
   and 4 cups whole milk
2 teaspoons Worcestershire sauce
6 dashes Tabasco sauce
4 tablespoons butter
1 tablespoon chopped parsley
salt and white pepper to taste
paprika
oyster crackers

1. Wash the clams thoroughly under cold water. Place in a large saucepan with 1 inch of water, bring to a boil, cover and cook 3 to 4 minutes until shells open. Drain and remove clams from the shells.
2. In a 4 quart soup pot, sauté salt pork until lightly browned. Add butter, chopped onion and celery, cook until translucent, 3-4 minutes.
3. Over low heat, stir in cream, Worcestershire sauce and Tabasco sauce. Add the clams and cook until heated through, but not boiling. Season with salt and pepper. Garnish with parsley.

The steamer clam is the most popular shellfish, except for the oyster, on both the Atlantic and Pacific coasts. Always associated with New England, 90-95% of the steamers used on the Massachusetts coast are eaten fried – full bellies are the favorite.

Fiesta Clam and Corn Chowder

Serves a crowd – 12 or more

$^1/_4$ pound bacon, cut in $^1/_2$ inch pieces
1 large onion, finely chopped
1 red onion, diced
1 green pepper, diced
6 medium red potatoes, unpeeled and diced
6 cups fish stock or clam juice (the fish bouillon cubes work fine)
2 sprigs fresh thyme
2 cups corn
2 pints chopped clams with the juice
2 cups half and half
2 teaspoons salt
$^1/_2$ teaspoon white pepper

1. Sauté bacon in a large heavy saucepan until crisp. Remove and add onion, red pepper, green pepper to pan. Sauté for 3 minutes and drain off any excess bacon fat from the pan.
2. Add potatoes, stock and thyme, bring to a boil and simmer, partially covered, for 20 minutes. Discard thyme.
3. Stir in the corn and clams, continue cooking for 15 minutes. Add the half-and-half, season with salt and pepper. Bring chowder back up to a light simmer before serving, being careful not to boil.

"The gods sent not corn for the rich men only."
                    – William Shakespeare

Clam Vichysoisse

Serves 10

4   large leeks
1   onion, diced
4   medium potatoes, Idaho or russet
1^1/$_2$ cups chicken stock
1^1/$_2$ cups chopped clams
3   cups clam broth
2   cups light cream
2   tablespoons chopped parsley
^{1}/$_2$ teaspoon salt
Tabasco sauce to taste
^{1}/$_2$ cup chopped scallions
croutons

**"Leeks to the Welsh, to Dutchmen butter's dear,
of Irish swains potato is the cheer."**
– John Gay

1. Remove root end and green tops from leeks. Split lengthwise and wash thoroughly. Slice into ^{1}/$_2$ inch pieces.
2. Place leeks, chopped onions and potatoes in a medium saucepan. Add chicken stock, chopped clams and clam broth. Simmer for 20 minutes or until potatoes are tender. Cool.
3. In a food processor fitted with a steel blade or a blender, puree in small batches until smooth. Return to the pan and bring to a simmer. Whisk in the cream, parsley, salt and a few dashes of Tabasco sauce to taste. Chill for at least 6 hours. Ladle into serving bowls and garnish with scallions and croutons.

Velvet Ginger Crab and Corn Soup

Serves 4 to 6

An Oriental starter.

2   cups fresh corn or
1   16-ounce package corn, thawed and divided
1   tablespoon corn starch
^{1}/$_4$ cup water
3   10-ounce cans chicken broth
1   teaspoon peeled minced ginger root
^{1}/$_2$ pound fresh crabmeat
^{1}/$_2$ cup scallions, chopped
^{1}/$_4$ teaspoon white pepper
1   teaspoon rice wine vinegar

1. In a food processor fitted with a steel blade, finely chop half of the corn. Combine cornstarch and water in a small bowl, stir well and set aside.
2. Combine chicken broth and ginger root in a large saucepan, bring to a boil. Add chopped corn, whole corn kernels, crabmeat and remaining ingredients. Return to a boil for 1 minute, reduce heat and simmer uncovered for 3 minutes.

Long Island Swordfish Cioppino   Serves 4

1¹/₂ pounds swordfish, cut into 2-inch cubes
6   slices bacon, diced
1   medium onion, chopped
1   cup diced celery
1   green pepper, chopped
¹/₂ cup chopped carrots
1   quart fish stock or clam juice diluted with an
    equal amount of water
2   tomatoes, peeled and chopped
2   tablespoons tomato paste
3   small potatoes, peeled and diced
¹/₂ teaspoon thyme
¹/₂ teaspoon basil
1   teaspoon salt
freshly ground black pepper
2   tablespoons minced parsley

1. Cook bacon in a large saucepan until lightly brown. Add swordfish, onion, celery, green pepper and carrot, sauté for 3 to 4 minutes until soft but not brown.
2. Add fish stock, tomatoes, tomato paste, potatoes and seasonings, bring to a boil and simmer for ¹/₂ hour until potatoes are tender. Sprinkle with additional parsley when serving.

Clam, Mushroom and Everything Else Chowder   Serves 4

¹/₂ cup butter
¹/₂ cup chopped celery
¹/₂ cup grated carrots
¹/₂ cup grated white turnip
2   tablespoons minced onion
1   12-ounce can minced clams
1   6-ounce can chopped butter-broiled
    mushrooms
¹/₂ teaspoon salt
¹/₈ teaspoon pepper
2   cups milk, heated
2   tablespoons corn starch
3   tablespoons cold water
¹/₂ cup heavy cream
chopped parsley

1. Melt butter in a saucepan. Add celery, carrots, turnip and onion. Sauté over low heat for 5 minutes until soft.
2. Add clams and mushrooms (including liquid from both cans), salt and pepper. Heat gently, do not boil. Gradually stir in hot milk.
3. In a small bowl, stir cornstarch and water together until smooth. Whisk into soup and cook until slightly thickened. Increase heat until just bubbling and add cream. To serve, sprinkle with lots of chopped parsley.

"Muse, sing the man that did to Paris go, that he might taste their soups and mushrooms know."

– William King

Back Bayou Seafood Gumbo   Serves 10 generously

4   tablespoons vegetable oil
3   cups diced okra
$^3/_4$ cup chopped celery
2   cloves garlic, minced
2   bunches scallions, chopped
2   tablespoons chopped fresh parsley
1   bay leaf
$^1/_2$ teaspoon thyme
salt and pepper to taste
few dashes Tabasco sauce
1   28 ounce can whole tomatoes
1   15 ounce can tomato sauce
2   cups medium shrimp, peeled
$1^1/_2$ cups fresh crabmeat
3   hard-shell crabs, boiled and cracked into
     pieces
cooked white rice

1. Put oil in a large heavy pot. Add okra and sauté for 2 minutes. Add celery, garlic, and pepper, cook until light brown. Stir in scallions and parsley, cook for 2 minutes longer.
2. Add bay leaf, thyme, salt, pepper, Tabasco sauce, tomatoes and tomato sauce. Add 1 quart of hot water and simmer for 20 minutes. Put the shrimp, crab and another quart of water in the pot, cook over medium-low heat for $^1/_2$ hour. Toss in the crabs and finish cooking for $^1/_2$ hour. Serve over rice in big soup bowls.

"If we don't have no more gumbo and no more jambalaya, what hell Cajun gon' eat that's any good, hein. Oh M'sieu, ça c'est awful!"
– Gumbo Ya-ya

Catch of the Day Fish Stew   Serves 16-20

4   pounds variety of firm fish cut into 3-inch
     pieces: cod, bass, eel, halibut or blackfish
$^1/_4$ cup olive oil
2   onions, chopped
4   cloves garlic, minced
2   leeks, washed and chopped
1   fennel bulb, sliced
4   tomatoes, chopped
1   8-ounce can tomato sauce
$^1/_4$ cup chopped fresh parsley
$^1/_2$ teaspoon cayenne pepper
2   cups dry white wine, fish stock or half of
     each
2   bay leaves
8   cups water
salt to taste

1. In a large, deep, heavy sauce pot brown fish in olive oil for 5 minutes. Add onions, garlic, leeks and fennel, sauté until softened and add remaining ingredients.
2. Simmer the soup for 1 hour or until the fish is cooked and the broth has reduced. Season with salt to taste and ladle into soup bowls, top with hot buttered croutons.

**"From the eel they formed their food in chief,
And eels were called the Derryfield beef;
It was often said that their only care,
And their only wish, and their only prayer,
For the present world and the world to come,
Was a string of eels and a jug of rum."**
**– History of New Hampshire,
Leonard Morrison, 1719.**

Noank Mussel Chowder   Serves 4

Mussels replace the traditional clams in this creamy-tasting soup.

4   pounds mussels, scrubbed, beards removed
1   medium onion, chopped
2   leeks, with green tops, chopped
4   strips bacon, chopped
1   tablespoon olive oil
4   potatoes, peeled and cut into $1/4$-inch pieces
2   carrots, peeled and grated
$1/2$ teaspoon salt
freshly ground black pepper
dash of Tabasco sauce
1   cup milk or cream
3   tablespoons chopped fresh parsley

"Chagu'n connain ça qua pé bouilli dans so chaudiere!"   – Old Creole saying

1. Place mussels in a heavy pot and add 3 cups of water. Cover and bring to a boil over high heat. Steam for 2 to 3 minutes, shaking pot several times until mussels open. Discard any that do not open. Cool, shell the mussels and set aside. Strain liquid through a cheesecloth or filter-lined sieve and reserve.
2. In a heavy saucepan, sauté onion, leeks and bacon in olive oil until vegetables are softened and bacon is crisp. Add mussel liquid, potatoes, carrots, salt, pepper and Tabasco sauce to taste. Simmer over low heat for 10 minutes or until potatoes are tender. Add milk or cream and mussels, heat through but do not boil. Sprinkle with parsley and serve.

Venetian Harbor Fresh Clam Soup   Serves 4

Try this when your summer tomatoes are at their peak.

6   tablespoons olive oil
2   teaspoons finely chopped garlic
$1/2$ cup dry white wine
1   cup water
3   pounds firm ripe tomatoes, peeled, seeded and chopped (Italian plum tomatoes are best)
2   dozen small hardshell clams
4   tablespoons chopped fresh flat leaf parsley
salt and freshly ground black pepper
toasted Italian bread
freshly grated Parmesan cheese

1. Heat the olive oil in a heavy 2 to 3 quart saucepan. Add the garlic and cook, stirring over medium heat for 30 seconds. Do not let the garlic brown. Pour in the wine, water and tomatoes, and bring to a boil. Reduce heat and simmer the sauce for 10 minutes.
2. Meanwhile, scrub the clams under cold water. When soup is ready, drop clams into the pot and cover. Cook for 10 minutes or until shells open. Serve in big soup bowls, sprinkle with parsley and pass the bread and grated cheese.

Oyster Bongo Bongo

Serves 8 to 10

An unusual and delicious party soup - dress it up with whipped cream and grated lemon zest.

4   tablespoons butter
4   shallots, minced
$^1/_2$ cup dry white wine
1   pint raw oysters
1   teaspoon salt
$^1/_4$ teaspoon white pepper
$^1/_2$ package (about 5 ounces) frozen chopped
    spinach
2   cups fish or chicken broth
4   cups light cream
2   tablespoons cornstarch
$^1/_4$ cup water
2   teaspoons Worcestershire sauce
dash of cayenne pepper

1. Melt butter in a heavy saucepan, add shallots and simmer a few minutes. Stir in the wine and bring to a boil. Cook until liquid is reduced by half.
2. Chop oysters and add to wine mixture with oyster liquid. Stir in salt and pepper and cook over medium heat for 4 to 5 minutes. Remove from heat.
3. In a separate saucepan, combine spinach and broth. Bring to a boil, reduce heat and cook until spinach is just tender. Add the light cream and combine the 2 mixtures. Cool.
4. In a blender or food processor, process the soup in several batches for 30 seconds. Return to soup pan over medium heat.
5. Dissolve cornstarch in cold water, stir into soup. Continue stirring until soup is thickened and thoroughly blended. Add remaining seasonings and serve hot in a warm tureen or in demitasse cups.

Seagoin' Steamers and Soup

Serves 8

If you love steamed clams – this is heaven.

2   quarts steamers (soft shell clams)
1   cup water
1   cup dry white wine
1   onion, chopped
3   stalks celery, chopped
1   carrot, chopped
6   cloves garlic, minced
3   bay leaves
1   tablespoon black peppercorns, crushed
4   tablespoons butter
juice of one lemon

1. Wash the clams in cold water and place in a large pot. Add water, wine, onion, celery, carrot, garlic, bay leaves and peppercorns. Cover and let simmer for 10 minutes until clams open.
2. Remove clams to serving bowls. Turn heat to high, whisk in the butter and lemon juice and pour hot over the clams.

Swedish Salmon Chowder   Serves 10

3   stalks celery, chopped
1   medium onion, chopped
3   garlic cloves, minced
5   tablespoons butter
2   16-ounce cans salmon
2   quarts water
4   fish flavored bouillon cubes
$2/3$ cup dry sherry
1   teaspoon thyme
1   teaspoon dill
$1/2$ teaspoon white pepper
2   teaspoons paprika
2   cups cubed potatoes
6   tablespoons flour
1   pint light cream
chopped parsley

1. Melt 2 tablespoons butter in a large saucepan. Add celery, onion and garlic, sauté for 3 to 4 minutes until translucent, about 5 minutes.
2. Remove any bones from salmon. Add salmon, including the liquid from the can, to the vegetable mixture. Add 2 quarts of water, bouillon cubes and sherry. Simmer uncovered for 10 minutes. Add potatoes and seasonings. Simmer until potatoes are tender.
3. In a separate saucepan, melt remaining 3 tablespoons of butter. Add flour and mix well. Add cream and cook until thickened and smooth, whisking constantly. Add half of the salmon mixture to the pan and stir briskly. Return to the soup pan and stir until blended. Serve garnished with fresh chopped parsley.

Scandinavian Summer Soup   Serves 8

Our foreign exchange student introduced us to this.

$1^1/2$ pounds shrimp, peeled, deveined and cooked
2   medium cucumbers, peeled, seeded and diced
2   tablespoons fresh dill, plus sprigs for garnish
2   teaspoons salt
$1^1/2$ teaspoons sugar
2   teaspoons prepared mustard
$1^1/2$ quarts buttermilk
salt and pepper

Cut shrimp into small pieces, about $1/2$-inch. Mix together with remaining ingredients and refrigerate at least overnight. Serve in chilled bouillon cups and garnish with dill sprigs.

Ocean House Fish Chowder for a Crowd Serves 20⁺

4 cups mixed chopped vegetables, onion, carrots, celery, green peppers
6 pounds fish fillets or steaks—haddock, tilefish, blackfish, salmon, scrod (avoid anything oily such as bluefish)
12 cups clam juice
6 cups water
1 tablespoon oregano
2 teaspoons marjoram
2 tablespoons Worcestershire sauce
salt and pepper
Tabasco sauce to taste
2 cups tomato sauce
$^1/_2$ cup chopped fresh parsley

1. Chop vegetables into $^1/_2$-inch cubes. Cut the fish into 1-inch cubes, any combination.
2. Place vegetables, clam juice, water and seasonings in a large pot. Simmer for 20 minutes until vegetables are almost cooked.
3. Turn down the heat, add fish and "poach" for 45 minutes. Add the tomato sauce and parsley, adjust seasoning. Simmer for 5 more minutes until heated through.

"One morning in the garden bed
The onion and the carrot said
Unto the parsley group:
'Oh, when shall we three meet again –
In thunder, lightning or in rain?'
"Alas,' replied in tones of pain
The parsley, 'in the soup.'"
– C. S. Calvery

The Devil's Shrimp Gumbo   Serves 4

A spicy hot winner.

$^1/_8$ pound salt pork, diced
$^1/_2$ cup onion, diced
1 cup fresh sliced okra
2 10-ounce cans whole tomatoes, crushed
1 teaspoon thyme
$1^1/_2$ teaspoons fresh ground black pepper
1 pound fresh medium shrimp
$^1/_4$ datil pepper - these are very hot but make the dish. If you have difficulty finding datil peppers, you may substitute the hottest peppers you can find. Taste the gumbo before adding too much.

1. In a medium saucepan, fry salt pork until golden brown. Add the onion and okra, cook for 10 minutes.
2. Add the remaining ingredients and simmer for 20 minutes, correcting seasoning at the end. The pepper will get hotter as this sits. Serve over white rice and garnish with lemon and parsley.

Oriental Chrysanthemum Bowle   Serves 6 to 8

Prepare everything ahead – great for after the theater.

2   quarts chicken stock
2   teaspoons salt
$1/4$ cup sherry
4   tablespoons soy sauce
1   teaspoon sesame oil
hot red pepper flakes to taste
2   tablespoons chopped cilantro
1   pound medium shrimp, cut in half
    lengthwise
oysters (2 to 3 per person)
clams (2 to 3 per person)
1   pound sea scallops
1   pound firm white fish cut into 2-inch chunks
    (2 varieties is best; salmon, cod, halibut)
2   chicken breasts, cut in thin strips
$1/4$ pound Chinese cellophane noodles (bean
    thread)
1   head bok choy (Chinese cabbage), finely
    shredded
1   pound fresh spinach, washed and stemmed
12 scallions, cut into 3-inch pieces
2   large chrysanthemums

1. Arrange raw seafood on a large platter in neat rows. Do the same with the vegetables to make an attractive presentation.

2. Bring chicken broth and salt to a boil in a large serving pot (a Mongolian hot pot or wok is traditional). Add sherry, soy sauce, sesame oil, hot pepper flakes and cilantro to bubbling broth. Provide guests with chop sticks and serving bowls. Invite guests to add raw ingredients to the broth and let cook until vegetables are tender crisp and seafood is opaque. Just before serving, scatter petals from the chrysanthemums on top of the steaming soup. Ladle some of the broth into each person's bowl as they serve themselves.

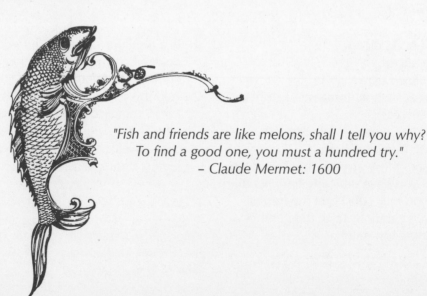

"Fish and friends are like melons, shall I tell you why?
To find a good one, you must a hundred try."
– Claude Mermet: 1600

Grand Central Oyster Stew for One   Serves 1

A train hopper's delight.

10 to 12 oysters, depending on your appetite
2   tablespoons clam juice
1   tablespoon Worcestershire sauce
1   tablespoon butter
$^1/_4$ teaspoon paprika
$^1/_8$ teaspoon celery salt
$^1/_2$ cup half-and-half
pat of butter
paprika

Oysters are like fine wine: it isn't the parent that determines its character, it's the environment in which it matures.
              – Encyclopedia of Fish Cookery

1. Shuck oysters, reserving the liquid. In a sauce pan, combine the reserved liquid, clam juice, Worcestershire sauce, butter, paprika and celery salt. Bring the liquid just to the boiling point over low heat and add the oysters and half and half.
2. Bring the liquid to the boiling point again, cooking the oysters until they plump up and the edges curl. Transfer the stew to a heated bowl and garnish with a pat of butter and a pinch of paprika.

Mussels with Thai Red Curry   Serves 6 as a first course

3   pounds mussels, scrubbed and beards removed
$^1/_4$ cup butter ($^1/_2$ stick)
5   plum tomatoes, peeled and chopped
2   tablespoons minced garlic
1   tablespoon chopped fresh ginger
2   14-ounce cans unsweetened coconut milk*
1   tablespoon (or more to taste) Thai red curry paste*
$^1/_3$ cup plus 2 tablespoons chopped fresh cilantro
$^1/_2$ teaspoon salt

* Available in Asian markets or in the Asian, Latin American section of some supermarkets

1. Melt butter in a large heavy pot over medium-high heat. Add tomatoes, garlic and ginger; sauté for 2 minutes until garlic is tender. Mix in coconut milk, curry paste, $^1/_4$ cup chopped cilantro and salt. Simmer for 5 minutes to blend flavors.
2. Add mussels to the pot, cover and cook until shells open, about 5 minutes (discard any mussels that do not open). Serve mussels in big bowls, pour sauce on top and garnish with remaining chopped cilantro.

Moules et frites (mussels and fries) are to a Belgian what a hot dog and hamburger are to an American. In Brussels, mussels are eaten raw at the sidewalk stands, finished off with fries and a glass of beer.

Steamed Mussels in Herbed Cream Sauce

Serves 2

Makes a hearty winter meal.

1½ pounds mussels
1 onion, chopped
2 tablespoons vegetable oil
2 garlic cloves, minced
2 tablespoons dry white wine
¼ cup heavy cream
2 tablespoons fresh bread crumbs
3 tablespoons snipped fresh chives or minced scallion greens
¼ cup snipped fresh dill
toasted French bread

1. Scrub the mussels well under cold water and scrape off the beards. In a kettle, cook the onion in the oil over moderately low heat, stirring, until it is softened. Add the garlic, the mussels, and the wine and steam the mussels, covered, for 3 to 5 minutes, or until they are opened. With a slotted spoon, transfer the mussels as they open to a heated dish and cover them with a hot dampened kitchen towel to keep them from drying out. Discard any unopened mussels.

2. Add the cream and the bread crumbs to the kettle, bring the liquid to a boil, and boil the mixture over high heat for 3 to 5 minutes, or until the sauce is thickened. Return the mussels to the kettle with the chives and the dill, stirring to coat the mussels with the sauce, and divide the mixture between 2 heated bowls and serve with French bread.

Chilled Shrimp and Cucumber Bisque

Serves 8

1 cup chopped onion
3 tablespoons butter
3 cups chicken stock
1½ cups peeled diced potatoes
1 teaspoon salt
½ teaspoon pepper
2 small cucumbers, peeled and seeded
1 pound cooked shrimp
1 cup cream
2 tablespoons chopped fresh dill

1. Sauté onion in butter until translucent. Add stock and potatoes, cook until potatoes are tender. Puree in blender or food processor and season with salt and pepper. Chill.

2. Coarsely chop shrimp and grate the cucumber, add to the chilled soup. Mix in the cream and dill, and taste to adjust seasoning. Refrigerate for at least 2 hours and serve in chilled cups with sprigs of fresh dill.

Santa Fe Seafood Stew

Serves 8 to 10

You can't beat the powerful aroma of this stew steaming.

6 large dried New Mexico chilies, seeded
2 large dried Ancho chilies, seeded
6 cups fish stock
2 tablespoons olive oil
1 large onion, diced
4 cloves garlic, minced
1 pound firm white fish (bass, halibut, snapper), cut into 1 inch chunks
2 dozen small hard shell clams
2 large crabs, 2 to 3 pounds, cleaned and quartered
1 pound red potatoes, diced
1 pound jumbo shrimp, unpeeled
1 tablespoon lime juice
$^1/_4$ cup chipped cilantro
lime slices for garnish

1. Soak chilies in 2 cups of fish stock for 30 minutes until softened. Place in a blender or food processor and blend to a smooth purée.
2. Heat olive oil in a large heavy saucepan, add onion and sauté for 3 to 4 minutes until translucent. Stir in garlic and cook for several more minutes; do not brown.
3. Add pureed chilies, remaining 4 cups of fish stock, fish and clams. Bring to a boil, reduce heat and simmer for 5 minutes. Add crab, potatoes and shrimp and cook until shrimp turns pink. Add lime juice, cilantro, and season with salt and pepper. Ladle into bowls and garnish with limes.

December 24th Crab Bisque

Serves 12

A tradition for holiday gatherings.

$^1/_2$ cup plus 2 tablespoons unsalted butter
2 pounds fresh lump crabmeat
2 cups whipping cream
$^1/_2$ cup Scotch
4 tablespoons flour
8 cups milk, warmed
dash of Tabasco sauce
salt and freshly ground black pepper

1. Melt $^1/_2$ cup butter in a large saucepan over medium heat. Add crab and sauté gently until heated through. Add the cream and cook until just hot, do not let the soup boil. Stir in the Scotch and remove from the heat.
2. Melt remaining 2 tablespoons of butter in a small saucepan. Add the flour and cook for 3 minutes, whisking constantly. Whisk in the hot milk, one cup at a time and continue cooking until sauce has thickened. Blend the sauce into the crab mixture, season to taste with Tabasco sauce, salt and pepper. Return to heat and warm before serving.

Tee Harbor Scallop Chowder

Serves 4

The best from a small Alaskan harbor.

4   medium potatoes, peeled and sliced (not chopped)
1   medium onion, chopped
1½ cups water
1   pound scallops (the fresher the better)
1   12-ounce can evaporated milk
6   tablespoons butter
salt and pepper
paprika

1. Place potatoes and onion in a saucepan with the water and bring to a boil. Reduce heat and simmer for 8 minutes, until the potatoes are still a little hard. Add the scallops and bring to a boil again. Cook for a few more minutes until the potatoes are done, but not mushy, and the scallops are tender but plump. Remove from heat and cool for 15 minutes.
2. Add the butter and stir until melted and add the evaporated milk; taste to adjust seasoning. Reheat, but do not boil, and serve, sprinkled with paprika. For a stronger scallop taste, make this the day before and reheat gently - a few reheats are best when you double this batch and there is a bowl left for the cook.

Montauk Mock Bouillabaisse

Serves 6 to 8

A Long Island Lighthouse specialty.

8   strips bacon, diced
1   medium onion, diced
2   cloves garlic, minced
2   1 pound 14-ounce cans whole tomatoes
1   cup white wine
2   cups fish stock (or water)
½ pound cod
½ pound bass or other firm fish
½ pound medium shrimp
½ pound scallops
1   6-ounce can chopped clams
½ teaspoon basil
1   bay leaf
salt and freshly ground pepper

In a large stockpot, sauté onion and garlic for 2 minutes. Add the remaining ingredients and cook over medium heat for ½ hour. Serve with crusty French bread.

Seafood Stew Salsa Verde

Serves 4

A meal in one dish, baked Spanish style

1 1/2 pounds haddock, bass, grouper or other
     firm white fish, cut into large chunks
12 clams
12 mussels
8 medium shrimp, cleaned
2 tablespoons olive oil
4 cloves garlic, minced
1 medium onion, finely diced
2 tablespoons flour
2 cups fish stock or clam juice
1 cup white wine
1/2 cup fresh chopped parsley
4 small potatoes
salt and pepper
1/2 cup peas

In a large ovenproof pot, sauté onion and garlic in the olive oil for 5 minutes. Add flour and blend well. Whisk in the fish stock and wine. Cook until lightly thickened. Put all of the seafood in the pot with the potatoes and parsley; season with salt and pepper. Bring to a boil and bake in a 400° oven for 25 minutes. Sprinkle with the peas before serving.

She-Crab Bisque

Serves 6 to 8

The spring tonic of South Carolinians.

2 cups blue claw crab meat - with the roe
1/4 cup finely minced scallions
1/2 cup butter
4 tablespoons flour
1 quart milk
1 teaspoon celery salt
1 tablespoon Worcestershire sauce
1/4 to 1/3 cup dry sherry, warmed
1/4 pint cream, whipped
paprika

1. Melt butter and add flour. Cook for 2 minutes over medium heat, stirring constantly. Remove from heat, add scallions, and slowly whisk in the milk until well blended.
2. Return to heat, add celery salt and Worcestershire sauce; simmer until creamy, about 10 minutes. Add the crab and cook for another 5 minutes. Spoon a little warmed sherry into individual soup cups or bowls (teacups and saucers look elegant) and top each with a spoonful of whipped cream and a sprinkle of paprika.

Seven Seas Christmas Stew

Makes 6 main dish servings

A celebration of seven different fish representing the seven sacraments.

2   tablespoons olive or salad oil
3   garlic cloves, minced
1   28-ounce can Italian plum tomatoes
2   8-ounce bottles clam juice
2   teaspoons dried parsley flakes
1   teaspoon dried basil leaves
$^1/_2$ teaspoon coarsely ground black pepper
$^1/_4$ teaspoon crushed red pepper
$^1/_2$ cup white wine
2   dozen littleneck clams
$1^1/_2$ dozen mussels
1   pound large shrimp
$^1/_2$ pound sea scallops
$^1/_2$ pound cleaned squid
$^1/_4$ pound flounder fillet
$^1/_4$ pound cod or scrod fillet
1   loaf Italian bread

Cod, "it has been calculated," wrote Alexandre Dumas, that if no accident prevented the hatchery of the eggs, and if each egg reached maturity, it would take only three years to fill the sea so that you could walk across the Atlantic Ocean on the backs of Cod.

About $1^1/_2$ hours before serving:

1. In 8-quart Dutch oven or saucepan over medium heat, cook garlic in oil until tender but not browned. Stir in tomatoes with their liquid, clam juice, parsley flakes, basil leaves, black pepper, and crushed red pepper; heat to boiling. Reduce heat to medium-low; cover and simmer 30 minutes, stirring occasionally. Add the wine.

2. Meanwhile, with stiff brush, scrub clams and mussels under running cold water to remove any sand; remove beards from mussels. Shell and devein shrimp; rinse with running cold water. Rinse scallops with running cold water to remove sand from crevices. Cut squid crosswise into $^1/_2$-inch thick slices. Cut flounder and cod into 1-inch chunks.

3. After sauce has simmered 30 minutes, add clams and mussels to pan. Over medium-high heat, cook, covered, until shells just begin to open, stirring occasionally, about 5 minutes. Stir in shrimp, scallops, squid, flounder, and cod. Over medium-high heat, heat to boiling. Cook 1 minute or until fish flakes easily when tested with fork and shrimp and scallops turn opaque throughout.

4. To serve, spoon stew into 6 large soup bowls. If you like, serve with Italian bread.

Babcock Clam Chowder

Serves 6 hungry adults

From an old recipe of my grandmother who lived in Stonington.

1   quart or more minced clams with juice
6   medium potatoes, peeled and diced
¹/₄ pound salt pork, finely diced
5   medium onions, peeled and diced
1   cup crumbled hard tack (pilot biscuit)
milk
8   tablespoons butter (1 stick)
1   pint cream
salt and pepper
paprika

1. Place potatoes in a large pot with 4 cups of water and boil until very soft. While potatoes are cooking, cook salt pork in a skillet until crisp. Add to the potatoes.
2. Add chopped onions to fat remaining in skillet and sauté until very soft, about 5 minutes. Add to the potatoes along with all of the pan drippings.
3. Soak 1 cup of crumbled hard tack in as much milk as it will absorb. Add tack and milk to the pot with the potatoes and stir well as the hard tack is prone to stick to pan. Stir in the clams and juice and simmer for 5 minutes.
4. Reduce heat, add the cream and butter, season with salt and pepper. When very hot, but not boiling, empty into a tureen, dot with more butter if desired and sprinkle with paprika. Serve with cornbread, hard tack and a salad.

Mussel Stew with Saffron and Cream   Serves 4

Be sure to provide bibs and finger bowls.

4 quarts mussels, beards removed
5 tablespoons butter
3 medium onions, chopped
1 clove garlic, minced
$^1/_2$ cup white wine
2 tablespoons brandy or cognac
pinch of saffron threads, steeped in 2 tablespoons hot water
$^1/_2$ teaspoon curry powder
pinch of cayenne pepper
salt and pepper
2 tablespoons flour
$^1/_2$ cup heavy cream
chopped parsley

1. Clean the mussels and place in a large pot. Add 2 cups water, cover and cook for 5 to 7 minutes until shells open. Discard the top shell of each and transfer to a serving dish, reserving the liquid. Keep warm (covered, in a low oven works fine).

2. Heat half the butter in a skillet. Add the onions and cook over low heat until soft and slightly brown. Add the garlic and cook another 30 seconds.

3. Pour in the wine and brandy, raise heat and ignite them. Add the saffron with its liquid, the spices and the pepper. Slowly pour in the mussel liquid, leaving behind any grit in bottom of pan. Boil to reduce for one minute.

4. Mix the remaining butter with the flour, making a paste. Just before serving, bring the mussel liquid and onions to a boil, whisk in the butter-flour mixture a little at a time, until the sauce coats a spoon. Add cream and simmer for 2 more minutes, adjust seasoning and pour over the mussels. Serve immediately with lots of chopped parsley.

Snapper Crab Stew

Serves 8 to 10

A family recipe, can be varied with shrimp or scallops.

$3/4$ cup finely chopped carrot
$3/4$ cup finely chopped celery
$3/4$ cup finely chopped onion
8 tablespoons (1 stick) unsalted butter
$1/4$ cup all-purpose flour
4 cups milk
4 cups heavy cream or half-and-half
$1/2$ bay leaf
1 tablespoon freshly ground black pepper, or to taste
1 teaspoon salt, or to taste
$1/8$ teaspoon cayenne pepper, or to taste
1 teaspoon Old Bay Seasoning, or to taste
1 tablespoon Worcestershire sauce
$1^1/2$ pounds lump crabmeat, picked over

1. In a kettle, cook the carrot, celery, and onion in butter over moderately low heat, stirring until the vegetables are softened. Add the flour, and cook the roux, stirring, for 3 minutes.
2. Add milk, cream, bay leaf, black pepper, salt, cayenne pepper, Old Bay Seasoning, and Worcestershire sauce, bring the mixture to a boil, and simmer it, stirring, for 8 to 10 minutes, or until it is thickened slightly.
3. Add the crabmeat, cook the mixture, stirring, for 1 minute, and discard the bay leaf.

Old Lyme Scallop and Corn Chowder

Serves 6 to 8

Use a fresh Niantic or other bay scallop in season.

2 tablespoons butter
1 large potato (Idaho or russet), peeled and diced to $1/2$-inch
$1/2$ cup minced onion
$1/2$ cup minced celery
$2^1/2$ cups corn, cooked if fresh, defrosted if frozen
4 cups milk
salt and freshly ground black pepper
1 pound scallops, cut in half if they are large
4 strips bacon, cooked and crumbled

1. Melt butter in a heavy pot over medium heat. Add potato, onion and celery and cook 5 minutes, stirring frequently.
2. Puree 1 cup of corn with 1 cup of milk in a blender. Add to the potato mixture in pot with remaining $1^1/2$ cups corn and 3 cups milk. Season with salt and pepper. Bring to a boil, reduce heat and simmer until potato is tender, about 20 minutes.
3. Add the scallops and cook 2 minutes until the scallops are <u>just</u> done. If made the day before, do not add the scallops until you are ready to reheat and serve. Ladle into warm bowls and sprinkle with crumbled bacon.

Nantucket Chef's Cioppino   Serves 8

From a School Street kitchen.

1   quart clams
1   cup dry red wine (such as Burgundy, Pinot Noir)
$^1/_2$ cup olive oil
1   large onion, chopped
2   cloves garlic, chopped
1   green pepper, chopped
$^1/_2$ pound mushrooms, chopped
4   ripe tomatoes, peeled, seeded and chopped
4   tablespoons tomato paste
2   cups red wine
1   teaspoon salt
1   teaspoon freshly ground black pepper
2   tablespoons finely chopped fresh basil or 1 teaspoon dried basil
1   sea bass or striped bass, about 3 pounds, cut into serving pieces, or 3 pounds thick fish fillets, cut into serving pieces
1   pound crabmeat
1   pound medium raw shrimp, shelled and deveined
3   tablespoons chopped parsley

1. Steam the clams in the 1 cup red wine until they open - discard any that do not open. Strain the broth and reserve.
2. Heat the olive oil in a deep 8-quart saucepan and cook the onion, garlic, pepper and mushrooms for 3 minutes. Add the tomatoes and cook 4 minutes. Add the strained clam broth, tomato paste, and 2 cups red wine.
3. Season with salt and pepper and simmer for about 20 minutes. Taste and correct seasoning. Add the basil and the fish, and just cook the fish through, about 3 to 5 minutes. Finally, add the steamed clams, crabmeat, and shrimp. Heat just until shrimp are cooked. Do not overcook. Sprinkle with parsley and serve.

Variations:
Cioppino with Mussels - substitute mussels for clams.
Cioppino with Oysters - substitute oysters for clams.

Seabury Clam and Corn Chowder   Serves 10 to 12

Just as popular at our Cape Cod house as in Maine.

4   cups potatoes, peeled and diced
1¹/₂ cups chicken stock
1   cup clam broth
4   slices bacon, diced
1   large onion, minced
2   cloves garlic, minced
¹/₂ red pepper, diced
¹/₂ green pepper, diced
1   stalk celery, diced
1   tablespoon Worcestershire sauce
1   tablespoon Old Bay Seasoning
1   tablespoon salt
1   teaspoon pepper
¹/₂ teaspoon thyme
3   tablespoons butter
3   cups milk
2   cups half-and-half
4   cups fresh or frozen corn
2   quarts ground quahogs

1. Bring potatoes, chicken stock, and clam broth to a boil in a large saucepan, until potatoes are just tender, about 10 minutes.
2. Cook bacon until browned, remove from pan. Add onion, garlic, peppers and celery, sauté for 5 minutes; combine with potatoes and add bacon.
3. Add seasonings, butter, milk, half and half and corn. Cook over low heat for 5 minutes. Add clams and simmer (don't boil) for another 5 minutes.

Charlotte Shrimp Bisque   Serves 8

A wonderful Deep South specialty.

¹/₄ pound (8 tablespoons) butter
1   large onion, finely diced
3   stalks celery, finely diced
2   cups water
4   cups whole milk
1   pound small-medium shrimp, peeled and deveined
1   tablespoon seasoned salt
black pepper
1   tablespoon chopped parsley
1   cup instant mashed potato flakes
paprika

1. Melt butter in a large saucepan. Add onion and celery and sauté over low heat until tender, about 5 minutes.
2. Add water and bring mixture to a boil. Add shrimp and simmer for 2 minutes. Stir in milk and seasonings, do not let boil. Whisk in the mashed potato flakes and remove from heat. The bisque will thicken as it sits. Serve hot with a sprinkle of paprika on top.

Joe's Sopa de Pescado (Spanish Style Fish Soup)   Serves 4

The recipe intends to evoke the type of fish soup served in the far northeast of Spain, but it was developed entirely by guesswork, authentic recipes not being available to me.

Despite the large number of ingredients, the cooking is very simple. The soup is a hearty dish, with a unique flavor. The liquid from the canned beans is an essential ingredient, giving body to the soup.

2   tablespoons olive oil
$^1/_2$ large Spanish onion, chopped
$^1/_2$ teaspoon sugar
$^1/_2$ green (bell) pepper, chopped
1   small hot green pepper, chopped
1   medium carrot, chopped
3   cloves garlic, chopped
$^1/_2$ cup apple juice
2   teaspoons Spanish paprika
1   teaspoon salt
1   19-ounce can white kidney beans
     ("cannellini")
1   8-ounce can tomato sauce
1   (double size) fish stock cube
2   chicken stock cubes
$^1/_4$ cup brandy
$^3/_4$ pound fresh tuna, cubed bite-size
$^1/_2$ teaspoon cracked black pepper

1. Heat oil in heavy, 4-quart saucepan. Add onion and sauté at medium heat until color begins to change; add sugar and continue to sauté until onion is golden. Dissolve stock cubes in 1 cup boiling water. Add peppers and carrot to onion. Continue to sauté, covering pan to let steam collect, but stirring frequently. When all vegetables begin to soften, add garlic. Continue to cook briefly, not letting garlic brown, then add apple juice and cook until liquid is almost completely reduced.

2. Add liquid only from canned beans, tomato sauce, paprika and salt and reduce heat. Simmer for 5 minutes, then transfer to food processor and puree for about 5 minutes until fine and smooth. Return to pan, add stock and enough water to make up about 1$^1/_2$ quarts. As the soup comes to a boil, add beans. Simmer for 20 minutes, to develop flavor and complete cooking. Add brandy, fish and black pepper, and water as necessary to make a total of 2 quarts of soup. Bring to a gentle boil and cook about 10 minutes, until fish is cooked, but still tender.

Serve with peasant style bread and wine or hard cider.

Shrimp and Kale Soup   Serves 2 to 4

This clear broth soup makes a very pretty presentation, especially in a soup plate. As a first course, in cups, the recipe will serve four; as a main course, two will eat it all.

1¹/₂ quarts water
1   teaspoon salt
3   to 4 cups fresh kale, torn in pieces, tough
      stems removed*
¹/₄ cup rice
3 chicken stock cubes
¹/₂ teaspoon onion powder
¹/₂ teaspoon ground ginger
¹/₄ teaspoon ground cumin
¹/₂ teaspoon coarse ground pepper
¹/₄ teaspoon hot red pepper flakes
¹/₂ teaspoon dried dill weed
12 medium shrimp
1¹/₂ tablespoons sherry

1. Bring water to a boil in 4-quart saucepan. Add rice, kale and salt. Dissolve chicken cubes in ²/₃ cup boiling water and add seasonings. Let rice and kale boil gently for 15 minutes, then add in the stock and seasonings. Check rice for doneness; about 15 to 20 minutes boiling time is required. When rice and kale are just tender (be careful not to overcook), add shrimp and sherry. Simmer about 1¹/₂ minutes to cook shrimp, which are done when they are pink and curled into circles.

* Kale is a fall vegetable and is rarely found in the market out of season. It can stand 15 or so minutes of boiling, but overcooking either the rice or the shrimp will ruin this soup.

Boston Baked Fish Chowder   Serves 4

Serve with plenty of Pilot crackers if available in your area.

1   pound haddock or cod fillets
2   large potatoes, peeled and sliced
¹/₄ cup celery tops
3   small onions, sliced
1   bay leaf
3   whole cloves
¹/₄ teaspoon dill seed
¹/₄ teaspoon white pepper
¹/₂ cup white wine
4   tablespoons butter
2   12-ounce cans evaporated milk
chopped parsley

1. Place all ingredients except milk and parsley in a 3-quart casserole. Bake for 45 minutes in a 375° oven until fish and potatoes are cooked through.
2. Heat milk to a simmer and pour over fish. Stir gently, ladle into bowls and sprinkle with parsley.

Around the World with a Can of Consommé   Serves 2

In Bombay:
They mix 2 teaspoons of curry with $1/4$ cup of cooked rice, spoon an equal amount into individual cups and fill with boiling hot consommé.

In California:
They bring to a boil 3 cups of consommé and 1 cup of tomato juice, 1 teaspoon sugar, $1/2$ teaspoon basil. They add to it 2 envelopes of unflavored gelatin soaked in $1/2$ cup vin rose or water. In each cup they place segments of fresh oranges, top with pink consommé, place it in the refrigerator to set. Served cold.

In China:
Just before serving, they break a raw egg into dainty transparent porcelain cups, and fill the cups with rapidly boiling consommé, and hurry to the table. It makes a particularly nice presentation when topped with a small rose or a few violets.

In England:
They top boiling hot consommé, served in cups, with small slivers of cooked beef, chicken, ham, or tongue. Prepare a mixture of 2 tablespoons parsley, add in $1/2$ teaspoon of marjoram, sprinkle a pinch in each cup.

In France:
They slice finely 6 to 8 spring onions, green and white parts. Add 2 to 4 tablespoons of sherry to boiling consommé, $1/4$ teaspoon tarragon, pour into cups and liberally garnish with the minced spring onions.

In Italy:
They place a large spoonful of finely grated Parmesan in the bottom of cups, top with 2 to 3 sprigs of rosemary and fill the cups with boiling hot consommé.

In Poland:
They bring to a boil 3 cups of consomme and drained juice of a can of shredded or diced beets and a pinch of caraway or anise seeds then place the beets in each plate and fill with boiling hot red consommé.

In Russia:
They layer tall stemmed glass with alternate spoonfuls of consommé, sour cream, and chopped greens. Top with caviar and serve with lemon.

Marty's Boatbuilding Stew

Makes about 32 servings

My wife and I have developed this recipe over the years while building wooden boats outside in the spring and fall. We have found there is no better taste than this stew and some grilled shrimp on a chilly evening while standing around a bonfire, after a hard day of boat building.

Should be served as a side dish with any outdoor seafood grilling party and is considered "brain food" for all wooden boatbuilding activities.

3 to 4 1-pound stewing hens, with bones removed, which have been slowly smoked.

3 pounds of slowly smoked beef roast (medium rare)

3 pounds of slowly smoked pork roast

1 pound of chopped garden-fresh scallions

3 pounds of white potatoes, chopped

12 medium-size fresh homegrown tomatoes (note: these need to be the darkest red available as this increases taste)

12 ears of fresh corn, cut off the cob (best to use 6 ears of yellow corn and 6 ears of white corn)

4 cups fresh green peas (or 2 10-ounce packages frozen)

4 cups fresh lima beans (or 2 10-ounce packages frozen)

2 cups fresh , coarsely chopped celery

2 cups fresh green beans, broken into very small pieces

1 large green pepper, chopped

2 cups fresh okra, cut in rounds

2 cups fresh black-eyed peas (or 2 cups frozen)

2 cups finely chopped carrots

2 turnips, finely chopped

2 small sweet potatoes, chopped

1$^1/_2$ 14-ounce bottles of catsup

1 10-ounce bottle of Worcestershire sauce

$^1/_2$ cup cider vinegar

$^3/_4$ cup lemon juice

4 teaspoons Louisiana hot sauce (not Tabasco sauce)

3 tablespoons salt

3 tablespoons pepper

1$^1/_2$ tablespoons Texas Pete hot sauce

$^1/_2$ cup sugar

1 teaspoon ground cloves

$^1/_2$ teaspoon cinnamon

1 bottle (12 ounces) Guinness Extra Stout Ale (note: it is important to use the 12-ounce bottle rather than from a can or tap)

Preparation:

1. First day smoke all the meat very slowly while adding water-soaked hickory to the 300° fire. This smoking process is extremely important.

2. Tear the chicken into very small pieces and cut up the rest of the meat very small as well.

3. Start vegetables cooking in a broth made up of chicken bouillon. I use about $^1/_3$ of a 4-ounce jar of chicken bouillon cubes in 10 cups of water. Combine first just the vegetables and broth in a large "preserving" kettle or roaster and cook until half done.

4. Add meat and all other ingredients. Bring to a boil, then immediately turn down to a simmer. Cook at a slow simmer for 8 to 10 hours being sure to stir occasionally to keep from sticking.

Caution: this stew is addicting. Can be served immediately, and any leftover can be frozen for future use.

Hint for smoking the meats... to obtain the best taste by holding in all of the natural juices, use a type of smoker called "The Big Green Egg", which is an Oriental kiln type smoker/cooker with a 3,000 year history.

Tree Trimming Soup

Serves 20 to 25

At the Palmer Inn in Noank, after a long day of decorating and entertaining, the holiday helpers are hungry. Now begins the fun of a homemade hot soup to warm us all.

4   tablespoons butter
4   carrots, chopped
4   celery stalks, chopped
5   scallions, including greens, chopped
10 cups chicken broth (6- to 13-ounce cans are fine)
6   $10^3/_4$ cans cream of potato soup
5   tablespoons picante sauce or salsa
3   cups water
2   tablespoons chopped fresh parsley
Tabasco sauce
freshly ground black pepper
8   ounces yellow sharp cheddar cheese, grated
8   ounces sour cream
3   tablespoons sherry (optional)

1. Melt butter in a large soup pot and cook carrots, celery and scallions until just tender. Stir in broth, soup, picante sauce, parsley and water. Season with a few dashes of Tabasco sauce and black pepper. Simmer over low heat for $1^1/_2$ hours, stirring frequently. This is best prepared a day ahead and chilled overnight.

2. Reheat soup slowly and add cheese, sour cream and sherry. Simmer until cheese is melted and soup is creamy. Serve sprinkled with paprika and accompanied by spiced dilly crackers or French bread.

Spiced Dilly Crackers:

This recipe is from Aunt Winky - one of the finest cooks of all times.

1   20-ounce box oyster crackers
$3/_4$ cup oil (vegetable or safflower)
1   tablespoon dill weed
2   tablespoons Parmesan cheese
1   package Original Ranch Dressing Mix

Mix oil and spices and then toss everything together. These may be made a day ahead – a great snack to take offshore packed in ziplock bags.

"While wine and friendship crown the board we'll sing the joys that both afford."
                              – John Dyer

THE BIG CATCH

Seared Scallops in Thyme Sauce   Serves 4 to 6

1½ pounds sea scallops
6 ounces bacon
1 tablespoon bacon drippings
1 medium leek, juliènned
⅓ cup white wine
2 teaspoons minced fresh thyme
2 teaspoons minced fresh parsley
1½ cups light cream
salt
white pepper

"And luscious scallops to allure the taste of rigid zealots to the delicious feast."
– John Gay

1. In a medium skillet, fry bacon until crisp. Remove from pan, drain and crumble. Reserve 1 tablespoon of bacon drippings in pan.
2. Add leeks and sauté for 2 minutes until tender. Add white wine and simmer until mostly evaporated, about 3 minutes.
3. Stir in thyme, parsley and cream and cook until slightly thickened. Season with salt and pepper, keep warm.
4. Heat a nonstick skillet or grill pan over high heat until very hot. Working in batches, sear scallops, about 2 minutes per side.
5. To serve, spoon a portion of sauce onto each plate, top with scallops and sprinkle with bacon.

Red Snapper Bake Niçoise   Serves 4

A reminder of a barge trip in the South of France.

4 6- to 8-ounce fillets of snapper
1 tablespoon olive oil
10 tiny white whole onions
4 cloves garlic, crushed
1 green pepper, sliced
1 pound tomatoes, peeled and chopped
1 teaspoon basil
1 teaspoon oregano
2 tablespoons tomato paste
½ cup white wine
20 pitted ripe black olives
4 anchovy fillets, finely chopped (optional)
4 ounces Feta cheese

1. Heat oil in a medium saucepan and add onions, garlic and green pepper. Sauté until wilted and lightly browned, 3 to 4 minutes.
2. Add tomatoes, basil, oregano, tomato paste and white wine. Remove from heat.
3. Place fish fillets in an ungreased 2 quart casserole dish. Pour sauce over the fish and bake for 15 minutes in a preheated 325° oven. Sprinkle olives, anchovies and Feta cheese over the fish and bake for an additional 10 minutes or until cheese has melted into the sauce. Serve in large bowls with sauce ladled over a bed of white rice.

Casserole of Fresh Tuna Provençal   Serves 4

4 fresh tuna steaks, 1 inch thick (about 2
    pounds)
6 medium onions, thinly sliced
8 medium plum tomatoes, peeled, seeded
    and sliced
4 lemons, peeled (save peel for another use)
    and cut the flesh into thin slices
2 tablespoons olive oil
2 heads Boston lettuce, shredded
2 cups white wine
2 bay leaves
salt and pepper
cornichons (baby French pickles)

**"In cooking fish, or fowl, or flesh
    Or any nice or dainty dish
With care peruse this useful book
    'Twill make you soon a perfect cook."
        – The Compleate English Cook: 1762**

1. In a heavy covered casserole dish, over
    medium heat, add 2 tablespoons olive oil
    and quickly brown the fish steaks on both
    sides. Remove from the pan.
2. Add half of the onion slices to the pan and
    sauté for a few minutes. Now make a "bed"
    for the fish, adding in neat layers half the
    tomato, half the lettuce and half of the
    lemon. Lay the fish on top and finish
    covering them with the same vegetable
    layers in reverse – lemons, lettuce, tomatoes
    and raw onions – ending with salt and
    freshly ground black pepper. Tuck a bay leaf
    in each corner.
3. Adjust the heat and simmer for 10 minutes.
    Add the wine and bring to a boil. Cover the
    pan and place in a 275° oven to cook
    slowly for about $2^1/_2$ hours. Serve with lots
    of crusty bread and cornichons.

Celebrity Pistachio Scrod   Serves 4

From a cruise on the *Horizon*.

4 6- to 7-ounce scrod or cod fillets
6 tablespoons softened butter
$^1/_2$ cup dry bread crumbs
$^1/_2$ cup pistachio nuts, shelled and chopped
2 teaspoons fresh tarragon
$^1/_4$ cup grated Parmesan cheese
salt
white pepper
juice of $^1/_2$ fresh lemon
$^1/_2$ cup flour
2 tablespoons olive oil
lemon wedges
tarragon sprigs

1. Combine butter, bread crumbs, pistachios,
    tarragon, and Parmesan in a small bowl and
    mix well. Season to taste with salt and
    pepper.
2. Squeeze lemon over fish fillets and dredge
    in flour on both sides. In a medium frying
    pan, sauté scrod for 4 minutes on each side
    and transfer to an oven-proof dish.
3. Top the fish fillets with the pistachio mixture
    and press down lightly. Bake in a 400° oven
    for 8 to 10 minutes until the topping is
    golden brown. Serve with additional lemon
    wedges and sprigs of tarragon.

Breed's Baked Sea Bass with Spicy Cornbread Herb Crust

Uncle Charlie's Arizona show-stopper.

Serves 8

8   6-ounce fillets of sea bass or halibut
1   large onion

Cornbread herb crust:
$^1/_2$ cup cornbread crumbs
$^1/_2$ cup dry bread crumbs
1   tablespoon minced parsley
2   teaspoons fresh thyme

Combine in a bowl and mix well.

Sundried tomato chili purée:
$^1/_2$ cup sundried tomatoes
1   lightly toasted Ancho chili pepper, seeded
    and stem removed
$^1/_2$ cup hot clam or fish stock
1   tablespoon Dijon mustard
1   teaspoon fresh lemon juice
$^1/_2$ roasted red pepper
1   tablespoon Balsamic vinegar
salt and pepper to taste

1. Combine tomatoes, chili, and clam or fish stock in a small bowl and let rest for 15 minutes to soften the tomatoes and chili.
2. Add to the blender with remaining ingredients and purée.
3. Season fish fillets with salt and pepper. Spread with tomato chili puree and top with 1 tablespoon of crust mixture per fillet.
4. Dice onion and spread on bottom of a lightly greased baking pan. Place fish on top of onions and bake in a preheated 375° oven for 15 to 20 minutes until fish is firm.

Herb Roasted Orange Salmon   Serves 4

4   8-ounce salmon fillets, skin on
2   tablespoons olive oil
$1/4$ cup fresh orange juice
finely grated zest of 1 orange
2   teaspoons minced garlic
1   teaspoon dried tarragon
1   teaspoon dried dill
pinch of salt
coarsely ground black pepper
2   teaspoons chopped chives

1. In a large bowl combine olive oil, orange juice and zest, garlic, tarragon, dill, salt and pepper.
2. Add salmon fillets and coat with the marinade. Toss the fish several times and marinate for 2 hours.
3. Place the salmon fillets, skin-side down, in an oven proof dish and pour the marinade on top. Bake in a preheated 450° oven for 10 minutes or until salmon is just cooked through. Remove to a hot serving platter and sprinkle with chopped chives.

Suffocated Sole   Serves 6

Once you try this you will keep coming back for the buttery juices.

fillets of sole, 1 or 2 per person, depending on size (about 2 pounds total)
8   tablespoons butter (1 stick)
4   medium onions
1   small bunch parsley, coarsely chopped
2   bay leaves
whole cloves
salt
freshly ground pepper

"Would it not be beneficial, were the average American to substitute fish for the everlasting steak and chop of a breakfast table?"
                    – Thomas Murray: 1888

1. Choose the right pot, preferably enameled cast iron, with an extremely tight fitting lid. Place pot on stove and melt 4 tablespoons of butter over medium heat. Add half the onion slices and half the parsley to the melted butter plus salt and pepper to taste.
2. Place the sole fillets in one layer on top of the onions. Place the remaining onion slices on top of the fillets, then the other half of the parsley. Dot with the remaining butter. Add bay leaves and 2 cloves on each fish fillet. Do not add any other liquid. The juices from the fish and vegetables will provide enough steam.
3. Bake in the center of a preheated 325° oven for 25 minutes (do not open), then check for doneness and cook another 10 to 15 minutes until fish is flaky and opaque. Serve with fresh mashed red skinned potatoes.

Clam Pan Roast with Sausage and Fennel   Serves 6

2   cloves garlic, minced
$^1/_2$ pound sweet Italian sausage, casing
    removed
$^1/_2$ pound Kielbasi cut into $^1/_2$-inch slices
12 small red potatoes, sliced
2   large bulbs fennel, trimmed and sliced
1   leek, cut in $^1/_2$-inch rounds
$^1/_2$ cup white wine
1$^1/_2$ cups clam juice
$^1/_2$ teaspoon freshly ground black pepper
$^1/_2$ teaspoon salt
3   pounds littleneck clams, scrubbed
2   large tomatoes, cut into 8 wedges each
$^1/_4$ cup coarsely chopped tarragon

"The savory adour blown
   Grateful to appetite more pleased my purse
Than smell of sweetest fennel."
              – John Milton

1. In a casserole over medium heat, cook garlic, sausage and Kielbasi until browned, about 5 minutes. Remove from pan and drain all but 1 tablespoon fat from the pan.
2. Arrange potatoes in pan and brown for 5 minutes. Turn with a spatula and brown on other side for 5 minutes. Spread fennel among potatoes and cook for 10 more minutes, stirring often.
3. Add leek, white wine, salt, pepper, and clam juice to pan. Cover with sausage mixture, add clams and cover. Cook over medium heat for 5 minutes. Add tomatoes and cook, covered until clams open, about 8 minutes. Sprinkle with tarragon and serve.

Baked Fish Cider Mill Style   Serves 4

Here in Mystic, we prefer Clyde's.

1$^1/_2$ pounds filleted firm white fish (cod,
    haddock or snapper)
3   shallots, finely chopped
1   tablespoon chopped savory
2   tablespoons chopped parsley
2   apples, peeled, cored and diced
salt and pepper
1   cup cider or apple juice
4   tablespoons butter
$^2/_3$ cup fresh white bread crumbs

1. Arrange the fish fillets in 1 layer in a well-buttered oven proof dish. Cover with the shallots, savory, parsley and apples. Season with salt and pepper. Pour over the cider or apple juice.
2. Melt the butter in a small pan and fry the bread crumbs until golden brown. Scatter over the top of fish and bake at 375° for 25 minutes until the fish is tender. Serve with crispy Johnnycakes or see Hushpuppy recipe in "Go With" chapter, page 225.

Sea Dog's Shrimp
Serves 4

1   pound cooked medium shrimp
1   lemon or lime, thinly sliced
1   small onion, thinly sliced

Marinade:
1   cup vegetable oil
$1/2$ cup cider or white vinegar
$1/3$ cup barbecue sauce
dash of Tabasco sauce
1   teaspoon Dijon mustard
1   tablespoon sugar
1   clove garlic, minced
1   teaspoon celery seeds
salt and pepper to taste

Layer shrimp, onion and lemon slices in a jar or bowl with a lid. Pour marinade over shrimp and refrigerate for 8 to 48 hours before serving. This stays well in a boat cooler for several days and tastes better the longer it sits. Serve over lettuce or in a sandwich with crusty French bread.

Warm Grilled Oriental Shrimp and Orange Salad
Serves 4

A Mason's Island summer barbeque favorite.

3   scallions, chopped
3   cloves garlic
$1/4$ cup vinegar
$1/4$ cup soy sauce
$1/4$ cup orange juice
1   tablespoon sesame oil
2   tablespoons Tabasco sauce
1   tablespoon chopped fresh ginger
$1^1/2$ pounds large shrimp, peeled
2 cups mixed salad greens
2   oranges, peeled and sectioned
1   medium red pepper, very thinly sliced
$1/4$ cup unsalted peanuts
toasted sesame seeds

1. In a food processor or blender, combine the scallions, garlic, vinegar, soy sauce, orange juice, sesame oil, Tabasco sauce and ginger. Process until smooth. Place the shrimp in a shallow baking dish and pour the marinade over it. Cover and chill for 4 hours or overnight.
2. Remove the shrimp from the marinade and grill over a hot fire for 3 to 4 minutes on each side (a grilling basket made especially for small seafood makes it easier to prevent "losing" a few shrimp through the grill).
3. Meanwhile, in a medium saucepan, bring the marinade to a boil for 10 minutes to reduce. Arrange the shrimp on the salad greens, top with the oranges and red peppers. Pour the dressing over the salad and sprinkle with peanuts and sesame seeds.

Savory Crab Cakes de Provence   Serves 6

8   ounces fresh lump crab meat
4   tablespoons butter
$^1/_3$ cup chopped scallions
1   clove garlic, minced
$^1/_2$ cup fresh bread crumbs
1   teaspoon Worcestershire sauce
1   tablespoon Dijon mustard
1   teaspoon Herbes de Provence
$^1/_4$ teaspoon white pepper
$^1/_2$ teaspoon salt
$^1/_4$ cup chopped parsley
1   egg, beaten
2   egg whites, beaten until frothy
fresh lavender

Herbes de Provence sauce:
$^1/_2$ cup chopped scallions
$^1/_2$ cup mayonnaise
$^1/_2$ cup sour cream
2   teaspoons Herbes de Provence
$^1/_4$ teaspoon salt
$^1/_4$ teaspoon white pepper

Mix all ingredients together and serve with the
  crab cakes.

1. Rinse crab meat and pick over, being sure
   to remove all cartilage. Melt 2 tablespoons
   butter in a skillet and sauté scallions and
   garlic until soft, about 3 minutes.
2. Stir in the bread crumbs, Worcestershire
   sauce, Dijon, herbs, salt, pepper, and
   parsley. Cook lightly for 3 minutes longer
   and remove from heat. Let the mixture cool.
   Gently fold in the crab, the beaten egg, and
   the beaten egg whites. Chill mixture in
   refrigerator for an hour.
3. Shape into 6 cakes. Melt remaining 2
   tablespoons butter in a medium skillet and
   sauté the crab cakes for 5 minutes on each
   side until crispy. Serve with sauce and
   garnish with sprigs of fresh lavender.

"Give me of spices, many:
And so blended that my
** palate tickles to taste them."**
** – William Shakespeare**

Fillet of Sole with Galiano Butter   Serves 6

2   pounds fillet of sole or flounder
$^2/_3$ cup slivered almonds
$^1/_2$ cup butter
$^1/_4$ cup Galiano liqueur
$^1/_4$ cup lemon juice
2   tablespoons fresh chopped dill
salt and pepper
lemon slices

1. In a large skillet, sauté almonds in butter
   until lightly toasted, push to the sides of the
   pan and add fish. Cook on one side for 5
   minutes until golden brown.
2. Turn fish, pour Galiano and lemon juice into
   pan, and baste the fish with the butter.
   Cook for 3 minutes, sprinkle with dill and
   season with salt and pepper. Arrange on a
   hot platter and garnish with lemon slices.

Red Snapper with Roasted Red Potatoes   Serves 4

1$1/2$ pounds red snapper, cut into 4 fillets (sea
    bass, cod or halibut may be substituted)
8   medium red potatoes, thinly sliced
1   onion, thinly sliced
3   cloves of garlic, minced
2   tablespoons olive oil
$1/2$ teaspoon salt
freshly ground black pepper
juice of 1 fresh lemon or 1 tablespoons lemon
    juice
1   tablespoon fresh chopped parsley
lemon wedges

1. Lightly coat a shallow roasting pan with
   nonstick cooking spray. Spread potatoes
   over the bottom of the pan, cover with
   onion, garlic, olive oil, salt and pepper. Toss
   to coat the vegetables. Bake in a 450° oven
   for 15 minutes or until potatoes begin to
   brown. Turn the potatoes and cook for
   another 10 minutes. Remove pan from the
   oven.
2. Place fish fillets, skin side down, on top of
   the potatoes. Sprinkle with lemon juice,
   parsley, salt and more pepper. Bake until the
   fish is opaque in the center, about 10 to 12
   minutes. Serve with lemon wedges.

Cane Garden Bay Sole with Bananas   Serves 4

Under the moonlight by Stanley's Welcome Bar.

8   medium fillets of sole (3 to 4 ounces per
    piece)
$1/2$ to 1 teaspoon curry powder to taste
salt and pepper to taste
$1/2$ cup flour (or enough to coat the fillets)
2   tablespoons oil
2   tablespoons butter
4   small bananas, cut lengthwise
juice of 1 lemon
1   tablespoon dark rum (optional)
2   tablespoons sliced almonds, lightly toasted
salt and pepper to taste

**Almonds, slivered and cooked, golden in butter,
are perfect on sautéed fillet of sole, served with
fresh asparagus spears.**

1. Sprinkle fish with curry powder and a pinch
   of salt and pepper. Dust fish with flour on
   both sides.
2. Heat oil in a large skillet and add 1
   tablespoon butter. Sauté fish over medium
   heat on both sides until lightly browned. Set
   aside and keep warm.
3. Add remaining 1 tablespoon of butter to
   pan and sauté bananas quickly for 1 minute.
   Put a half banana over 2 fish fillets and
   sprinkle with almonds. Squeeze lemon and
   rum, if desired, into pan and scrape up any
   pan juices to top the fish. This can be held
   in a 300° oven for up to a half hour.

Spiced Salad of "Fruits de Mer"   Serves 6

1   pound firm steak fish (swordfish, salmon, halibut, shark, etc.)
$^3/_4$ pound fresh sea scallops
$1^1/_2$ teaspoon coriander seeds
2   bay leaves, crumbled
1   tablespoon sugar
$^1/_4$ teaspoon whole allspice
$^1/_4$ teaspoon dried thyme
$^1/_2$ teaspoon black peppercorns
$1^1/_4$ cups rice wine vinegar
1   cup water
$^1/_3$ cup olive oil
5   scallions, thinly sliced
1   medium carrot, thinly sliced
Bibb lettuce
spinach leaves
minced fresh chives

1. Cut fish into 1 inch cubes and quarter scallops if they are large. Combine coriander, bay leaves, sugar, allspice, thyme, peppercorns, vinegar and water in a saucepan and simmer, covered, for 10 minutes.
2. Add the olive oil and seafood, turn heat to high. When liquid comes to a simmer, remove pan from heat. Don't cook any further even though you might be tempted. Pour ingredients into a 1 quart canning jar or other medium container and let cool. Cover and refrigerate for at least 3 days or up to 5 days, stirring periodically. To serve, arrange greens, scallions and carrots on a plate. Spoon some of the seafood salad onto the lettuce, drizzle the dressing over all and sprinkle with chives.

Starr Swordfish Portugaise   Serves 4

A Lisbon classic.

4   8-ounce swordfish steaks
3   tablespoons olive oil
1   cup chopped scallions
1   teaspoon Tabasco sauce
2   teaspoons minced garlic
3   cups chopped tomatoes or 1 28-ounce can tomatoes, drained and chopped
2   tablespoons capers
1   tablespoon red wine vinegar
1   bay leaf
2   whole cloves
1   teaspoon Worcestershire sauce
salt and pepper to taste
chopped fresh parsley

1. Sauté scallions in oil for 3 minutes until soft. Add remaining ingredients and simmer for 30 minutes, stirring occasionally.
2. Place swordfish in a large baking dish and pour over sauce. Bake in a 375° oven for 20 minutes until browned and bubbly. Sprinkle with lots of chopped parsley and whole steamed baby red potatoes.

Nast Family Salmon Patties with Caper Sauce   Serves 6

1   14-ounce can salmon or $^3/_4$ pound fresh
    salmon, cooked and flaked
1$^1/_2$ cups corn flake crumbs
2   eggs, slightly beaten
$^1/_2$ teaspoon salt
freshly ground black pepper
2   tablespoons chopped parsley
4   tablespoons minced onion
3   tablespoons butter or vegetable oil

Caper sauce:
$^1/_2$ cup sour cream
$^1/_4$ cup mayonnaise
2   to 3 teaspoons chopped capers, as you like
2   teaspoons grated onion
juice of $^1/_2$ lemon
salt and pepper

1. If using canned salmon, drain, reserving
   liquid. Remove skin and bones and place in
   a medium mixing bowl. If using fresh
   salmon, poach for 10 minutes in lightly
   salted water, cool, drain (reserving $^1/_2$ cup
   liquid) and flake.
2. Add $^1/_2$ cup corn flake crumbs, salmon
   liquid, eggs, salt, pepper, parsley and
   chopped onions. Mix thoroughly and shape
   into 12 flat patties, 2$^1/_2$ inches in diameter.
   Coat with remaining crumbs.
3. Heat butter or vegetable oil in a large frying
   pan and cook patties for 2 to 3 minutes on
   each side until golden. Drain on paper
   towels and serve with the caper sauce on
   top.

"Steamers" (Steamed Soft Shell Clams)   Serves 4 as an appetizer or 2 as an entrée

4   tablespoons ($^1/_4$ cup) unsalted butter
6   garlic cloves, or to taste, minced
4   pounds small soft-shelled clams, scrubbed
    well and rinsed well
6   scallions, chopped
1   cup milk

1. In a kettle, melt the butter over moderate
   heat and add the garlic, clams, 3 cups
   water, and the scallions. Bring the liquid to a
   boil, covered, and steam the clams, shaking
   the kettle once or twice, for 5 to 10
   minutes, or until the shells are opened.
   Transfer the clams with a slotted spoon to
   heated individual bowls, stir the milk into
   the broth remaining in the kettle, and ladle
   the broth mixture into individual bowls.
2. Serve the bowls of broth with the bowls of
   clams. To eat the clams, remove them from
   the shell, peel the dark membrane from the
   necks, and dip the clams in the broth.

Maine Blueberry-Mint Scallops   Serves 4

In Bar Harbor, we just pick the berries and mint by the kitchen door.

1$^1/_2$ pounds sea scallops
1 egg
2 egg yolks
1 tablespoon Dijon mustard
$^1/_4$ cup blueberry vinegar (raspberry may be
   substituted)
salt, fresh pepper
1 tablespoon minced fresh mint
2 cups light salad oil
fresh blueberries
mint sprigs
a variety of lettuce greens

1. Rinse scallops and place in a saucepan. Cover with water, add a pinch of salt and bring to a simmer. Cook for one minute. Remove saucepan from the heat and let scallops cool to room temperature in the poaching liquid. Drain scallops and refrigerate.

2. In a blender or food processor, combine egg, egg yolks, Dijon mustard, vinegar, salt, pepper and mint. Blend for 1 minute. With motor on, drizzle oil in a slow steady stream until incorporated. Cover and refrigerate.

3. To serve, arrange a few salad greens on a plate and mound scallops in the center. Spoon blueberry vinegar mayonnaise over and around scallops but do not mask completely. Sprinkle berries on plate and garnish with mint sprigs.

Wamphaussuc Point Bluefish Broil   Serves 4-6

1 bluefish fillet, 1$^1/_2$ to 2 pounds
2 tablespoons fresh lemon juice
2 tablespoons mayonnaise
$^1/_2$ cup Parmesan cheese
$^1/_4$ cup melted butter
3 tablespoons finely chopped onion
dash of salt
Tabasco sauce to taste
paprika
fresh dill sprigs

1. In a small bowl, mix all ingredients together, except fish, paprika and dill. Put bluefish on a baking sheet and cover with the sauce. Sprinkle with paprika.

2. In a preheated broiler, cook fish for 8 to 10 minutes, depending on the thickness, until it flakes with a fork. Remove to a serving platter and surround with dill.

**"This dish of fish is too good for any but anglers or
   very honest men."**
                                   – Izaak Walton

Smoked Salmon Salad with Caper Dill Vinaigrette   Serves 6

6   ounces smoked salmon (any other smoked
     fish may be used, tuna, trout or haddock)
12 slices French bread, $^1/_2$ inch thick
$^1/_3$ cup olive oil
2   tablespoons white wine vinegar
2   tablespoons chopped red onion
$^1/_4$ cup chopped dill
2   tablespoons capers
salt and freshly ground black pepper to taste
a variety of mixed small greens - endive,
     spinach, or mesclun
small pickled onions for garnish

1. Slice the fish very thin or flake, if it is that
   variety. Toast the baguettes until golden and
   brush with olive oil while they are still warm.
2. Whisk the remaining olive oil into the
   vinegar in a small bowl. Add the red onion,
   dill and season with salt and pepper.
3. Arrange the fish on the toasted baguette
   croutons. Top each portion with $^1/_2$
   teaspoon of the vinaigrette. Toss the
   remaining vinaigrette with the greens and
   arrange on a platter. Top with the fish
   croutons and scatter pickled onions overall.

**"To procure sleep: wash the head in a concoction
of dill seed, and smell of it frequently."**
     – The Ladies Indispensable Companion: 1854

Picnic French Tuna Baguette   Serves 6

$^1/_4$ cup olive oil
2   tablespoons red wine vinegar
1   teaspoon dried oregano
1   tablespoon chopped fresh parsley
$^1/_4$ teaspoon crushed red pepper
dash of salt
1   16-inch long loaf French or Italian bread
1   7-ounce jar roasted red peppers, drained
1   12$^1/_4$-ounce can chunk white tuna, drained
1   2-ounce can flat anchovies, drained
12 olives, black or green, sliced
4   thin slices red onion
lettuce leaves
1   tablespoon capers

1. In a small bowl, whisk together first 5
   ingredients and season with salt to taste.
   Slice bread horizontally in half and drizzle
   dressing on cut sides of bread.
2. Arrange roasted red peppers on bottom
   piece of bread, top with tuna and
   anchovies. Next, add olives, red onion and
   capers, finishing with lettuce. Put top on
   loaf and wrap tightly in foil for at least 1
   hour before slicing. This can also be lightly
   crisped up in a 325° oven for 10 minutes.

**"There, stay thy haste
And with this savory fish
Indulge thy taste."**
                    – John Gay

Curried Shrimp and Summer Vegetable Pilaf   Serves 6

1½ pounds medium shrimp, cooked, peeled,
   and deveined
¼ cup fresh lemon juice
2   small onions, thinly sliced
2   scallions with green tops, chopped
2   large tomatoes, peeled, seeded and diced
½ cup chopped cucumber
2   cloves garlic, minced
½ teaspoon dried thyme or 1½ teaspoons
   fresh chopped thyme
½ teaspoon salt
fresh ground pepper
pinch cayenne pepper
3   tablespoons butter or vegetable oil
1   teaspoon curry powder
1   6-ounce package rice pilaf mix, prepared
   according to directions, or 2 cups of your
   own recipe
½ cup petite peas
lettuce leaves

1. Toss together shrimp, lemon juice, onions,
   scallions, tomatoes, cucumber, garlic,
   thyme, salt, pepper and cayenne pepper.
   This can be done ahead and refrigerated
   overnight or up to 12 hours.
2. Prepare pilaf mix. In a separate medium
   saucepan, heat butter or oil, add curry
   powder. Simmer over low heat for 5
   minutes, stirring several times. Add pilaf,
   peas, and reserved shrimp mixture and toss.
   Serve hot or at room temperature
   surrounded by garden lettuce leaves.

Tipsy Tarragon Shrimp   Serves 4

From a Pomfret caterer.

1½ pounds medium shrimp, peeled and
   deveined
6   tablespoons butter
4   tablespoons minced scallions
2   cloves garlic, minced
2   teaspoons tarragon
2   tablespoons fresh parsley, chopped
½ cup dry vermouth
1   tablespoon capers
½ fresh lemon

1. Melt butter in a medium skillet. Add
   scallions and garlic, sauté for 3 minutes
   being careful not to brown. Add the shrimp
   and cook another 3 minutes until pink.
2. Add the tarragon, parsley and vermouth and
   reduce over high heat for a few more
   minutes. Turn off stove, toss in the capers
   and squeeze the fresh lemon over all. Serve
   with lots of white rice.

Hillandale Shrimp Jambalaya

Serves 6

From the famous Brew Kitchen.

1¹/₂ pounds large shrimp, peeled
3 tablespoons butter
¹/₂ cup chopped onion
1 clove garlic, minced
2 cups consommé
2 cups chicken broth
1 cup chopped and seeded plum tomatoes
2 tablespoons parsley - a few sprigs for garnish
¹/₈ teaspoon ground cloves
¹/₂ teaspoon thyme
1 bay leaf
¹/₂ teaspoon chili powder
¹/₈ teaspoon cayenne pepper
¹/₂ teaspoon salt
¹/₄ teaspoon pepper
1 cup uncooked long grain rice

1. Melt butter in a medium saucepan, add onion and garlic, sauté until soft. Add liquids, tomatoes, and seasonings, bring to a boil. Stir in rice, cover and simmer for 30 minutes.
2. Toss in the shrimp and cook for 10 more minutes. Put cover back on and let rest for 5 minutes before serving and garnish with parsley sprigs.

Bridge Club Hot Shrimp and Artichoke Bubble

Serves 6 for lunch or 4 for dinner

1 pound medium shrimp, peeled, tails removed
8 tablespoons butter (reserve 2 tablespoons for mushrooms)
¹/₂ pound fresh mushrooms
4 tablespoons flour
³/₄ cup milk
³/₄ cup heavy cream
¹/₄ cup dry sherry
1 tablespoon Worcestershire sauce
salt and pepper to taste
dash cayenne pepper
1 14-ounce can artichokes, drained and cut in half
paprika

1. Melt 2 tablespoons butter in a medium saucepan and sauté mushrooms for 2 minutes, set aside.
2. Add 6 remaining tablespoons of butter to pan, whisk in the flour and slowly add the milk and cream. Cook until thickened, about 3 to 4 minutes and add sherry and Worcestershire sauce. Season to taste.
3. Put artichokes in the bottom of a 2 quart baking dish, scatter shrimp on top and finish with sautéed mushrooms. Pour cream sauce into dish, sprinkle with paprika, and bake at 375° for 30 minutes.

Rollin' Sole Rolls

Serves 10

Customize this your own way.

5   large fillets of sole (4-6 ounces)
2   tablespoons butter
1   cup finely chopped mushrooms
1   cup fresh bread crumbs
$^1/_8$ teaspoon celery salt
dash of nutmeg
dash of paprika
1   teaspoon chopped chives
1   teaspoon chopped parsley
$^1/_2$ cup white wine

1. Melt butter and sauté mushrooms for 2 minutes. Add bread crumbs, seasoning and white wine and mix well.
2. Lightly butter 10 muffin cups. Cut each sole fillet in half lengthwise and line up on the counter with the white side down. Divide mushroom stuffing evenly over fillets and roll up, starting with the small end. Place one roll in each cup and lightly cover with foil. Bake at 375° for 20 minutes. To remove from pan, run a knife around each fillet and serve on individual plates. May be garnished with:
   • a plump raw oyster
   • a large cooked shrimp, butterflied
   • a dollop of hollandaise sauce, lemon wedges sprinkled with fresh parsley

Inbakad Lax – Salmon in Crust

Serves 4-6

1-1$^1/_2$ pounds salmon fillets, skinned
1   recipe for single layer pie crust or 1 refrigerated pie shell
$^1/_3$ cup melted butter
2   cloves garlic, minced
1   tablespoon tarragon
1   tablespoons chervil
2   tablespoons fresh parsley, chopped
1   lemon, cut in wedges

**"That I may reach that happy time
   The kindly Gods I pray,
For all the peas and salmon in prime
   upon the last of May?"**
                    – William Makepeace Thackeray

1. Place salmon on a lightly buttered baking sheet. Roll out pie crust to fit fillet and fold over the fish, crimping edges all around the bottom as you would do on a pie. Make several slits in the top.
2. Melt butter in a small saucepan, add garlic, tarragon and chervil. Pour over salmon in crust, brushing to cover surface. Bake in a 400° oven for 20 to 25 minutes. Let rest for 5 minutes before serving. Sprinkle with chopped parsley and surround with lemon wedges.

Mussel Coquille St.-Jacques

Serves 4

A switch from the traditional dish – superb!

2 pounds mussels
1 onion, finely chopped
2 cloves garlic, minced
2 cups dry white wine
1 teaspoon crushed peppercorns
4 tablespoons butter
4 tablespoons flour
$1/4$ cup heavy cream
salt and pepper
chopped parsley
$1/2$ cup buttered bread crumbs

1. Place onion, garlic, white wine and peppercorns in a large pot. Boil over medium heat for 10 minutes to reduce by approximately one half.
2. Meanwhile, wash mussels and remove beards. Toss them into the boiling wine, cover, reduce heat and cook for 5 minutes or until mussels open. Remove mussels and take the meats out of the shells. Strain broth into a medium bowl.
3. Melt the butter in a small saucepan, add the flour over low heat. When the mixture begins to bubble, add the mussel liquid. Cook the sauce for 5 minutes, stirring; add the cream. Stir in the mussels, season to taste with salt and pepper. Transfer mixture to 4 scallop shells or individual casserole dishes, sprinkle with parsley and bread crumbs. Broil for 1 minute until golden brown and bubbling.

Tinkers Tuna Salad Toss

Serves 4

A different take-along for the beach.

1 6 ounce can white tuna, drained
$1/3$ cup mayonnaise
2 tablespoons relish, sweet red or green
1 teaspoon mustard
$1/2$ cup celery, chopped
1 medium tomato, chopped
$1/2$ cup red onion, chopped
2 scallions, chopped
1 apple, diced
$1/2$ cup shredded cheddar cheese
2 tablespoons capers, drained
fresh ground pepper
paprika

Flake tuna in a medium bowl and add remaining ingredients. Serve on lettuce leaves, in a sandwich, or as a terrific tuna melt for a crowd.

81

Bookstore Baked Stuffed Bluefish II
Serves 6-8, depending on size of fish

Those Seaport Store gals are back at it again.

1 whole bluefish, 4 to 6 pounds
2 tablespoons butter, melted
1 cup white wine, divided

Wild rice stuffing:
4 tablespoons butter
1 small onion, minced
$^1/_2$ cup mushrooms, sliced
4 strips bacon, cooked and crumbled
1 cup cooked wild rice
$^1/_2$ teaspoon thyme
2 tablespoons fresh chopped parsley
salt and pepper to taste

1. Clean fish, leave on head and tail if you like, but remove gills. Place on a large baking sheet.
2. Melt 4 tablespoons butter in a skillet and sauté onions and mushrooms 3 to 4 minutes until lightly browned. Crumble in the bacon, toss with the cooked rice and $^1/_2$ cup white wine. Add the thyme and parsley, salt and pepper to taste.
3. Fill body of fish with stuffing and secure opening with skewers. Brush outside with melted butter and cover tightly with aluminum foil. Pour remaining $^1/_2$ cup wine into the pan. Bake at 425° for 40 to 50 minutes or until fish flakes with a fork. Serve whole fish on a large platter or plank, surrounded by more fresh parsley sprigs.

Swordfish Skewers Souvlakia
Serves 6

When the grill is long put away, a taste of summer.

2 pounds swordfish
$^1/_4$ cup olive oil
$^1/_3$ cup vermouth or dry white wine
3 tablespoons lemon juice
$^1/_2$ teaspoon salt
1 teaspoon oregano
3 cloves garlic, minced
$^1/_8$ teaspoon red pepper flakes
2 scallions, finely chopped
$1^1/_2$ cups cherry tomatoes
1 red onion, quartered and separated
$1^1/_2$ dozen fresh bay leaves, or dried which have been soaked in water to soften
1 lemon, cut in wedges

1. Mix together in a bowl the oil, vermouth, lemon juice, salt, oregano, garlic, red pepper flakes, and scallions. Cut fish steaks into $1^1/_4$ inch cubes and place in the marinade, cover and chill several hours, turning once or twice.
2. On skewers, alternate the fish, tomatoes, onion and bay leaves. Baste with the marinade and place on a broiler pan. Broil for 6 to 8 minutes on each side, basting several times. Can also be barbecued over medium hot coals. Accompany with lemon wedges when serving.

Pan-Seared Halibut with Rosemary Vinaigrette   Serves 6

2   pounds halibut or other firm white fish
    (haddock or scrod)
flour seasoned with salt and pepper
1/4 cup olive oil
1/4 cup white wine vinegar
4   cloves garlic, minced
2   teaspoons fresh rosemary or 1/2 teaspoon
    dried rosemary, crumbled
3   tablespoons butter

1. Dip fish fillets in the seasoned flour, coating both sides lightly. Heat olive oil in a large skillet and sauté the fish, turning to brown both sides. Remove to a hot platter.
2. Add vinegar, garlic and rosemary to the pan. Stirring, scrape up the drippings and let cook down slightly. Swirl in the butter until melted and spoon the sauce over the fish.

Quiambaug Quahog Hash   Serves 4

From the Quiambaug House in Mystic, a brunch specialty.

3   medium potatoes, peeled and diced
1   dozen large chowder clams or 16 ounces of
    fresh chopped clams
1   2-inch thick slab of salt pork, diced
2   stalks celery, chopped
3/4 cup chopped scallions
4   tablespoons cream
1/2 teaspoon salt
1/2 teaspoon black pepper
1/2 teaspoon thyme

1. In boiling salted water, cook diced potatoes until just tender. Drain and set aside.
2. Scrub clams under cold water. Place in a pot with 1 inch water and steam over medium heat for 15 minutes until shells open. Remove from broth, shuck clams and chop the meat coarsely. Mix with potatoes, cream and seasoning. Mix well.
3. In a heavy-bottomed skillet, fry salt pork for several minutes until lightly brown. Add celery and scallions and cook until tender. Add the potato-clam mixture and stir well to combine everything in the pan. Fry until edges are crispy and brown, turning several times. You may need to add a little oil around the edges if it begins to stick. Make sure it is crusty on both sides. Great served with catsup or tartar sauce.

Charles W. Morgan Clam Pie

Serves 4 to 6

2 8-ounce cans minced clams
4 slices bacon
1 small onion, chopped
1 unbaked 9-inch pie shell
4 eggs
1 cup heavy cream
salt and pepper

**"Unless some savory at the bottom lie,
Who cares for the crinkling of the pie?"
– William Makepeace Thackeray**

1. Drain the clams and reserve the liquid. Fry the bacon until crisp, drain and crumble. Sauté the onion in the bacon fat until just soft.
2. Sprinkle the bacon in the pie shell. Add the sautéed onion. Spread the minced clams over the onion.
3. Beat the eggs and clam liquid together. Add the cream and a pinch of salt and pepper. Beat until well mixed and pour over clams. Bake in a hot oven, 450°, for 10 minutes. Reduce temperature and bake for 25 to 30 minutes until firm to the touch. Cool slightly before cutting.

Salmon with Basil Zinfandel Sauce

Serves 4

White Zinfandel is such a rage, have plenty chilled on hand.

4 6-ounce salmon fillets
1 egg, beaten
$^1/_3$ cup milk
$^3/_4$ cup seasoned bread crumbs
2 tablespoons butter

Zinfandel sauce:
6 tablespoons butter
2 large shallots, chopped
small handful julienned basil
4 ounces white Zinfandel wine
juice of 1 lemon
6 ounces heavy cream
salt and pepper
1 tomato, seeded and chopped

1. Make egg wash by whisking together the egg and milk. Dip salmon in egg wash and lightly dredge with crumbs. Sauté in butter on medium-high heat, approximately 3 minutes on each side until golden brown. Keep warm.
2. Sauté shallots in 2 tablespoons butter until soft. Add wine, lemon juice, half the basil and let reduce until thickened. Add cream and again reduce until thickened. Remove from heat. Swirl in remaining 4 tablespoons butter, 1 tablespoon at a time, mixing thoroughly. Add rest of basil and adjust seasoning. Pour sauce over fish and garnish with chopped tomato.

Scallops with Ginger Pepper Cream   Serves 4

1¹/₂ pounds scallops
salt and pepper
3   tablespoons butter
¹/₂ cup chopped red pepper
¹/₂ cup chopped green pepper
4   tablespoons chopped shallots
¹/₂ cup white wine
1   teaspoon lime juice
2   teaspoons fresh grated ginger
1   medium tomato, seeded and chopped
6   ounces heavy cream
1   tablespoon chopped cilantro or parsley

"Yes, by Saint Anne, and ginger shall be not i' the mouth, too."   – William Shakespeare

1. Pat scallops dry and season with salt and pepper. Melt the butter in a sauté pan, add the red pepper, green pepper and shallots. Sauté 2 to 3 minutes until just soft but not browned.
2. Add the white wine, lime juice, ginger and scallops to the pan. Gently poach the scallops for several minutes until just opaque. Remove scallops from pan and keep warm.
3. Reduce the pan juices, add the cream and reduce for 2 more minutes. Stir in the tomato and scallops, season to taste and sprinkle with cilantro or parsley.

Open-Faced Tuna Niçoise Sandwich   Serves 4

Adapted from a Martha Stewart show.

4   ¹/₂-inch thick tuna steaks (4 to 5 ounces)
1   lemon
¹/₄ cup Italian parsley
3   tablespoons olive oil
4   anchovies, chopped
2   tablespoons capers, chopped
2   cloves garlic, minced
2   teaspoons fresh rosemary, chopped
1   tomato, chopped
salt and pepper
4   ¹/₂-inch slices of Italian bread, cut from the center of the loaf
chopped lettuce

1. Grate zest from lemon and squeeze juice into a bowl. Add parsley, 2 tablespoons olive oil, anchovies, capers, garlic, rosemary and tomato. Season with salt and pepper.
2. Place tuna steaks in a shallow non-reactive dish and cover with the marinade. Coat well and let stand for 1 hour, turning several times.
3. In a large skillet, heat remaining 1 tablespoon of oil. Place tuna in pan and cook over medium-high heat for 3 minutes. Turn fish over, pour marinade over top and cook for 3 more minutes, swirling the juices around in the pan.
4. Cover each slice of bread with a bed of chopped lettuce, top with tuna and spoon juices over the sandwich.

Sherried Seafood à la King

Serves 4 to 6

A New Year's Eve Noank tradition.

2$^1/_2$ cups mixed cooked seafood (scallops, crab, lobster, shrimp, etc.)
4   tablespoons butter
1   small onion, diced
1   green pepper, diced
4   tablespoons flour
1   cup milk
1   cup cream
1   teaspoon paprika
$^1/_3$ cup sherry
salt
few dashes of Tabasco sauce
4   tablespoons chopped pimento
chopped parsley
buttered toast points

1. Heat butter in a medium saucepan. Add onion and green pepper, sauté for 3 to 4 minutes until soft but not brown.
2. Stir in flour and mix well. Whisk in milk and cream, cook until thickened over medium heat, stirring constantly. Reduce heat, add sherry, seafood, seasonings and pimento. Simmer for a few minutes until sauce is pink and bubbly. Serve over toast points, and sprinkle with chopped parsley.

Bay Street Scallops Pernod

Serves 6

1$^1/_2$ pounds bay scallops
4   tablespoons butter
8   ounces mushrooms, sliced
3   tablespoons flour
1   cup dry white wine or vermouth
$^1/_2$ cup milk
1   tablespoon fresh tarragon
2   tablespoons Pernod
salt and pepper
6   prepared puff pastry shells (available in the frozen food section at most stores)
fresh parsley, chopped

1. In a medium pan, sauté mushrooms and scallops over high heat in 2 tablespoons of butter until lightly browned, about 5 minutes. Remove from pan.
2. Melt remaining 2 tablespoons of butter in pan and stir in the flour and mix well. Whisk in the wine and milk, stir until slightly thickened. Add the tarragon and Pernod, season to taste with salt and pepper.
3. Return the scallops and mushrooms to the pan and simmer lightly. Spoon into puff pastry shells and sprinkle parsley all around the plate.

Pilgrims visiting the Shrine of St. James bear scallop shells as a token of their faith. In France, the shellfish is known as "Coquille Saint-Jacques."

Baked Shrimp Tacos Tampico

Serves 6

Best served with Spanish rice and an avocado salad.

3 tablespoons oil plus 2 tablespoons for frying tortillas
1 pound medium shrimp, peeled and deveined
4 small red bliss potatoes or other waxy potato, cooked and diced
1 medium onion, thinly sliced
1¼ pounds tomatoes, seeded and chopped, or 2 cups of canned, drained and crushed
1 4-ounce can diced green chilies
2 tablespoons chopped parsley or cilantro, plus extra sprigs for garnish
1 teaspoon cumin
salt and pepper
12 6-inch round corn tortillas
²/₃ cup sour cream
1 cup grated Monterey Jack or cheddar cheese

1. Heat 3 tablespoons of oil in a large skillet, add shrimp and potatoes. Cook over medium-high heat for 4 to 5 minutes until shrimp are cooked and potatoes lightly browned. Remove mixture to a bowl.

2. In the same pan, add the onion to the remaining drippings and cook for 5 minutes. Add the tomatoes, chilies, parsley or cilantro, cumin and salt and pepper; simmer for 10 minutes and adjust seasoning if you need to. Add a few spoonfuls of the sauce to the shrimp potato mixture just to coat.

3. Heat the remaining 2 tablespoons oil in a skillet and fry the tortillas, one at a time, lightly on both sides. Drain well.

4. Put a large spoonful of the potato-shrimp mixture on each tortilla. Roll up loosely. Put a little of the tomato sauce on the bottom of a 9-by-13-by-3 inch baking dish and spread around. Place the tacos over all. Top each taco with a dollop of sour cream and sprinkle the cheese on top. Bake for 20 minutes in a 375° oven until heated through and bubbling. Take care not to overcook or let sit too long - the tacos should be soft but not disintegrating. If you make this ahead, wait to finish with the sauce, sour cream and cheese right before baking. Garnish with parsley or cilantro sprigs.

Take-Along Seafood Casserole

Serves 6

Perfect when you need a traveling entrée.

$^1/_2$ pound cooked shrimp or lobster
$^1/_2$ pound scallops
$^1/_2$ cup mayonnaise
$^2/_3$ cup milk
1   10$^1/_4$-ounce can cream of shrimp soup
$^1/_2$ pound mushrooms, sliced and sautéed in 1
    tablespoon butter
1   tablespoon fresh basil, chopped
1   tablespoons fresh parsley, chopped
salt and pepper
2   cups very thin egg noodles, uncooked
$^1/_2$ cup grated cheddar cheese

1. In a large bowl, mix mayonnaise, milk and cream of shrimp soup. Add mushrooms, seafood, seasonings and noodles. Pour into a lightly-buttered 2 quart casserole, cover and refrigerate overnight.
2. Before baking, remove casserole from refrigerator and let come to room temperature. Sprinkle with cheddar cheese and bake at 350° for 45 minutes.

Castilla Tuna Salad

Serves 6 to 8

Best made in the morning to take on the boat or to a picnic.

2   6-ounce cans white tuna, drained
12 stuffed green olives, chopped
1   cucumber, seeded and chopped
2   tomatoes, seeded and chopped
$^1/_3$ cup chopped red onion
1   green pepper, chopped
2   cloves garlic, minced
2   tablespoons chopped parsley
salt and pepper
2   tablespoons olive oil
1   tablespoon red wine vinegar
lettuce leaves
hardboiled egg
capers

1. Flake tuna in a large bowl. Add olives, cucumber, tomatoes, red onion, pepper, garlic, parsley, toss with olive oil and vinegar. Add a little more olive oil depending on your taste and season with salt and pepper.
2. Serve very cold on lettuce leaves. Garnish with hard-boiled egg and sprinkle with capers.

Crispy Curried Shrimp

Serves 4

1½ pounds large shrimp, peeled and deveined
4 tablespoons flour
2 teaspoons curry powder
¼ teaspoon cayenne pepper
salt to taste
4 tablespoons olive oil
2 bunches scallions, cut into 2-inch pieces
lemon wedges

**"Our shrimps to swim again as when they lived,
in a rare butter made of dolphin's milk
whose cream does look like opals."**
– Ben Johnson

1. In a bowl, mix flour, curry powder, cayenne pepper and salt. Add the shrimp and toss to coat well.
2. In a large heavy skillet, heat oil over moderately high heat and sauté shrimp about 3 minutes. Toss in the scallions and sauté for 2 more minutes until everything is nicely browned and tender. Serve shrimp with lemon wedges and fluffy white rice.

Topsy Turvy Tuna Bake

Serves 8

3 6-ounce cans white meat tuna, drained
2½ cups macaroni (elbows or shells)
3 tablespoons butter
½ cup minced onion
1 green pepper, chopped
2 cloves garlic, minced
salt and pepper
3 cups grated sharp cheddar cheese (8 ounces)
3 eggs, beaten
¾ cup milk
2 tablespoons chopped parsley

**"Where so ready a nature its cookery yields
    Macaroni and Parmesan grows in the fields:
Little birds fly about with a true pheasant taint
    And the geese are all born with a liver
        complaint."**
– The Land of Cocagne

1. Cook macaroni according to package directions, drain.
2. Melt butter in a small saucepan and sauté onion, green pepper and garlic until soft; season with salt and pepper.
3. In a large bowl, toss macaroni with cheese and add tuna. Mix in sautéed onion, pepper, and garlic and pour into a lightly greased 2 quart casserole. Pack mixture down gently.
4. Combine beaten eggs with milk and pour over macaroni. Bake in a 350° oven for 1 hour until macaroni is golden and custard is set. Cool for 15 minutes before serving. Enjoy!

Saugatuck Salmon in Pastry Extravaganza

Serves 6

1   1½-2 pound salmon fillet, cut into 6 pieces about 2 inches by 4½ inches, skinned
1   10-ounce package spinach, washed, stems removed
1   17-ounce package frozen puff pastry sheets, thawed and chilled
1   egg, beaten with 1 tablespoon water
6   large sprigs of fresh dill

Dijon Dill sauce:
4   tablespoons Dijon mustard
2   tablespoons white wine vinegar
1   tablespoon fresh dill, chopped
1   tablespoon sugar
⅓ cup vegetable oil
salt and pepper

Whisk all ingredients together in a small bowl, season with salt and pepper to taste and serve with the salmon.

a samon pye

"Take a joule of samon season it with peper, salt, and ginger; cloves, and mace, and butter; so bak it tender, then draw it; and fill it with butter and eat it when it is cold with vineger; but if you eat it hott; put in a caudle of verjuce, egge, butter, and suger."

– **Lady Sheldons Receipt: The Compleat Cook**

1. Bring 2 cups of water to a boil in a large skillet. Add salmon and poach for 5 minutes. Remove from pan with a slotted spatula, remove skin and chill. This may be done the day before.
2. Place spinach in a medium saucepan with ¼ cup of water, cover and lightly wilt for 2 minutes. Drain well.
3. Cut both sheets of puff pastry on the fold lines as you unwrap it, making 6 long pieces. Cut a 1-inch piece off of each end, make a fish shape with a sharp knife.
4. On a lightly floured surface, roll out pastry into a rectangle long enough to enclose each piece of fish. Wrap or "encloak" the salmon fillets in the spinach leaves, top with a sprig of dill and wrap in the puff pastry sheets. Crimp the edges to seal well and place each packet on a lightly-greased baking sheet, seam side down. Brush egg wash mixture on top and "glue" pastry fish on each. Bake in a preheated 400° oven for 25 minutes until golden brown. Serve with Dijon Dill sauce under each fillet.

Schooner *Heritage* Fish Bake

Serves 4-6

"I do it for the glory," quotes the chef.

2   pounds fish fillets (haddock or cod)
1   tablespoon fresh chopped parsley or 1
    teaspoon dried
1   tablespoon fresh chopped rosemary or 1
    teaspoon dried
1   tablespoon fresh thyme or 1 teaspoon dried
black pepper
3   tablespoons butter
1   cup dry white wine
lemon wedges

1. Lightly butter a baking pan just large
   enough to hold the fish (about 9-by-13
   inches). Place fish in pan and sprinkle with
   herbs and lots of freshly ground black
   pepper.
2. Dot the fish with butter and pour the wine
   around fish. Bake in a 400° oven for 15 to
   20 minutes, depending on the thickness of
   fish. Serve with parslied boiled potatoes.

**"Of all the fish that swim or swish
in ocean's deep autocracy,
There's none possess such haughtiness
as the codfish artistocracy."**
– Wallace Irwin

Shrimp Under Fire

Serves 6

Broil some fresh pineapple slices to serve with this dish.

2   pounds large shrimp, peeled and deveined,
    leaving tails intact
4   tablespoons butter
$1/3$ cup dark rum, plus 2 tablespoons for
    igniting
$1/4$ cup minced parsley
1   tablespoon lemon juice
2   cloves garlic, crushed
$1/2$ teaspoon salt
$1/8$ teaspoon freshly ground black pepper

1. Cut shrimp lengthwise, not quite through
   and butterfly or flatten slightly.
2. Melt butter in a large skillet. Add $1/3$ cup of
   rum, parsley, lemon juice and garlic. Add
   shrimp and sauté for 4 to 5 minutes until
   shrimp turns pink. Splash remaining 2
   tablespoons rum over shrimp, season with
   salt and pepper, shake pan and ignite
   immediately at the table. Swirl shrimp in the
   pan and spoon over white rice.

Halibut in Chili Lime Sauce

Serves 4

A creative Spice Islands combination.

4   6- to 8-ounce halibut fillets (sea bass, old wife or similar firm white fish)
2   tablespoons olive oil
4   celery stalks, chopped
1   large onion, chopped
1   cup white wine or stock
1   28-ounce can whole tomatoes
2   4-ounce cans chopped green chilies
$1/4$ cup fresh lime juice
grated zest of one lime
$1/4$ cup chopped parsley
4   cloves garlic, minced
pinch of dry basil
freshly ground pepper
Tabasco sauce
parsley sprigs for garnish
lime slices

1. Heat olive oil in a deep large skillet over medium heat. Add celery and chopped onion. Cook until soft, about 5 minutes, do not brown.
2. Increase heat, add wine or stock, tomatoes, chilies, lime juice and zest, chopped parsley, garlic, basil and pepper. Reduce heat and simmer for 30 minutes. Slide the fish into the pan and simmer gently until cooked through, 9 to 10 minutes per 1 inch of thickness. Garnish with lime slices, sprinkle with Tabasco, and top with parsley sprigs.

Downeast Clam Hash

Serves 6

Makes a hearty Sunday brunch.

2   cups peeled and chopped potatoes
$1/4$ cup butter
1   medium onion, minced
2   cups chopped cooked clams (big, meaty quahogs are best)
salt and freshly ground black pepper
$1/2$ cup heavy cream
chopped parsley

1. Boil potatoes in salted water for 5 minutes until just slightly tender, drain.
2. Melt butter in a large heavy skillet and sauté onion until lightly browned. Add potatoes and clams; mix well. Press mixture down in pan and let it brown for 10 minutes.
3. Pour cream over and let it settle in. Cook hash over very low heat for 15 minutes. Serve with either cocktail sauce, tartar sauce or topped with a poached egg. Sprinkle with chopped parsley.

Majestic Connecticut River Shad Bake

Serves 6

When May rolls around, every Saturday there is a "Shad Plank" in either Old Saybrook or Essex, Connecticut. The shad, caught the night before, are nailed to thick oak planks, and held in place with strips of salt pork. The fishermen build an oak bonfire and set the planks in the sand with the fish facing the flames – then the tall stories begin. And, of course, the Connecticut River shad roe is considered the world's best.

1   3-pound dressed shad, boned and cleaned
1   pair shad roe
$^1/_2$ pound crabmeat
2   slices white bread, crumbled
salt and pepper
2   tablespoons butter
1   medium onion, thinly sliced
4   strips bacon
fresh chopped parsley

1. Wash and dry fish thoroughly, place in a shallow foil-lined baking pan (this helps the clean-up). Open fish.
2. Mash roe, spread over bottom of cavity. Cover with the crabmeat and bread crumbs. Dot with butter and season with salt and pepper.
3. Close fish over stuffing and sprinkle top of fish lightly with salt and pepper. Place onion slices, then bacon strips on top of fish; loosely cover with foil. Bake in a 350° oven for 45 to 50 minutes or until fish flakes nicely with a fork.

Starr Scalloped Scallops

Serves 6

This is an easy impressive holiday or company dish for special occasions. It can be made larger or smaller as you wish.

1   cup soft fresh bread crumbs
1   cup finely crushed Ritz cracker crumbs
$^3/_4$ cup melted butter
scallops or oysters, at least 2 quarts
salt and pepper
nutmeg
$^1/_2$ cup cream

1. Mix bread crumbs, cracker crumbs and butter. Put half on bottom of an 8-by-13 inch casserole. Place scallops or oysters on top of bread crumbs, sprinkle with salt, pepper and a little nutmeg.
2. Pour cream around edges of casserole, not directly on top of scallops. Sprinkle with remaining crumbs and bake at 350° for 45 minutes.

Sea Bass en Papilotte

Serves 6

An exquisite party presentation for any whole medium sized fish.

1   2$^1/_2$ to 3-pound bass, gutted and cleaned, leave the head on if you wish
1   head leaf lettuce, shredded
2   tablespoons olive oil
salt and pepper
sprigs of fresh basil
1   cucumber, peeled and cut into balls
$^1/_4$ cup dry vermouth or white wine
$^1/_2$ cup heavy cream
2   tablespoons chopped parsley

**"In ordinary life you must be economical;
When you invite guests, you must be lavish!'
– Chinese Proverb**

1. Spread a large sheet of heavy duty foil on a baking sheet. Cover half of it with lettuce and sprinkle with olive oil, season with salt and pepper. Top with the fish and push the basil sprigs inside the body cavity.
2. Surround the fish with the cucumber balls, sprinkle the fish with wine and pour cream on top. Season with a bit more salt and pepper, garnish with parsley, and fold the foil over to enclose the fish completely, pinching the edges firmly to seal. Cook in a 350° oven for 30 to 45 minutes, depending on the size of the fish. Bring the foil fish package to the table and open it in front of your guests. The aroma is intoxicating!

Bengal Shrimp Curry

Serves 4

A curried-citrus flavor makes this an interesting main course.

16 large shrimp, peeled, deveined and butterflied, leaving the tail on
4   tablespoons butter
2   tablespoons cognac or brandy
grated rind of 1 orange
juice of 1 orange plus $^1/_2$ cup
2   tablespoons brown sugar
1   tablespoon curry powder
$^1/_2$ cup chopped scallions
pinch of salt and pepper

1. Melt butter in a skillet and sauté shrimp for 3 minutes until pink. Add cognac and carefully ignite, stir in orange rind.
2. In a small bowl, combine orange juice, brown sugar, curry powder, scallions, and salt and pepper. Mix well and pour over the shrimp.
3. Cook until sauce has reduced slightly, being careful not to overcook the shrimp. Serve over couscous or white rice.

Salmon in Pyjamas

Serves 6

An original adaptation from a favorite English inne.

6 5-ounce salmon fillets, skinless (about 6-by-2-by-1-inch)
12 sheets of puff pastry (if frozen, defrost)
8 tablespoons butter (1 stick)
2 large red peppers, julienned
1 large leek, white and pale green parts only, cut into match stick-size strips
1/2 cup dry white wine
1/2 teaspoon crushed red pepper
1/2 teaspoon salt
1/2 cup thinly cut fresh basil

"He raiseth ramparts of immortal crust."
– Ben Johnson

1. Melt 2 tablespoons butter in a large skillet over medium-high heat. Add peppers and leek and sauté until just tender, about 5 minutes. Add wine and crushed red pepper to skillet. Simmer until liquid evaporates, season with salt and stir in basil. Remove from heat.
2. Melt remaining 6 tablespoons butter in a small pan. Place one sheet puff pastry on work surface (keep remaining sheets under a damp dish towel). Brush with some of the melted butter, top with second sheet and brush with butter. Place one salmon fillet on pastry sheet, 5 inches from short end. Top with 1/4 cup of the vegetable mixture.
3. Fold 5 inch end section of puff pastry over the salmon and fold in sides. Roll up, forming a rectangular packet. Place on a large baking sheet and brush all over with melted butter. Repeat with remaining pastry sheets, salmon fillets, vegetables and melted butter. Can be prepared up to 6 hours ahead, covered and refrigerated.
4. Bake in a 400° oven for 35 to 40 minutes until pastry is golden brown and salmon is cooked through.

Fresh Salmon in the Oven

A quick idea.

In a glass casserole, barely cover the bottom with half white wine and half water. Place salmon down, brush top with oil or butter, salt and pepper, dill if you like, and cover with any kind of lettuce leaves. This is the secret. For 1 pound of salmon, bake at 400° for 18 minutes. It's great for company because it can be prepared in advance. Serve by itself or with any sauce such as dill sauce. Try it once and you'll be hooked!

Chili of the Sea
Serves 4

An after-the-race favorite at Off Soundings.

1 1-pound 12-ounce can chopped tomatoes
$^1/_2$ cup catsup
1 medium onion, diced
1 medium green pepper, diced
2 cloves garlic, minced
1 cup clam juice
1 teaspoon Tabasco sauce
1 tablespoon chili powder
2 teaspoons cumin
$^1/_2$ pound medium shrimp
$^1/_2$ pound crabmeat
2 4-ounce cans chopped clams
salt and pepper to taste
hot cooked white rice

1. Simmer tomatoes, catsup, onion, green pepper, garlic, clam juice and seasonings in a medium saucepan for 15 minutes, stirring several times.
2. Add the shrimp, crabmeat and chopped clams, simmer for 10 minutes. Season with salt and pepper. Serve over hot rice.

Green Goddess Shrimp
Serves 4

From a fabulous and famous Stonington hostess.

$1^1/_2$ pounds large shrimp, peeled and deveined
slice of lemon
pinch of salt
2 tablespoons olive oil
1 small onion, minced
2 cloves garlic, minced
1 cup minced parsley
$^1/_4$ cup white wine
pinch of saffron
cayenne pepper
12 pitted green olives, chopped
$^1/_2$ teaspoon Dijon mustard
juice of $^1/_2$ lemon
1 teaspoon wine vinegar
$^1/_3$ cup olive oil

1. Cook shrimp in salted water with lemon slice and salt for 4 minutes until pink. Drain, rinse under cold water and set aside.
2. Heat olive oil in a saucepan and sauté onion and garlic until soft. Add the parsley, wine, saffron, cayenne pepper, and the 12 chopped olives. Simmer for 3 minutes and purée in a blender or food processor.
3. Make the vinaigrette. Mix mustard, lemon and vinegar well, whisk in the oil until thoroughly blended. Slowly add the olive-parsley mixture to the vinaigrette, whisking as you combine them. Pour over the shrimp and chill for at least 2 hours. Serve over crispy salad greens.

Salmon Melt in Avocado Half   Serves 6

$^1/_2$ cup mayonnaise
2   tablespoons lemon juice
1$^1/_2$ cups salmon, cooked and flaked
1   tablespoon capers, chopped
2   hardboiled eggs
$^1/_2$ cup cheddar cheese, shredded
3   large avocados, halved and seeded
lemon juice
$^1/_2$ cup fresh bread crumbs
1   tablespoon melted butter
fresh garden greens

1. Mix mayonnaise with lemon juice in a small saucepan. Add salmon, capers, eggs and cheese; heat through.
2. Brush avocados with lemon juice and fill with the salmon mixture. Combine bread crumbs with melted butter, sprinkle over filled avocado halves. Place under the broiler until crumbs are lightly browned. Serve on a bed of fresh garden greens.

"Rivers, bound to the Artic,
Journey many a day,
A shoreline gift with eddies,
Where speckled salmon play."
Author Unknown

The Anchorage Shrimp Thermidore   Serves 4 to 6

1   cup long grain rice
6   tablespoons butter
1   pound medium shrimp, peeled and
     deveined
1   cup very thinly sliced celery
1   cup mushrooms, quartered
4   tablespoons flour
1   teaspoon salt
dash pepper
1$^1/_2$ cups half-and-half
$^1/_2$ cup grated cheddar cheese
paprika

1. Place rice in a medium saucepan. Add 2 cups water, cover and cook, without stirring, for 20 minutes.
2. Meanwhile, melt butter in a large sauté pan. Add shrimp, celery and mushrooms. Cook until shrimp is pink and vegetables are just tender, about 5 minutes, remove from pan.
3. Add flour to the remaining butter in the pan along with salt and pepper. When well blended, whisk in the cream and cook until thickened. Gently fold in the shrimp, peppers and mushrooms.
4. Pour the rice into a lightly buttered 2$^1/_2$ quart casserole, cover with shrimp mixture and cheese. Dust with paprika. Bake at 350° for 25 minutes until bubbly and brown.

Crab and Peppers Mesclun   Serves 4

2¹/₂ cups crabmeat
6   tablespoons olive oil
¹/₂ cup thinly sliced green pepper
3   red peppers, thinly sliced or 2 4-ounce jars
    roasted red peppers
2   tablespoons chopped scallions
2   tablespoons tomato sauce
¹/₂ teaspoon salt
Tabasco sauce
2   tablespoons chopped fresh parsley

1. Heat olive oil in a large skillet. Add peppers and scallions, sauté for 3 minutes. Stir in the tomato sauce, salt and Tabasco sauce. Cook for 3 minutes.
2. Gently fold in the crabmeat and simmer for 10 minutes, stirring occasionally. Sprinkle with parsley and serve with, or on top of, boiled root vegetables - tiny potatoes, carrots, yams, etc.

Shrimp with Cajun Tabasco Butter   Serves 4

Serve this over freshly cooked grits that have been flavored with chopped scallions.

8   tablespoons (1 stick) butter, at room
    temperature
¹/₄ cup chopped fresh chives or scallions
4   teaspoons crab boil, ground in a spice
    grinder or food processor
1¹/₂ teaspoons Tabasco sauce
dash of salt
1   cup sliced red onion
1   red or green bell pepper, sliced
1   to 1¹/₄ pounds large shrimp, peeled and
    deveined
¹/₃ cup vermouth

1. Prepare the Cajun butter by mixing butter, chives or scallions, crab boil, Tabasco sauce and a dash of salt. This may be prepared 2 days ahead, covered and refrigerated.
2. Melt 2 tablespoons Cajun butter in heavy large skillet over medium-high heat. Add onion and bell pepper and sauté until almost tender, about 5 minutes. Push vegetables to side of skillet and melt 2 more tablespoons of Cajun butter. Add shrimp and sauté until just cooked through, about 3 minutes. Mix shrimp and vegetables together and season with salt.
3. Divide shrimp among plates, add vermouth to skillet and boil 1 minute. Gradually whisk in remaining Cajun butter until just melted. Pour sauce over shrimp.

Hot Crab Croque Monsieur   Serves 6

Great for brunch, lunch, or a light supper.

12 slices white bread, crusts removed
2 cups lump crabmeat
6 thick slices fresh tomato
6 slices Swiss cheese
3 eggs, lightly beaten
2 cups milk
1 teaspoon Worcestershire sauce
1 tablespoon chopped parsley
salt and pepper to taste

1. In a greased 9-by-13-inch baking dish, place 6 slices of bread. Spread the crabmeat evenly over bread slices, top with tomatoes, cheese and remaining bread.
2. Combine eggs, milk and seasonings. Pour over sandwiches, cover and refrigerate for at least 2 hours or as long as overnight. Bake at 350° for 30 minutes until puffed and brown.

"Bread and cheese be two targets against death."
– William Shakespeare

Braised Cod with Golden Onions   Serves 4

Team the cod with mashed sweet potatoes.

4 6-ounce cod fillets
3 tablespoons butter
2 large onions, thinly sliced
$^1/_2$ teaspoon dried thyme, crushed
1 bay leaf
salt and pepper
$^2/_3$ cup whipping cream
$^1/_2$ cup dry white wine
2 tablespoons chopped fresh chives

**"And this is good old Boston
    The home of the bean and cod,
Where the Lowells talk only to Cabots,
    And the Cabots talk only to God."**
– Fannie Farmer

1. Melt butter in heavy medium skillet over medium-high heat. Add sliced onion and cook until golden and soft, stirring frequently, about 10 minutes. Add thyme and bay leaf to skillet and cook until mixture is fragrant, about 1 minute.
2. Season cod fillets with salt and pepper and place on top of onions. Add whipping cream and white wine and swirl skillet to blend liquids. Bring liquids to simmer. Reduce heat to medium-low. Cover skillet and braise cod fillets until just cooked through, about 7 minutes.
3. Using spatula, transfer cod fillets to medium-size platter. Boil sauce until slightly thickened, about 1 minute. Season fish to taste with salt and pepper. Discard bay leaf. Spoon sauce over fish. Garnish with chopped chives and serve.

Pan-Fried Grenoble-Style Haddock   Serves 2

Such simple ingredients – the texture contrast is elegant.

2 1-inch slices French bread, toasted, buttered and cut into $1/2$ inch croutons
1 large lemon
2 6 to 8-ounce haddock fillets (or scrod)
$1^1/2$ tablespoons flour
$1/4$ teaspoon salt
1 tablespoon vegetable oil
4 tablespoons butter
1 tablespoon capers
chopped fresh parsley

1. Toast French bread and set aside. Cut lemon in half and section flesh as you would a grapefruit, dice coarsely.
2. Dredge fish in flour and sprinkle with salt. In a medium size skillet, heat oil and 2 tablespoons butter until just sizzling and add the fish. Cook for 4 to 5 minutes until golden brown; turn and crisp the remaining side. Top the fish with the lemon dice, add the remaining 2 tablespoons of butter to the pan along with the capers and croutons. Sauté for 30 seconds to heat through and serve on warm plates, spooning the caper butter and croutons over the fish. Sprinkle with lots of parsley before serving.

Crispy Crumbed Herb Flounder   Serves 2

From the files of an Herb Society of America member.

1 pound flounder fillets, or 2 pieces per person
$1^1/2$ cups fresh bread crumbs
$1/2$ teaspoon salt
freshly ground black pepper
1 teaspoon dried thyme
1 teaspoon dried oregano
1 teaspoon dried dill
1 tablespoon dried parsley
1 teaspoon garlic powder
2 eggs, beaten, or $1/2$ cup egg substitute
2 tablespoons butter or margarine
2 tablespoons vegetable oil
$1/2$ cup white wine
4 orange slices, halved, twisted and secured with a parsley sprig

1. Place bread crumbs, salt, pepper, thyme, oregano, dill, parsley and garlic powder in a food processor. Grind until blended but still coarse. Place on a shallow plate.
2. Dip the flounder into the beaten egg and then in the seasoned crumbs. Heat the butter or margarine and oil in a large skillet and add the flounder. Cook over medium heat for 4 to 5 minutes on each side until crispy and brown. Pour the wine around the sides of the pan, swirl to mix well. Serve the flounder with the wine butter poured on top. Garnish with orange slices.

Swordfish in Maltese Caper Sauce

Serves 4

2 pounds swordfish steaks, cut into 4 serving pieces
4 tablespoons olive oil
3 large onions, very thinly sliced
1 pound plum tomatoes, coarsely chopped
$1/2$ cup tomato paste
2 tablespoons chopped fresh parsley
4 tablespoons capers, drained
1 tablespoon fresh lemon juice
salt and freshly ground black pepper

1. Heat 2 tablespoons olive oil in a sauté pan and cook the onions for 10 minutes until golden brown. Add the tomatoes, cook for 15 more minutes, stirring occasionally. Mix in the tomato paste, parsley, capers, lemon juice and season with salt and pepper.
2. Meanwhile, heat the remaining 2 tablespoons olive oil in another large skillet, add the swordfish steaks and cook over medium-high heat until cooked to taste, 4 to 5 minutes per side, depending on thickness. Serve the swordfish with the caper sauce ladled on top and accompany with Canary rice.

Canary rice:
1 lemon
1 teaspoon butter or olive oil
1 cup long-grained white rice
$1/2$ teaspoon ground dried turmeric
2 cups chicken stock or water
2 tablespoons chopped fresh parsley

Grate the rind and squeeze the juice of the lemon. Over low heat, melt the butter or oil in a saucepan. Stir in the rice and turmeric and sauté until the rice grains are transparent, about 3 minutes. Add the stock or water, lemon rind, lemon juice and cover. Bring to a boil, reduce heat to low and steam for 15 minutes. Fluff with a fork, sprinkle with parsley and serve with the swordfish.

Baked Bluefish au Poivre

Serves 4

So simple, the best bluefish ever.

4 6-ounce bluefish fillets, skinned
4 tablespoons fresh lemon juice
2 cloves garlic, minced
1 teaspoon olive oil
salt to taste
1 tablespoon cracked black peppercorns
4 slices lemon
parsley for garnish

1. Place bluefish in a 9-by-14 inch baking dish. Sprinkle 2 tablespoons of the lemon juice over fish, rub with a little garlic and oil. Press half of the peppercorns into the fish.
2. Turn fillets over and repeat on the other side. Place a lemon slice on each piece of fish and bake for 20 to 30 minutes at 400°, depending on the thickness of the fish. Garnish with parsley and pour the pan juices on top.

Sea Scallops in Tomato Garlic Cream   Serves 4

1¹/₂ pounds sea scallops
4   tablespoons butter
4   cloves garlic, minced
3   plum tomatoes, diced
1   cup heavy cream
salt and white pepper
¹/₂ cup flour
¹/₂ cup fresh chopped watercress plus sprigs for
garnish

**"An exquisite and poignant sauce, for which I'll
say unto my cook, 'There's gold, go forth and be a
knight'."**

– Ben Johnson

1. Sauté garlic in 2 tablespoons butter over low heat. Do not brown. Add the tomatoes and sauté for 2 minutes. Add cream, salt and pepper and simmer until sauce has thickened, about 5 minutes.
2. Season scallops with salt and pepper and toss with the flour. Using a separate large skillet, melt remaining 2 tablespoons of butter and brown the scallops for 3 to 4 minutes, depending on the size of the scallops. Stir scallops several times, but do not overcrowd the skillet. Pour the tomato sauce over the scallops, add the watercress and heat until warm. Serve immediately and garnish with watercress sprigs. This dish is excellent with buttered pasta or egg noodles.

Tuna "on the Slate"   Serves 4

In Italy the tuna is seared directly on a thin piece of slate over an open fire.

4   tuna steaks, 6-8 ounces
extra virgin olive oil
salt and freshly ground black pepper
1¹/₂ cups fresh bread crumbs
1   lemon, quartered
¹/₃ cup flat leaf Italian parsley

1. Rub tuna steaks with oil and season generously with salt and pepper. Dredge on both sides with bread crumbs and refrigerate for 1 hour.
2. Heat a large heavy skillet or griddle over high heat for 3 minutes.
3. Add fish, reduce to medium and cook for 2 to 3 minutes until nicely browned, turn and season again with salt and pepper. Continue cooking for 4 to 6 minutes until tuna is just cooked through. The secret to this dish is a quick hot sear so that the fish is still a little pink. Place steaks on plates, squeeze lemon over each and sprinkle with chopped parsley.

Clam Pizza Puttanesca

Makes 8 6-inch pizzas

"The Lady of the Night"

1 recipe pizza dough, or other commercially bought dough
corn meal
4 cups thinly sliced plum tomatoes (8 tomatoes)
$^1/_2$ pound shucked fresh clams (about 4 dozen) or 2 10-ounce cans, drained
6 tablespoons capers, drained
1 2-ounce can anchovies, rinsed and coarsely chopped
$^1/_3$ cup ripe black olives, chopped
$^1/_2$ teaspoon red pepper flakes
1 cup grated Parmesan cheese
olive oil

1. Preheated oven to 500° or the highest setting. Place a pizza stone or an inverted baking sheet on the lowest rack of the oven. Divide dough into eight pieces and form into rounds.
2. Arrange $^1/_2$ cup tomatoes over each round of dough. Sprinkle with $^1/_4$ cup clams, 2 teaspoons capers, 1 teaspoon anchovies, 1 teaspoon olives and a pinch of red pepper. Top with the Parmesan cheese. Drizzle with olive oil.
3. Working 2 at a time, place pizzas on a cornmeal dusted pizza wheel or another baking sheet. Carefully slide pizzas onto the heated pizza stone or baking sheet and bake 12 to 14 minutes or until the bottom is crisp and brown. Repeat with remaining dough and toppings.

Quick Rise Pizza Dough:

This can be done in a food processor to cut down on kneading time.

4 $4^1/_4$ cups all-purpose white flour
2 packages Rapid-Rise yeast
2 teaspoons salt
1 teaspoon sugar
2 teaspoons olive oil
$1^3/_4$ cups water

In a large mixing bowl, stir together 3 cups flour, yeast, salt and sugar. In a small saucepan, heat $1^3/_4$ cups water and oil, until hot to the touch. With a wooden spoon, gradually stir the oil and water mixture into the flour. Beat until well mixed. Gradually add enough of the remaining flour to make a firm, soft dough. Turn onto a lightly floured surface and knead 8 to 10 minutes, or until smooth and elastic. Cover with plastic and let rest for 10 minutes before forming pizzas. (The dough can be made ahead, punched down, enclosed in a large plastic bag and refrigerated overnight. Bring to room temperature before using).

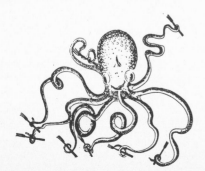

Lemon Piccata Bluefish

Serves 4

A Mystic angler's secret.

2 pounds fresh bluefish fillets
8 tablespoons butter (1 stick)
1 medium onion, finely chopped
$^1/_2$ cup celery leaves, finely chopped
juice of 2 lemons
$^1/_2$ teaspoon salt (optional)
$^1/_8$ teaspoon cracked black pepper
2 tablespoons chopped fresh parsley
2 tablespoons capers, drained
paprika
lemon wedges

1. Lightly grease or spray with nonstick cooking spray a 9-by-14-inch baking dish. If on the boat, line dish with foil and then spray for a quick clean-up. Place fillets, skin side down, in prepared pan.
2. Melt butter in a small saucepan and sauté onion and celery until tender, add lemon juice. Simmer for 1 minute and season with salt and pepper. Add parsley and capers and cook for another minute. Pour butter over fish and bake in a 400° oven for 15 to 20 minutes until fish flakes with a fork. Sprinkle with paprika and serve with lemon wedges.

Scallop Bake Provençal

Serves 4

As served on a canal vacation.

1$^1/_2$ pounds scallops
$^1/_2$ cup flour
salt and pepper
2 tablespoons butter or olive oil
2 cups diced tomatoes, drained
$^1/_4$ cup chopped scallions
2 cloves garlic, minced
$^1/_2$ cup dry white wine
2 tablespoons chopped fresh parsley
$^3/_4$ cup bread crumbs
$^1/_2$ cup Parmesan cheese

1. Toss scallops with flour, salt and pepper in a bowl. Heat butter or oil in a skillet and sauté scallops for 4 minutes or until nicely browned.
2. Add tomatoes, scallions, garlic, wine and parsley and simmer over medium-high heat until sauce has thickened, another 3 to 4 minutes. Pour into a lightly greased 2-quart casserole, sprinkle with bread crumbs and cheese. Brown under a preheated broiler until bubbly and browned. If not serving immediately, this can be finished in a 425° oven for 10 minutes.

Shrimp in Coconut Milk with White Rice (Camarones con Coco)   Serves 6

This recipe comes from the northern part of Colombia where I grew up. In those days, the fresh coconut would be split with a machete, the meat removed and grated by hand to squeeze out the milk. I have adapted the recipe to today's busier times.

White rice:
3   cloves garlic
2   tablespoons light vegetable oil or olive oil
2   cups long-grain rice
3   cups water
salt

1^1/$_2$ tablespoons light vegetable oil or olive oil
3   cloves garlic, peeled and mashed
1   cup dry white wine (optional)
2^1/$_2$ teaspoons sea salt
1   teaspoon white pepper
1   14-ounce can unsweetened coconut milk
1^1/$_2$ pounds large shrimp, peeled and deveined
1^1/$_2$ tablespoons fresh lime juice
3   tablespoons fresh cilantro, chopped

1. In a pot, sauté garlic in oil. Do not brown the garlic (garlic can become bitter tasting if it's browned). Add the rice and immediately add water. Add salt to taste, stir well and bring to a boil over high flame. Boil until the water has evaporated from the surface. The rice will be moist and pock marks will show at the surface. Turn the heat down as far as it will go without turning it off. If necessary, place the pot on a trivet over the heat. Cover and let it steam for 20 minutes. Do not remove the cover. Do not stir during this time. After 20 minutes, remove the cover and stir the rice with a fork. It should be dry, light and puffy. If it is soggy or wet, you have used too much water.

2. Meanwhile, prepare shrimp. Heat the oil and garlic in a sauté pan for a minute. Do not brown the garlic. Add wine, salt, pepper, and coconut milk and simmer very slowly for about 3 minutes. Add lime juice and shrimp. Cook and stir over a low flame until the shrimp turn pink, about 3 to 5 minutes. Do not overcook! Stir in the cilantro and serve immediately over fluffy white rice. A salad of lettuce, red onion and orange and a red wine vinaigrette go well with this dish.

3 Fast Ways to Fix Fish for One

Use 4- to 6-ounce fish fillet or steak of your choice, season and microwave on high 4-5 minutes until opaque. Let stand, covered, 2 minutes.

Mexican: Top fish with 1 tablespoon bottled salsa. Sprinkle with 1 tablespoon shredded cheddar or Monterey Jack cheese. Microwave as above, covered with waxed paper.

Deviled: Top fish with 1 tablespoon creamy mustard blend (like Dijonnaise). Sprinkle with 2 teaspoons seasoned dried bread crumbs, then with paprika. Microwave covered with waxed paper.

Amandine: Cook fish covered with plastic wrap. In 1-cup glass measure, microwave 1 tablespoon sliced almonds and 1 teaspoon margarine or butter on High $1^1/_2$ to 2 minutes until browned, stirring halfway through cooking. Stir in 1 teaspoon lemon juice, spoon over fish.

Monkfish Medallions Americaine   Serves 6

A classic dish - "poor man's lobster"

$2^1/_2$ to 3 pounds monkfish, trimmed and cut
    into 2-inch thick pieces
$^1/_4$ cup olive oil
4 small onions, thinly sliced
4 shallots, minced
2 cloves garlic, minced
4 tablespoons cognac or other brandy
1 $2^1/_4$-ounce can tomato paste
1 $13^1/_4$-ounce can plum tomatoes, crushed
1 cup white wine
1 teaspoon thyme
1 bay leaf
salt and freshly ground black pepper
cayenne pepper
chopped parsley for garnish

1. Heat the oil in a large saucepan. Add the onions, shallots and garlic and cook until softened. Add the monkfish and cook over high heat until browned, turning once. Add the cognac and ignite, shaking the pan.
2. Mix the tomato paste with the crushed tomatoes and wine. Pour over the fish and add the thyme, bay leaf, salt, pepper and cayenne pepper to taste. Cook over gentle heat for 15 to 20 minutes until the fish is tender. Discard the bay leaf and spoon the monkfish and sauce into a warmed serving dish and sprinkle with parsley.

Sherried Rosemary Shrimp   Serves 4

1½ pounds medium shrimp, unpeeled
⅓ cup olive oil
2   tablespoons fresh rosemary, chopped
¼ teaspoon oregano
6   cloves garlic, chopped
salt and pepper to taste
1   cup sherry
¼ cup chopped parsley

1. Heat olive oil in a skillet and add rosemary, oregano, garlic, salt and pepper. Add shrimp and sauté over high heat, stirring constantly for 3 to 4 minutes until pink.
2. Pour sherry over shrimp, add wine and cover for 5 minutes, reducing heat. Ladle into bowls with lots of the shrimp broth and sprinkle with fresh parsley.

Camden Cold Curried Apple Shrimp   Serves 6

1½ pounds large shrimp, peeled and deveined
1   cup white rice
6   scallions, chopped
salt and pepper
2   medium-size apples
4   tablespoons butter
1   large onion, chopped
3   stalks celery
4   tablespoons flour
2   tablespoons curry powder
2   cups chicken broth
⅓ cup light cream
½ cup toasted almonds
chopped parsley
chutney

1. Cook shrimp in a pot of boiling salted water for 3 minutes until just firm and pink. Cool immediately under cold running water, drain and set aside.
2. Cook rice in 2 cups of water, covered for 15 minutes. Remove to a bowl. When cooled, toss with scallions and season with salt and pepper.
3. Peel and core apples, cut into ½-inch chunks. Melt 2 tablespoons butter in a saucepan, add apple, chopped onion and celery. Sauté for 3 to 4 minutes until soft. Add remaining 2 tablespoons of butter to pan, stir in flour and curry powder. Over medium heat, add chicken broth and simmer for 10 minutes, stirring occasionally. Cool and place in a blender or food processor. Process for 30 seconds until smooth but still a little chunky. Add cream and combine well. Adjust seasoning with salt and pepper if needed. This may all be done ahead and refrigerated.
4. To serve, pile shrimp in the center of a large chilled platter and surround with cold rice. Pour part of the sauce over shrimp and serve with toasted almonds and chopped parsley and add a dash of chutney on the side.

Broiled Scrod with Blue Cheese Melt   Serves 4

4   6-ounce scrod fillets, or other firm white
    fish (haddock, halibut, etc.)
$^1/_2$ cup dry vermouth or white wine
1   tablespoon melted butter or margarine
dash salt and pepper
$^1/_2$ cup fresh bread crumbs
4   tablespoons crumbled blue cheese
1   tablespoon minced fresh chives
lemon wedges

1. Place fillets in a glass dish, pour vermouth over the fish and marinate for 1 hour. Drain off vermouth.
2. Coat a broiler pan with cooking spray and place fish on the pan. Brush with melted butter, sprinkle with salt and pepper. Broil fish 4 inches from heat source for about 5 minutes. Turn fillets over, top with bread crumbs, sprinkle with chives and cheese. Broil for an additional 3 to 5 minutes until fish is golden and cheese is bubbly. Serve with lemon wedges.

Sherried Shrimp and Chilies   Serves 4 to 6

From the Mexican pavillion – an Epcot vacation.

$1^1/_2$ pounds medium shrimp, peeled and
    deveined
1   cup flour
1   teaspoon salt
$^1/_2$ teaspoon black pepper
$^1/_2$ cup peanut oil
3   green jalapeño chilies, seeded and cut into
    matchlike strips 1-inch long and $^1/_8$-inch
    thick
1   medium red pepper, cut into julienne strips
$^1/_2$ cup pale dry sherry
2   tablespoons finely chopped fresh parsley
lime wedges for garnish

1. Combine flour, salt and pepper in a paper or plastic bag. Add shrimp and shake to coat evenly. Remove the shrimp from the bag and shake to dust off excess flour.
2. Heat oil in a large skillet over medium heat until a light haze forms. Add the shrimp and sauté for 4 to 5 minutes until lightly browned. Stir in the chilies and peppers, tip the skillet and pour in the sherry. Carefully ignite and slide pan across the heat until the flames die down. Serve with white rice, sprinkle with parsley and garnish with lime wedges.

Sunday Shrimp and Cheese Strata
Serves 6

A wonderful brunch or luncheon dish, served with a fresh fruit salad always is a hit.

8   slices good quality white bread
1   cup grated cheddar cheese
1   pound small or medium shrimp, cooked, peeled and deveined
$1/2$ cup chopped green pepper
6   tablespoons melted butter
4   eggs, beaten
$1/2$ teaspoon dry mustard
$1/2$ teaspoon salt
$1/4$ teaspoon pepper
1   teaspoon Worcestershire sauce
2   cups milk

1. Tear bread into bite-size pieces. Lightly grease a 2-quart casserole and layer shrimp, green pepper, bread cubes and cheese. Pour melted butter over the top.
2. In a bowl, lightly beat the eggs with the dry mustard, salt, pepper, Worcestershire sauce and milk. Pour the mixture over the casserole, cover with plastic wrap and refrigerate for at least 3 hours or as long as overnight.
3. Bake in a preheated 350° oven for 25 to 35 minutes until puffed and browned.

Senate Seafood Lasagna
Serves 6-8

From the kitchen of our State Representative from Mystic - a hit on election night.

1   medium onion, chopped
2   tablespoons butter
1   8-ounce package cream cheese
1   egg, beaten
1   15-ounce container ricotta cheese
$1^{1}/_{2}$ teaspoons basil
$1/8$ teaspoon black pepper
$3/4$ pound scallops
$1/2$ pound cooked shrimp (reserve 4)
$1/2$ pound crab meat
2   10-ounce cans cream of mushroom soup
$2/3$ cup white wine
$1/2$ cup grated Parmesan cheese
9   lasagna noodles, cooked and drained
$2/3$ cup shredded mozzarella cheese

1. Melt butter in a large saucepan and sauté onion until just soft. Stir in cream cheese, egg, ricotta cheese, basil and pepper and cook 2 minutes until cream cheese has melted down. Remove from heat.
2. Chop scallops if large and combine with shrimp, crabmeat, soup, wine and Parmesan; mix well.
3. Arrange 3 noodles in a 9-by-12-by-1-inch baking dish and cover with seafood mixture. Layer 3 more noodles and top with the cheese mixture; finishing with the remaining 3 noodles. Sprinkle with mozzarella and remaining 4 shrimp, cut in half to make 8 pieces. Cover with foil and bake at 325° for $1^{1}/_{4}$ hours. Let stand for 15 minutes before serving.

Oriental Sesame Shrimp Salad   Serves 10

This may also be made by substituting grilled or poached chicken breasts (4 whole breasts, skinned and cut into $1/4$-inch wide strips).

2   pounds shrimp, cooked, peeled and deveined
1   sweet red pepper, cored, seeded, and cut into julienne strips
1   small jicama, peeled and cut into julienne strips
1   can (5 ounces) water chestnuts, drained and halved
5   scallions (green onions, white part and 2 inches green), cut into julienne strips
4   dozen snow peas, trimmed, stringed, and blanched briefly in boiling water
$3/4$ cup toasted cashews
2   tablespoons minced fresh parsley plus sprigs for garnish
2   cloves garlic, minced
$1/2$ cup bottled teriyaki sauce
$1/4$ cup sesame oil
$1/4$ cup safflower oil
2   tablespoons sesame oil
2   tablespoons rice vinegar
2   tablespoons dry sherry
1   tablespoon brown sugar
2   teaspoons ground coriander
few drops hot chili oil (optional)
3   tablespoons toasted sesame seeds
1   10-ounce can Oriental baby corn, drained, for garnish

1. In a large bowl, combine pepper, jicama, water chestnuts, scallions, peas, cashews, shrimp and chopped parsley.
2. Whisk remaining ingredients until well blended and pour over shrimp mixture. Toss well and refrigerate for at least 2 hours. When ready to serve, mound on a lettuce lined platter surrounded with baby corn and sprigs of parsley.

Baked Haddock à la Ritz Carlton   Serves 6 to 8

Mother has won 5 prizes over the years with this simple recipe. In 1939, at the age of 19, she had just started working at Shawmut Bank in Boston. She would stay in town after work and walk downtown to the Boston Edison Night Cooking School for 7 o'clock classes and back over to North Station for the last train back to Melrose.

3   pounds haddock fillets
4   tablespoons butter
2   eggs, beaten
1   teaspoon salt
dash of pepper
2   tablespoons fresh lemon juice
$^1/_2$ cup finely chopped onion
$^1/_2$ cup chopped dill pickle
paprika
1   pound Brussels sprouts, cooked
1   bunch sliced beets, cooked, peeled and
    sliced

Place fillets in a lightly buttered 2-quart baking dish. In a small saucepan, melt the butter and remove from heat. Whisk in the eggs, salt, pepper, lemon juice, onion and pickle. Spread mixture evenly over the fish. Sprinkle with paprika and bake for 30 minutes in a 375° oven until bubbling. Serve on a warmed platter with a border of cooked buttered Brussels sprouts and sliced beets.

Eva's Swedish Fish Casserole   Serves 4

From a cousin in Sweden – her specialty.

4   6 to 8-ounce cod fillets
2   tablespoons butter or margarine
2   large onions, chopped
$^3/_4$ cup mayonnaise
3   cups cream
$^2/_3$ teaspoon brown mustard
$^1/_2$ cup chopped parsley, reserve some for
    garnish
salt and pepper
$^2/_3$ cup fresh bread crumbs
paprika

1. Place cod in a lightly greased 2-quart casserole. Melt butter in a saucepan and sauté onions until soft. Add mayonnaise, cream, mustard and parsley. Season to taste with salt and pepper.
2. Pour sauce over fish and sprinkle with bread crumbs and paprika. Can be assembled early in the day and refrigerated. Bake in a hot 375° to 400° oven for 25 minutes until bubbly and brown. Sprinkle with reserved chopped parsley and serve simply with boiled or mashed potatoes, as this has lots of sauce.

Alex's Butterflied Coconut Shrimp

Serves 4

Always asked for on those home-from-college weekends.

1 pound large shrimp, peeled and deveined, leaving tail on
¼ cup flour
½ teaspoon salt
½ teaspoon dry mustard
1 egg
2 tablespoons cream of coconut (cream may be substituted)
¾ cup flaked coconut
½ cup bread crumbs
oil for frying (peanut oil is best, as it does not smoke)

1. Split shrimp along back side (the curved side). In one bowl, combine flour, salt, and dry mustard. In another bowl, beat egg and combine with cream of coconut.
2. Mix coconut and bread crumbs. Dip each shrimp first into flour mixture, then egg and coat with the coconut crumbs. Refrigerate until ready to cook.
3. Heat 2 inches of oil in a deep skillet (about 350°). Add half the shrimp and fry for 2 minutes, turning once. Do not crowd the pan. Cook remaining shrimp and drain on paper towels. Keep warm in oven until ready to serve with a bowl of Oriental Chive dressing for dipping.

Oriental Chive dressing: Makes 1 cup
3 tablespoons soy sauce
½ teaspoon Tabasco sauce
2 cloves garlic, crushed
½ teaspoon sugar
½ cup olive oil
1 tablespoon sesame oil
2 tablespoons rice or white vinegar
2 tablespoons chopped fresh chives
½ teaspoon ground black pepper

Whisk all ingredients together in a bowl until consistency is smooth. This makes a wonderful accompaniment to other dishes such as chicken, pasta salads, and as a dip for crisp vegetables.

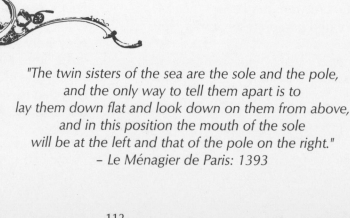

*"The twin sisters of the sea are the sole and the pole,
and the only way to tell them apart is to
lay them down flat and look down on them from above,
and in this position the mouth of the sole
will be at the left and that of the pole on the right."
– Le Ménagier de Paris: 1393*

Pan Seared Red Snapper in Ginger Broth   Serves 2

Serve this in those oversized blue and white Chinese soup bowls.

2 6-ounce red snapper fillets (or other white fish), with skin on
$1/2$ medium bok choy
2 teaspoons Asian sesame oil
2 teaspoons vegetable oil
1 carrot, scored lengthwise and cut into thin "pennies"
1 $1/2$ inch piece of ginger root, peeled and minced
1 clove garlic, minced
$1/4$ cup white wine
2 cups low salt chicken broth
1 teaspoon sugar
2 scallions, cut into 2-inch julienne strips
$1/2$ teaspoon cornstarch
$1/2$ teaspoon curry powder
fresh cilantro sprigs

1. Cut leaves from bok choy stalks, keeping leaves and stalks separate. Slice leaves thin and cut stalks diagonally into $1/2$-inch slices.

2. In a large heavy saucepan, heat 1 teaspoon of each oil together over moderately high heat until hot but not smoking and stir-fry bok choy stalks, carrot, garlic and ginger root 1 minute. Add wine, broth and sugar and simmer, covered, 5 minutes. Add bok choy leaves and scallions and simmer, covered, 3 to 5 minutes, or until tender. Season broth with salt and pepper and keep warm, uncovered.

3. Pat fish dry and rub cornstarch and curry powder into skin of each fish fillet. Halve each fish fillet on the diagonal.

4. In a 9-inch nonstick skillet, heat remaining 2 teaspoons oil together over moderately high heat until hot but not smoking and sauté fish, skin sides down and pressing flat occasionally with a metal spatula, until golden, about 2 minutes. Turn fish and sauté until just cooked through, about 2 minutes more. Divide broth and vegetables between 2 bowls and top with fish, skin sides up. Garnish each serving with coriander sprigs.

Isle of Tresco Mackerel

Serves 4

Prepared from what was on board while sailing the Isles of Sicily.

4 fillets of mackerel, Spanish, East Coast or Wahoo
2 tablespoons olive oil
1 onion, diced
1 cucumber, peeled, seeded and chopped
$1/2$ cup cream
1 cup beer
1 teaspoon chervil
1 teaspoon tarragon
1 tomato, chopped
dash of Tabasco sauce

1. Heat olive oil in a large skillet and brown fish on both sides for 3 to 4 minutes. Remove from pan. Add onion and cucumber, sauté until translucent. Stir in cream, beer, seasonings and tomato. Bring mixture to a medium simmer and add browned fish. Cook for 10 minutes, basting until mackerel flakes with a fork.

"Mackerel scales and mares' tails make lofty ships carry low sails."
— **John Irving**

Old World Stuffed Calamari

Serves 6 to 8

Always a part of our Italian holiday menu.

2 to 3 pounds small squid, cleaned
$1/2$ cup olive oil
2 medium onions, chopped
8 cloves garlic, chopped
1 tablespoon each fresh oregano, basil, salt and freshly ground black pepper
1 28-ounce can crushed tomatoes with sauce
1 6-ounce can tomato paste
2 cups water
2 cups fresh bread crumbs
$1/2$ cup grated Parmesan or romano cheese
$2/3$ cup chopped fresh parsley, plus sprigs for garnish
2 eggs, beaten

1. Heat half the oil ($1/4$ cup) in a heavy saucepan and cook onions and 6 cloves garlic over medium heat until soft. Add oregano, basil, salt and pepper, tomatoes, tomato paste, and water; simmer for 1 hour, stirring occasionally.
2. Meanwhile, combine bread crumbs, cheese, eggs and remaining garlic and parsley; mix well. Season with a little salt and pepper and stuff squid with bread crumb mixture. Secure tops with toothpicks.
3. Heat remaining olive oil in a large skillet and brown squid on both sides, about 3 to 4 minutes (do this in small batches). Drain on paper towels. When all the squid is cooked, add to the tomato sauce and cook for 20 minutes longer. Garnish with parsley sprigs and serve over hot pasta or polenta.

Shirley's Seafood Supreme

Serves 6 to 8

From an old friend – a 20 year favorite.

1   pound medium shrimp, peeled and
     deveined
$^1/_2$ pound lobster meat or crab
$^3/_4$ pound sea scallops
8   tablespoons butter
$^1/_4$ cup flour
$1^1/_2$ cups milk
2   tablespoons dry vermouth
salt and pepper
1   cup fresh bread crumbs
$^1/_3$ cup Parmesan cheese
paprika

"Crowd not your table;
    Let your number be
Not more than seven,
    Never less than three."
        – William King

1. Melt 4 tablespoons butter in a skillet, add seafood and sauté for 2 minutes. Sprinkle flour in pan, mix well, and slowly stir in the milk. Cook over medium heat for several minutes until sauce has thickened. Add the vermouth and season to taste with salt and pepper. Pour into a lightly greased 2- to 3-quart casserole.
2. Melt remaining 4 tablespoons of butter, add bread crumbs to pan and brown lightly. Mix with the cheese and spread on top of the seafood mixture. Sprinkle generously with paprika and bake at 350° for 20 to 25 minutes. Serve with a green salad, crusty bread and a nice dry white wine.

Smoky Broiled Spanish Mackerel

Serves 6

This is equally good cooked in a hinged wire grill basket over a charcoal fire.

2   pounds Spanish mackerel fillets
$^1/_3$ cup soy sauce
3   tablespoons melted butter or margarine
1   tablespoon liquid smoke
2   cloves garlic, minced
$^1/_2$ teaspoon ground ginger
freshly ground black pepper
parsley sprigs for garnish

1. Rinse and dry fish. Skin fillets and cut into serving-size portions. Combine remaining ingredients and mix well.
2. Place fish on a well-greased broiler pan and brush with sauce. Broil about 3 inches from the source of the heat for 4 to 5 minutes. Turn carefully and brush with the sauce. Broil for 4 to 5 minutes longer, basting with the sauce. Remove to a warm platter and garnish with parsley.

Fisher's Island Seafood Casserole

Serves 6 to 8

A festive buffet entrée.

3/4 pound fresh sea scallops; if large, cut in half
1/2 pound medium shrimp, peeled and deveined
1/2 pound crabmeat (fresh or frozen)
6 tablespoons butter
1 small onion, finely chopped
1/4 cup flour
1 teaspoon salt
1/8 teaspoon white pepper
1 to 1 1/2 teaspoons Old Bay seasoning
1 1/2 cups milk
2 tablespoons dry sherry
1 1/2 cups fresh bread crumbs
1/3 cup shredded cheddar cheese

"The true essentials of a feast are only fun and food." — **Oliver Wendell Holmes**

1. Melt 4 tablespoons butter in a saucepan and sauté onion for 2 minutes. Add scallops, shrimp and crabmeat, cook for another 3 to 4 minutes. Remove from pan with a slotted spoon, leaving butter and juices behind. Stir flour, salt, pepper and Old Bay Seasoning into butter and slowly whisk in the milk. Cook until thickened, remove from heat and add sherry.
2. Gently fold the seafood into the sauce and either spoon into a large casserole or individual baking dishes or shells. Melt the remaining 2 tablespoons butter and mix with bread crumbs and cheese. Top casserole with crumb mixture and bake in a 350° oven for 20 to 25 minutes until browned and bubbly. May be held in a low oven for up to an hour before serving.

Finnan Haddie Delmonico

Serves 4

1 pound finnan haddie fillets (smoked haddock)
2 cups heavy cream
2 tablespoons butter
1 teaspoon lemon juice
cayenne pepper
4 sliced hard-boiled eggs
toast points
minced parsley
paprika

"It was a glorious supper. There were kippered salmon, and Finnan Haddock, and a lambs head." — **Charles Dickens**

1. Poach finnan haddie in simmering water for 5 minutes, drain and flake.
2. Combine cream, butter, lemon juice and cayenne pepper to taste in a saucepan and heat to a simmer. Add fish and hard-boiled eggs. Cook gently for 5 minutes.
3. Place toast point (at least 4 per person) in large soup bowls and spoon fish overtop. Sprinkle with parsley and paprika. Serve to an appreciative audience with side dishes of boiled new potatoes and asparagus.

Brazilian Broiled Shrimp (Camaroes a Paulista)   Serves 4

An adaptation from a trip to the coastal town of Sao Paulo.

1¼ pounds jumbo shrimp (16) peeled and deveined
2   teaspoons olive oil
½ teaspoon salt
¼ teaspoon freshly ground black pepper
½ cup fresh lime juice (3 limes)
1   small onion, minced
2   cloves garlic, minced
1   tablespoon minced cilantro, plus few sprigs for garnish
shredded lettuce

1. Toss shrimp, oil, salt and pepper. Arrange on a foil-lined baking sheet.
2. Mix lime juice, onion, garlic, and cilantro in a medium-size bowl, set aside.
3. Broil shrimp 4 inches from the heat for 2 minutes on each side until just pink and opaque. Immediately toss with the lime juice mixture and serve warm on a bed of shredded lettuce, garnished with cilantro leaves.

Acorn Squash Shrimp Boats   Serves 2

From Marblehead with style.

1   large acorn squash
3   tablespoons butter or margarine
2   tablespoons brown sugar
2   tablespoons dry sherry
salt and freshly ground black pepper
¾ pound medium shrimp, peeled and deveined
1   small onion, diced
¼ teaspoon dry mustard
¼ cup grated sharp cheddar cheese
¼ cup grated Parmesan cheese

1. Cut squash in half lengthwise (bow to stern), scrape out seeds, and place in a shallow baking dish. Mix brown sugar and sherry and divide between the squash halves. Dot each with 1 tablespoon butter and season with salt and pepper. Cover tightly with foil and bake in a 375° oven for 45 minutes or until meat is soft. Baste once or twice during cooking time.
2. Melt 2 tablespoons of butter and sauté onion until soft, about 5 minutes. Add shrimp and cook until pink. Stir in dry mustard and cheddar cheese, cooking until cheese is melted. Pile mixture into squash halves and top with Parmesan cheese. Return to oven and bake until bubbly and brown.

Savory Shrimp with Cheese Grits   Serves 8

From a Cambridge kitchen to summer in Niantic.

1¹/₂ pounds cooked medium shrimp (if frozen, defrost)
1¹/₂ cups grits
1   cup grated cheddar cheese
salt and pepper
¹/₂ pound butter (2 sticks)
8   ounces mushrooms, sliced
2   bunches scallions, chopped
1   carrot, sliced
4   tablespoons flour
2   cups vegetable broth
chopped parsley
8   slices bacon, cooked until crisp, drained and crumbled

1. Cook grits according to package directions. Add 1 stick of butter, cheddar cheese, and salt and pepper to taste. Place in a double boiler to keep warm.
2. Make a roux: in a small saucepan, melt 4 tablespoons of butter. Add flour and cook several minutes, stirring constantly. This should have bubbled but not browned. Add broth and cook until thickened.
3. Melt remaining 4 tablespoons of butter in a large saucepan and sauté mushrooms, scallions and carrot until tender. Add shrimp and sauce; cook until heated through, about 4 to 5 minutes. Serve shrimp over hot grits, sprinkle with parsley and garnish with bacon.

Ginger Soy Scallops   Serves 4

A part of our favorite Oriental dinner with fried rice and vegetable egg foo yong.

1   pound sea scallops
2   tablespoons soy sauce
1   tablespoon dry sherry
2   teaspoons cornstarch
2   tablespoons chopped fresh ginger
2   tablespoons vegetable oil, preferably peanut oil
3   cloves garlic, chopped
¹/₄ pound bok choy, cut into 3-inch lengths
1   red pepper, julienned
2   scallions cut on the bias into 2-inch pieces
1   cup pea pods
sesame oil

1. Combine soy sauce, sherry, cornstarch and ginger. Add scallops, mix well and put aside for 15 minutes.
2. Preheat a wok or large deep frying pan and add 1 tablespoon oil. Stir for 1 minute, turn heat up to high and add bok choy, pepper, scallions and pea pods. Stir fry until vegetables are almost cooked, about 1 to 2 minutes.
3. Add the remaining 1 tablespoon of oil, a few dashes of sesame oil, the scallops and marinade; stir fry for 2 minutes until mixture is thickened and scallops are opaque.

The Well-Dressed Bluefish

Serves 6 to 8

Artistically prepared.

1. Prepare your favorite fish for baking: clean and scale, leaving fins and head on. To stuff or not to stuff, your option. Place on a baking sheet in a 350° oven for about 45 minutes or remove 15 minutes before it is done. Turn oven to 450°.
2. Next, prepare your favorite pie crust (no sugar). Roll out into a piece larger in size than your fish. With 2 broad spatulas, drape the crust over the fish, tucking it around the body. Using a sharp knife, cut "scales" as shown and make a circle around the eye. Brush crust with milk and return fish to oven until crust is nice and brown.

3. Carefully place dressed fish on a heated platter and garnish with curly parsley sprigs, lemon wedges and a stuffed olive for the eye. From your garden, a must: Make a necklace of small daisies or nasturtiums.

P.S. If you try baking the fish on a piece of cheesecloth or foil, it makes removing from the baking sheet much less stressful.

Seared Tuna with Garlic Buds

Serves 2

Don't be timid, the garlic settles down as it cooks.

4 tablespoons extra virgin olive oil
2 8-ounce tuna steaks or bass fillets (1 inch thick)
12 large garlic cloves, sliced
8 fresh thyme sprigs (left whole)
3 tablespoons fresh lemon juice
2 chopped scallions
2 tablespoons chopped fresh parsley

1. Heat 2 tablespoons oil in a heavy large nonstick skillet. Season fish generously with salt and pepper. Add to skillet and sauté until just cooked through, about 5 minutes on each side. Transfer fish to warm plates.
2. Add remaining 2 tablespoons oil to pan and cook garlic with the thyme until golden, about 4 minutes. Add lemon juice and simmer until liquid thickens slightly. Add scallions and parsley, heat thoroughly and spoon sauce over fish. Serve with crispy bread to soak up the garlic broth.

Curried Shrimp with Peaches   Serves 4

An inspiration after a day in the orchard.

1$^1/_2$ pounds medium shrimp, peeled, deveined
    and cooked
3 tablespoons butter
1 medium onion, chopped
1 stalk celery, chopped
1 tablespoon curry powder
$^1/_2$ teaspoon salt
$^1/_8$ teaspoon white pepper
3 tablespoons flour
3 tablespoons sherry
1$^1/_2$ cups milk
3 to 4 fresh peaches, pitted, peeled and sliced
$^1/_2$ cup fresh or frozen peas, cooked
2 tablespoons toasted coconut
chopped fresh parsley

1. Melt butter in a saucepan and sauté onion and celery until translucent, about 5 minutes. Add curry powder, salt, pepper and flour; mix well. Slowly whisk in the sherry and milk. Cook, stirring, over medium heat, until sauce thickens.
2. Add shrimp to sauce, bring to a simmer for 3 to 4 minutes, until heated through. Gently fold in the peach slices and peas and cook for a few more minutes before serving. Spoon curry over rice, sprinkle with toasted coconut and chopped parsley.

A Georgia Fish Bake   Serves 4 to 6

From our Georgia Banks beach house – a Sunday standard.

1 pound cooked grouper, flaked (any other
    mild fish, or even crabmeat, may be used)
1$^1/_2$ cups crushed Ritz crackers
1 cup diced celery
1 cup finely chopped onion
$^1/_3$ cup melted butter
$^1/_2$ cup milk
1 teaspoon dry mustard
$^1/_2$ teaspoon salt
$^1/_3$ cup chopped fresh parsley
2 tablespoons white wine
$^1/_2$ cup chopped green pepper
cayenne pepper
1 cup grated sharp cheddar cheese
paprika

Combine fish with cracker crumbs, celery and onion. Moisten with butter and milk and add dry mustard, salt, parsley, wine, green pepper, and a dash of cayenne pepper. Place in a lightly greased 2-quart casserole, sprinkle with cheese and paprika. Cover with aluminum foil and bake for 20 minutes in a 400° oven. Uncover, and bake for 10 more minutes until cheese is golden brown.

Spanish Calamari Salad
Serves 8 to 10

Serve on a decorative platter as part of a seafood buffet.

3   pounds fresh or frozen squid, cleaned and cut into ¹/₂-inch rings
¹/₂ cup olive oil
6   cloves garlic, minced
1   cup chopped fresh parsley
1   small red onion, thinly sliced
2   stalks celery, chopped
1   10-ounce package mushrooms, sliced
4   tablespoons fresh lemon juice
¹/₂ cup each green and black olives
2   tablespoons capers, drained
¹/₄ cup red wine vinegar
¹/₄ cup olive oil
salt and pepper
1   to 2 hot red cherry peppers (optional)

1. Put olive oil in a skillet and sauté garlic for 1 minute, do not brown. Add squid and ¹/₂ cup parsley and simmer about 20 minutes until squid becomes tender. Remove to a large bowl and cool.
2. Add remaining ¹/₂ cup parsley, sliced red onion, celery, mushrooms, lemon juice, capers, and olives. Toss with vinegar and oil, season to taste with salt and pepper. Serve on a bed of lettuce and sprinkle hot red pepper on top.

Pecan Smothered Fillet of Sole
Serves 4

4   large sole fillets, 5 to 6 ounces each or any other firm white fish, scrod, haddock or halibut
1   cup buttermilk (the dry mix is fine but reconstitute with milk)
black pepper to taste
¹/₂ teaspoon salt
1¹/₂ teaspoons garlic powder
flour
4   tablespoons butter
¹/₂ cup pecans, broken
2   teaspoons fresh lemon juice
2   tablespoons fresh chopped parsley

1. Season the buttermilk with pepper, salt and garlic powder. Dip fillets in buttermilk and then dredge them in flour. Shake off excess.
2. Melt 3 tablespoons of butter in a large skillet and sauté over medium-low heat until fish is golden brown.
3. Melt remaining 1 tablespoon butter in a small pan and lightly toast pecans, about 3 minutes. Stir in lemon juice. Spoon over fish fillets and sprinkle with parsley.

Libby's Crab Imperial   Serves 6

As popular now as it was in the '60's.

1   pound lump crabmeat
$^1/_2$ cup chopped green pepper
$^1/_2$ cup chopped pimento
3   slices white bread, crusts removed
2   eggs, beaten
1   cup mayonnaise, regular or lite
1   teaspoon Worcestershire sauce
1   teaspoon dry mustard
1   teaspoon paprika ($^1/_2$ teaspoon for crab mixture,$^1/_2$ teaspoon for top)
$^1/_2$ teaspoon dill or tarragon, your choice
juice of $^1/_2$ lemon
pinch of cayenne pepper

1. If using lump crabmeat, be sure to pick over carefully, removing any cartilage, placing meat in a medium bowl. Add green pepper and pimento. Crumble in bread slices. Mix lightly with a fork.
2. Fold in eggs, mayonnaise and remaining ingredients, mixing well. Pour into a buttered $1^1/_2$ quart casserole. soufflé dish, or individual ramekins. Sprinkle with remaining paprika and bake in a 400° oven for 15 to 20 minutes until puffed and brown.

**"Of mordant mustard add a single spoon,
Distrust of condiment that bites too soon."
                    – Sydney Smith**

Baked Grouper with Bread Crumbs

As much wine or fish as you have on hand.

In a glass casserole, barely cover the bottom with half white wine and half water. Place grouper down and cover the top with mayonnaise, bread crumbs, and salt and pepper. Bake a 1-pound piece for 18 minutes at 400°. Then place under the broiler for about 2 minutes to make bread crumbs crispy. It's fast and easy and has a lot less fat than fried grouper!

Baked Pompano Tarragon

In a glass casserole, barely cover the bottom with half white wine and half water. Place pompano, skin side down, and cover top with oil or butter, salt and sprinkle tarragon (dried or fresh). Bake at 400° for 10 minutes. For a change, instead of tarragon and salt, try splashing on some soy sauce. It's fast, easy and delicious!

LUXURIOUS LOBSTER

Lobster Salad with Tarragon Vinaigrette   Serves 4

A perfect end to a Nantucket day. Cook your lobster in the morning and invite your guests for 6 o'clock.

2    $1^1/_2$ to $1^3/_4$-pound lobsters
2   shallots, minced
2   teaspoons chopped fresh tarragon
2   teaspoons chopped fresh parsley
$^1/_4$ teaspoon salt
$^1/_4$ teaspoon pepper
$^1/_2$ cup olive oil
3   tablespoons fresh lemon juice
2   tablespoons white wine vinegar
1   large head bibb lettuce
fresh tarragon sprigs
a variety of summer tomatoes - yellow, red, cherry or heirloom
edible flowers such as nasturtium, violet, or chive blossoms

1. In a large pot, bring 1 inch of water to a boil. Plunge lobsters, head first, into water, cover, return to a boil and simmer 10 minutes; drain and cool.
2. Break off large claws and legs. Crack claw and leg shells using a lobster or nut cracker. Remove meat and set aside.
3. Break off tails, cut shell of tail segments lengthwise on the underside. Remove meat, cut into $^1/_2$ inch pieces and chill.
4. Combine shallot, tarragon, parsley, salt and pepper, oil, lemon juice, and vinegar in a wide mouth jar, cover and shake until well blended.

To serve: arrange leaves of lettuce in the middle of individual plates. Divide lobster meat equally and drizzle with the vinaigrette. Arrange tomatoes, flowers and tarragon sprigs around the outside of the plate, making a colorful border.

Broiled Lobster with Herb Sabayon   Serves 4

An exquisite double combination of flavors – so French!

4   1¹/₄ pound lobsters
¹/₃ cup brandy
1   egg yolk
¹/₂ cup heavy cream
2   tablespoons fines herbes - finely chopped
    parsley, tarragon, chives, chervil
8   tablespoons melted butter
salt and white pepper

"If your lobster be alive, tye it to the spit, roast and baste it half an hour, and toast the end of it."
– E. Moxon

1. Holding the claws down with one hand, split the lobster down the middle with a sharp knife. Halve, then cut lengthwise and remove the sac and intestinal track.
2. Arrange the lobsters on a large baking sheet, cover with foil and bake in a 350° oven for 15 minutes or until shells are pink.
3. Meanwhile, combine the egg yolk and cream in a heavy saucepan. Beat the mixture vigorously and constantly over very low heat until it is foamy and light. Do not allow sauce to boil. Fold in the herbs and set aside.
4. Remove the lobsters from the oven, sprinkle with the brandy and coat with the herb sabayon sauce. Return to the oven uncovered to brown. Serve each lobster with a bowl of the seasoned melted butter for dipping.

Ramekins of Maine Lobster   Serves 6 as an appetizer

Meat of 1 large Maine lobster, 1¹/₂ to 2
    pounds, cooked and coarsely chopped
2   tablespoons butter
1   shallot, minced
4   mushrooms, sliced
2   tablespoons flour
1   cup milk or half-and-half
2   tablespoons sherry
¹/₂ teaspoon paprika
salt and pepper
buttered bread crumbs
grated Parmesan
chopped parsley

1. Heat the butter in a small pan, add shallot and mushrooms, sauté for 2 minutes. Stir in flour and mix well.
2. Slowly whisk in the milk, add the sherry and cook until thickened. Stir in the lobster meat and paprika, season with salt and pepper. Divide the mixture into 6 ramekins or scallop shells, top with buttered crumbs and Parmesan. Brown under a preheated broiler until bubbling and golden, sprinkle with parsley before serving.

"Toast a toast as big as you have an occasion for."
– Old Cookery Book

Lobster Curry, Gorda Style   Serves 6

A Bitter End memory or was it Marina Key?

4   1$^1/_2$- to 2-pound rock or spiny lobsters, no
    claws
2   tablespoons olive oil
6   ounces butter
1   onion, finely chopped
1   green pepper, finely chopped
3   tablespoons curry powder
1   teaspoon turmeric
2   tablespoons tomato paste
1   apple, peeled and finely chopped
$^1/_4$ cup grated coconut
$^1/_2$ cup white wine
1$^1/_2$ to 2 cups fish stock or clam juice
$^2/_3$ cup heavy cream
3   tablespoons chutney
3   tablespoons chopped scallions

1. Cut the tails from the lobsters and quarter.
   Heat oil and butter in a large skillet and add
   lobster pieces, onion and green pepper.
   Sauté until vegetables are light brown,
   about 5 minutes.
2. Transfer to a heavy casserole and add curry
   powder, turmeric, tomato paste, apple,
   coconut and white wine. Pour in enough
   stock to cover, season to taste and bake in a
   350° oven for 30 minutes.
3. Take out the lobster and keep warm. On the
   stovetop, reduce liquid by one half, add the
   cream and continue cooking for another 5
   minutes. Stir in the chutney. Serve in large
   bowls with hot white rice and sprinkle with
   scallions.

**"Do you put cayenne in your curry tarts in India,
Sir?"   – W. M. Thackeray**

Flaming Lobster with Cognac Cream   Serves 2

A special Valentine's Day presentation.

1   large lobster, 2$^1/_2$ to 3 pounds
4   tablespoons butter
1   shallot, minced
minced parsley
salt and pepper
$^1/_2$ cup cognac, warmed
4   tablespoons heavy cream

1. Split lobster in half lengthwise, remove sac
   and intestinal track. Place on an ovenproof
   baking dish just large enough to hold the
   lobster. Mix butter with shallot, parsley, salt
   and pepper and spread over lobster. Bake in
   a 450° oven for 15 minutes.
2. Remove from oven, pour warmed cognac
   over and flame. Pour cream over and return
   to oven to blend juices. Serve one half
   lobster for each person and pour cognac
   sauce over the body.

**"My soul tasted that heavenly food, which gives
me new appetite."**

**   – Dante**

The Bride's Lobster Strudel   Serves 16

A big hit at a summer bridal luncheon on the terrace.

$^1/_4$ cup butter ($^1/_2$ stick)
3   tablespoons flour
1   cup warm milk
$^1/_4$ cup grated Gruyere cheese
2   tablespoons heavy cream
$^1/_4$ teaspoon dry mustard
salt and white pepper
2   cups cooked lobster meat
1   cup cooked shrimp, chopped
1   cup sole or flounder, cooked and flaked
$^3/_4$ cup chopped mushrooms, sautéed in 2
     tablespoons butter
16 phyllo leaves
$^3/_4$ cup butter ($1^1/_2$ sticks)
1   cup fresh bread crumbs

1. In a saucepan, melt $^1/_2$ stick of butter, stir in the flour, and cook the roux over low heat, stirring for 3 minutes. Remove the pan from the heat and add warm milk in a steady stream, whisking vigorously until the mixture is thick and smooth. Simmer the sauce for 3 minutes, stir in the Gruyere cheese, heavy cream, dry mustard, salt and white pepper to taste. Cook the sauce until the cheese is melted and remove to a large bowl. Refrigerate for 1 hour. When sauce has cooled, gently fold in the lobster meat, shrimp, sole and mushrooms.

2. Have the phyllo leaves ready and covered with a damp towel to keep them from drying out as you work. Brush 4 of the leaves with melted butter, sprinkle with a little of the fresh bread crumbs and stack them. Spread a strip of the seafood mixture (about $^3/_4$ cup) 2 inches from the edge of one of the long sides of the buttered phyllo. Fold in the sides of the leaves to contain the mixture and roll up the leaves jelly-roll fashion. Continue to make rolls with remaining phyllo, butter, and filling in the same manner. Transfer the rolls to a buttered baking sheet, seam side down, and brush the tops with melted butter. These may be frozen at this point and defrosted in the refrigerator before baking.

3. Bake the rolls in a preheated 350° oven for 40 to 45 minutes or until they are crisp and golden. Let the strudel stand for 5 minutes before cutting. Serve on individual plates, surrounded with fresh fruit and sprigs of mint, then pass the champagne.

Lobster à la Marseilles

Serves 4

Marie-Thérèse Louis de Savoie-Carignan, Princess de Lamballa and director of the household of her friend Marie-Antoinette is said to have fainted away when she saw a lobster. "She closed her eyes and remained motionless for a half an hour!"

1½ pounds fresh lobster meat or the meat
    from 4 small 1-pound lobsters
4   tablespoons butter
2   shallots, finely chopped
8   large mushrooms, sliced
1½ cups fresh tomato, seeded and chopped
salt and pepper
2   tablespoons chopped fresh parsley
buttered and toasted slices of crusty French
    bread

1. In a medium saucepan, melt 2 tablespoons of the butter. Add the shallots and mushrooms; sauté until just tender, about 3 minutes.
2. Add the tomatoes and season to taste with salt and pepper. Cook over medium heat for 5 minutes, stirring several times. Add the lobster meat and the remaining 2 tablespoons butter. Bring to a simmer to warm lobster and melt the butter.
3. Ladle into large bowls, surround each dish with French bread tucked into the broth and sprinkle with parsley.

Hong Kong Lobster Rolls with Rosemary Ginger Vinaigrette

Serves 4

3   large zucchini, trimmed
2   cooked 8-ounce lobster tails, shelled, halved
    lengthwise and thinly sliced crosswise or
    8 cooked large shrimp, halved lengthwise
¾ cup sprouts (alfalfa, daikon, watercress)
24 1-inch pieces thinly sliced pickled ginger

Vinaigrette:
3   tablespoons soy sauce
2   tablespoons wine vinegar
1   tablespoon sherry
2   tablespoons honey
1½ tablespoons minced fresh ginger
1½ tablespoons minced fresh rosemary
½ teaspoon crushed red pepper
½ cup vegetable oil

1. Place 1 zucchini on a work surface. Using a vegetable peeler, cut zucchini into thin ribbons about 5 inches long and 1½ inches wide. Repeat with remaining zucchini, making a total of 12 ribbons.
2. Divide lobster meat equally, placing a piece on the end of each zucchini ribbon. Top with sprouts and pickled ginger. Starting at filled end, roll each piece of zucchini into a cylinder. Place seam side down on a paper towel-lined baking sheet. Cover and chill for at least 2 hours.
3. Prepare vinaigrette by whisking everything except the oil in a medium bowl to blend. Gradually add oil. To serve, pour vinaigrette into a small bowl, place in center of a platter and surround with lobster rolls.

Bedeviled Lobster Tails

Serves 4-6, depending on the size of the tails

Not everyone has access to fresh lobster – this truly fits the bill.

6 4-6 ounce frozen lobster tails, thawed
$^1/_2$ teaspoon lemon-pepper seasoning
2 scallions, chopped
1 stalk celery, finely chopped
2 tablespoons butter or margarine
1 tablespoon flour
$^1/_8$ teaspoon dry mustard
1 teaspoon Worcestershire sauce
1 tablespoon chopped fresh parsley
$^3/_4$ cup light cream
1 6-ounce can crabmeat, drained, flaked and
   cartilage removed
4 tablespoons fresh bread crumbs
salt and pepper
3 tablespoons melted butter
paprika

1. Rinse lobster tails, as they are often packed in a salted water. Using kitchen shears or a sharp knife, cut in half lengthwise through the top shell, turn and finish separating by cutting through the bottom shell. Make a little slit lengthwise through the meat (this keeps the tail from curling up). Sprinkle with lemon-pepper and set aside.

2. Melt 2 tablespoons of butter in a small saucepan and sauté scallions and celery until tender but not brown. Add the flour, mustard, Worcestershire sauce and parsley. Whisk in the cream and cook until thickened and bubbling, about 2-3 minutes. Remove from heat and gently fold in the crabmeat and bread crumbs. Season to taste with salt and pepper and cool for a half hour.

3. Spoon the crabmeat mixture into the split lobster tails and drizzle with the melted butter and sprinkle with paprika. Bake in a 375° oven for 10-12 minutes until stuffing is nicely browned.

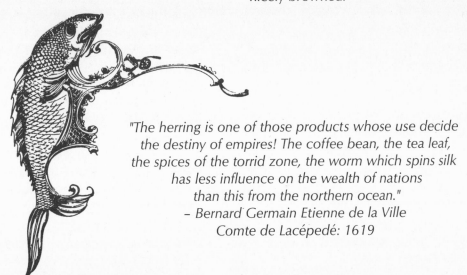

"The herring is one of those products whose use decide the destiny of empires! The coffee bean, the tea leaf, the spices of the torrid zone, the worm which spins silk has less influence on the wealth of nations than this from the northern ocean."
– Bernard Germain Etienne de la Ville
Comte de Lacépedé: 1619

Lobster and Sweet Corn Soup   Serves 4

This is a prize-winning main course – well worth the time.

4   1 to 1¹/₄-pound lobsters
4   tablespoons butter
¹/₂ cup fennel, finely diced
¹/₂ cup diced pancetta
2   medium leeks, chopped
1   cup dry white wine
¹/₂ cup heavy cream
1   jalapeño pepper, seeded and diced
4   cups corn kernels (6 ears)
freshly ground pepper
1   tablespoon fresh tarragon
¹/₄ cup parsley, chopped
¹/₂ cup buttered croutons

1. Fill a large stockpot with 2 inches of water, add 1 teaspoon of salt and bring to a boil. Put the lobsters in the water, head first, cover and cook for 5 minutes or until they turn red. Remove from the pot to cool and reserve the cooking water.

2. Remove the claws and knuckles and twist off the tail of each lobster. Split the tail lengthwise and remove the meat. Discard the black intestinal vein and cut the meat into ¹/₂ inch pieces along with that from the claws and knuckles.

3. Return the lobster shells to the liquid in the pot and simmer over medium heat for 20 minutes. Strain into a bowl and let stand for 10 minutes. Pour off and reserve 6 cups of the liquid, leaving behind any grit at the bottom.

4. In a large saucepan, melt 2 tablespoons of the butter. Add the pancetta and cook over low heat until browned, about 5 minutes. Add the fennel and cook until wilted; transfer the pancetta and fennel to a plate.

5. Add the remaining 2 tablespoons of butter to the pan. Stir in the leeks and sauté for 5 minutes. Add the wine and reduce over medium heat for 4 minutes.

6. Stir in the reserved lobster stock, cream, jalapeño and season with salt and pepper to taste. Add the corn and simmer until tender, about 10 minutes.

7. Add the fennel, pancetta, lobster meat, tarragon and parsley, bring to a low boil to warm thoroughly. Spoon into bowls and top with buttered croutons.

Candlelight Champagne Lobster Risotto Serves 2

2 tablespoons butter
$^1/_4$ cup chopped scallions
$^2/_3$ cup short grain Arborio rice
1 cup champagne
1 14$^1/_2$-ounce can chicken broth
$^1/_2$ pound fresh lobster meat
$^1/_4$ cup frozen petite peas
1 tablespoon freshly chopped parsley
salt and pepper to taste
$^1/_4$ cup freshly grated Parmesan cheese

1. Over medium heat, melt butter in a 2-quart saucepan. Add scallions and sauté for 1 minute. Add rice and cook, stirring constantly for 2 minutes until lightly golden.
2. Reduce heat to low and add the champagne, $^1/_2$ cup at a time, cooking until it has been absorbed each time. Add the broth in the same manner, $^1/_2$ cup at a time, stirring often, about 15 minutes.
3. Gently fold in the lobster meat, peas and parsley, seasoning with salt and pepper to taste. Add the Parmesan and serve immediately.

Linguine alla Lobster Serves 4

A quick and easy dish that stretches a small amount of lobster.

2 1-pound lobsters, steamed or boiled for 10 minutes, cooled with claw and tail meat removed
or 2 4- to 5-ounce fresh or frozen lobster tails
$^1/_2$ pound linguine
1 28-ounce can crushed tomatoes
3 tablespoons olive oil
2 tablespoons tomato paste
1 teaspoon sugar
3 cloves garlic, minced
$^1/_4$ cup minced fresh parsley, preferably flat-leafed
1 teaspoon fresh chopped basil, few sprigs for garnish
$^1/_4$ cup cognac or brandy
salt and freshly ground black pepper
Parmesan cheese, freshly grated

1. Cook linguine in a large pot of boiling salted water. Drain in a colander, cover and keep warm.
2. In a skillet, simmer tomatoes, oil, tomato paste, sugar, garlic, parsley and basil over low heat for 20 minutes. Remove lobster meat from shell and chop coarsely. Add to the sauce and cook for 5 minutes. Stir in cognac and toss with linguine. Serve and sprinkle with Parmesan, garnish with basil sprigs.

Lobsters Grilled with Seaweed   Serves 4

Wrapped in foil, this imparts a wonderful smoky taste.

4   1- to 1^1/$_2$-pound lobsters
seaweed
clams and mussels (optional)

Deviled butter:
12 tablespoons butter (1^1/$_2$ sticks)
1   teaspoon Worcestershire sauce
1   tablespoon Dijon mustard
juice of 1 lemon or 2 tablespoons freshly
    squeezed
2   tablespoons chopped fresh parsley
freshly ground black pepper

Melt butter in a small saucepan. Whisk in
Worcestershire sauce, Dijon, lemon juice and
parsley. Season to taste with black pepper and
serve with lobsters.

1. With a sharp knife, pierce the heads of the
   lobster on the back side from the claws
   forward. Take a large sheet of heavy duty
   aluminum foil long enough to enclose one
   of the lobsters and spread a layer of
   seaweed in the center. Arrange the lobster
   on the seaweed and cover it with another
   layer of seaweed. Tuck a few clams and
   mussels around the outside if you have
   them. Fold up the foil to the middle, crease
   and wrap the lobster, enclosing completely.
2. Grill the lobsters on a rack over an open fire
   or on a barbecue grill for 15 minutes. Turn
   and cook for another 15 minutes. Remove
   and discard foil and seaweed. Split the
   lobsters lengthwise and serve with deviled
   butter.

**"Ah! Who has seen the lobster rise, clap her broad
wings, and soaring claim the skies?"**
– Jonathan Swift

Captain Linda's Lobster Dip   Serves 10 (makes 2^1/$_2$ cups of dip)

**A wonderful way for everyone to get a taste of the "leftover" lobster onboard the schooner
"Heritage" from Rockland, Maine.**

1   cup fresh lobster meat, chopped
    (approximately the meat of 3 1-pound
    lobsters)
^{1}/$_2$ cup mayonnaise
1   cup sour cream
^{1}/$_2$ teaspoon garlic powder
1   teaspoon horseradish
^{1}/$_2$ teaspoon Worcestershire sauce
dash of salt and pepper

Mix sour cream, mayonnaise and seasonings.
Add salt and pepper to taste. Gently stir in the
lobster and refrigerate for at least one hour.
Serve with crackers for dipping.

Lobster Jambalaya

Serves 6

You might add a few oysters here - this dish can be prepared in a hot chafing dish or blazer.

1 pound fresh cooked lobster meat, cut into bite-size pieces
3 tablespoons butter
$^1/_4$ cup cooked ham, chopped
$^1/_4$ cup chopped onion
$^1/_2$ cup chopped green pepper
2 tablespoons flour
2 cups canned tomatoes
$^1/_2$ teaspoon salt
dash of Tabasco sauce
3 cups cooked white rice
$^1/_4$ cup chopped fresh parsley

1. Melt butter in a large saucepan and sauté ham, green pepper and onion for 2 to 3 minutes. Add flour and cook for another 2 minutes stirring constantly.
2. Add salt, Tabasco sauce, tomatoes and cook until sauce is thickened. Stir in lobster meat, rice and chopped parsley and heat until bubbling.

Lobster Diavolo

Serves 4

A New Orleans-style favorite.

2 2$^1/_2$-pound lobsters
6 tablespoons butter
$^1/_2$ cup chopped scallions
2 cloves garlic, minced
$^3/_4$ cup sliced mushrooms
1 bay leaf
1 teaspoon tarragon
2 cups canned Italian plum tomatoes, drained
$^1/_4$ cup white wine
salt and pepper
$^1/_2$ cup buttered bread crumbs
chopped fresh parsley

1. In a large pot, boil lobsters in 1 inch of water for 10 minutes, until shells are bright red; cool under running water. Cut in half lengthwise and remove meat from bodies and claws. Reserve shells.
2. Melt butter in a large saucepan and sauté scallions, garlic and mushrooms for 3 to 4 minutes until just soft. Add bay leaf, tarragon, tomatoes, and white wine. Simmer for 10 minutes until sauce has reduced and thickened. Add lobster meat, season with salt and pepper and reheat until bubbling. Divide lobster and sauce between the 4 reserved shells, top with crumbs and bake for 10 minutes in a 375° oven. Serve 1 half to each guest, sprinkled with chopped parsley.

Cape Cod Lobster Pies

Serves 4

A Campbell House specialty.

6   tablespoons butter
6   tablespoons flour
1   cup milk, warmed
2   cups half-and-half, warmed
1   pound fresh lobster meat
1   teaspoon paprika
$^1/_3$ cup sherry
pinch cayenne pepper
2   tablespoons fresh chopped parsley
$^1/_2$ teaspoon salt

Lobster pie topping:
$^3/_4$ cup fresh bread crumbs
4   tablespoons ($^1/_2$ stick) butter, melted
$^1/_2$ cup finely crushed potato chips
2   tablespoons freshly grated Parmesan cheese
$^3/_4$ teaspoon paprika

In a medium bowl, combine all ingredients and
blend thoroughly. Use to top lobster pies or
any other seafood casserole.

1. In a 2-quart saucepan, melt 4 tablespoons
   butter over low heat. Add flour and cook,
   stirring, for 2 to 3 minutes. Whisk warm milk
   and half-and-half into flour mixture and
   simmer for 10 minutes until thickened.
2. In a separate sauté pan, melt remaining 2
   tablespoons of butter. Add lobster meat,
   sprinkle with paprika and cook over low
   heat for 5 minutes, until butter is nice and
   pink. Add sherry, a pinch or 2 of cayenne
   pepper, chopped parsley and salt. Gently
   fold lobster butter into cream sauce and
   spoon into 4 individual casserole dishes.
   Sprinkle with topping, a little more paprika
   and bake in a 375° oven for 12 to 15
   minutes until brown and bubbly.

Bourbon Street Lobster

Serves 4

$1^1/_2$ pounds fresh lobster meat, diced
1   red bell pepper, cut into thin strips
1   green bell pepper, cut into thin strips
4   tablespoons butter
1   cup white wine
1   cup cream
1   tablespoon Cajun seasoning
2   tablespoons chopped parsley
chopped scallions
paprika

1. Melt butter in a sauté pan. Add peppers and
   sauté for a few minutes. Stir in the lobster
   meat and Cajun seasonings and cook for
   another 2 minutes until butter is nice and
   pink.
2. Reduce heat, add the white wine, cream
   and parsley and simmer until sauce has
   thickened. Serve over white rice topped
   with a few chopped scallions and a dusting
   of paprika.

Taj Mahal Lobster

Serves 2

A remembrance from a trip to India.

2   1$^1/_2$-pound lobsters
the pulp from $^1/_2$ fresh coconut, or $^1/_3$ cup
   unsweetened coconut
1   fresh hot green chili, seeded
2   garlic cloves, minced
$^1/_2$-inch piece fresh ginger root, peeled
6   stems fresh coriander with leaves, plus
   sprigs for garnish
2   tablespoons Balsamic vinegar
$^1/_4$ teaspoon salt
1   tablespoon olive oil
2   lemon twists or slices

1. Steam the lobsters in 1 inch of boiling salted water for 10 minutes. When cool enough to handle, split them open and remove the tail, claw, and knuckle meat. Snip off the legs.
2. To make the sauce, combine the coconut, garlic, chili, ginger root, coriander, vinegar and salt in a food processor and blend to a paste. To serve, arrange lobster meat in the center of 2 serving plates, spoon sauce on top and drizzle with olive oil. Arrange the legs around the border of each plate and garnish with cilantro sprigs and lemon.

Seaman's Baked Stuffed Lobster

Serves 2

From a lobster fisherman's wife over 30 years ago - a party favorite.

2   1$^1/_2$-pound lobsters
1$^1/_2$ cups Ritz cracker crumbs
2   tablespoons freshly grated Romano cheese
$^1/_2$ teaspoon oregano
$^1/_2$ teaspoon basil
1   tablespoon fresh chopped parsley
salt and pepper
oregano
dash of Tabasco sauce

1. Split lobsters in half lengthwise on the underside. Remove sac and intestinal vein. Leave any tamale or roe in cavity. Crack the claws and slit the inner shell of the tail in 3 places to prevent curling.
2. Toss the remaining ingredients together and fill each lobster body. Dot with a few pieces of butter and sprinkle with paprika. These may be made ahead, covered and refrigerated. To bake, place in a 400° oven for 20 minutes and serve with bowls of hot lemon butter with a dash of Tabasco sauce.

Oyster Bar Lobster Stew

Serves 4

If you love lobster, nothing better, nothing simpler.

1   pound fresh lobster meat, cut into chunks
6   tablespoons butter
6   cups half-and-half
salt and white pepper
4   slices white bread, buttered and toasted,
    crusts removed
paprika
freshly chopped parsley

1. Melt butter in a large saucepan. Add lobster and gently sauté for 2 to 3 minutes until butter is nice and pink.
2. Add cream and simmer for 5 minutes. Season with salt and pepper.
3. Remove half of the lobster meat to a small bowl. Ladle stew in 4 serving dishes and float a piece of toast on each bowl, top with reserved lobster meat and sprinkle with paprika and parsley.

South of the Border Lobster

Serves 4

A summer feast – serve with ears of fresh corn on the cob.

4   $1^1/_2$ pound lobsters
8   tablespoons (1 stick) butter
2   cloves garlic, minced
juice of 2 limes
$1/_4$ cup fresh cilantro, chopped
$1/_2$ teaspoon cumin
dash of Tabasco sauce

1. In a large pot, bring 2 inches of water to a boil with a pinch of salt. Add the lobsters, cover and steam for 10 minutes.
2. While the lobsters are cooking, melt butter in a small saucepan. Sauté the garlic for one minute being careful not to brown.
3. Add the lime juice, cilantro and cumin, seasoning with Tabasco sauce to taste. Divide the dipping sauce into 4 small bowls and serve with the lobster.

PASTA & PORPOISES

Shrimp and Linguine Salad with Feta   Serves 8

An elegant but easy make ahead dinner.

1   pound linguine
$^1/_2$ cup olive oil
2   cloves garlic, chopped
2   tablespoons fresh lemon juice
2   tablespoons wine vinegar
$^1/_2$ cup chopped parsley
$^1/_2$ cup chopped basil
salt and pepper
1   bunch watercress, coarsely broken up
$^1/_4$ cup pitted black olives, sliced
3   tomatoes, cut into wedges or 16 cherry
    tomatoes, halved
$1^1/_2$ pounds medium shrimp, cooked, peeled
    and deveined
4   ounces Feta cheese

1. Cook the linguine in boiling salted water until just tender. Drain and rinse with cold water.
2. In a large bowl, whisk olive oil, garlic, lemon juice and vinegar. Add basil, parsley, salt and pepper, watercress, olives, linguine and shrimp and toss until well coated. Arrange on a large platter, with tomatoes around the outside and crumble cheese over the top.

"God sends meat and the Devil sends cooks."
– John Taylor, 1630

Anchorage Shrimp and Feta Salad   Serves 6 to 8

All the way from an Alaskan Seaport member.

4   cups cooked and cooled shell or short spiral
    pasta
$1^1/_2$ pounds small shrimp, cooked
$^1/_2$ cup crumbled Feta cheese
$^1/_2$ cup chopped scallions
1   cup green peas, cooked
2   cups finely chopped fresh spinach
2   cloves garlic, minced
$^1/_4$ cup finely chopped fresh parsley
$1^1/_2$ teaspoons fresh thyme
1   tablespoon finely chopped fresh basil
$^1/_4$ teaspoon freshly ground black pepper
salt
$^1/_3$ cup white wine vinegar
$^1/_3$ cup olive oil

1. In a large bowl, mix the pasta, shrimp, Feta cheese, scallions, peas and spinach.
2. Combine remaining ingredients in a small jar and shake well. Drizzle over the salad and toss gently. Refrigerate for an hour before serving.

Mediterranean Pasta Salad   Serves 8 to 10

For a summer party, prepare everything early in the day and toss before serving.

1   pound rotini or other small pasta, cooked
    and drained
1¹/₂ pounds medium shrimp, cooked and
    peeled
1   large green pepper, cut into strips
1   large yellow pepper, cut into strips
1   large red pepper, cut into strips
1   basket cherry tomatoes, halved, about 18 to
    20
8   ounces Feta cheese, cubed
¹/₃ cup Greek olives, pitted and chopped
1   tablespoon capers, drained
2   tablespoons chopped fresh basil
2   tablespoons chopped fresh parsley

Herb dressing:
²/₃ cup olive oil
3   tablespoons red wine vinegar
2   tablespoons chopped fresh basil
4   scallions, chopped
¹/₄ cup grated Parmesan cheese
¹/₄ teaspoon freshly ground black pepper
pinch of salt

1. Combine all ingredients in a food processor
   or blender and purée until smooth.
2. In a large bowl, mix all salad ingredients and
   gently toss with dressing. Serve on a
   decorative platter garnished with basil and
   parsley sprigs. This is equally delicious
   chilled or at room temperature.

"An olive, capers, or some better — salad."
                    – Ben Johnson

Risotto with 2 Tuna Sauces   Serves 8 to 10 as a primi piatti or first course

Sauce #1:

2   cloves garlic, cut in half
3   tablespoons olive oil
2   cups peeled plum tomatoes
1   tablespoon chopped fresh basil
1   6^1/$_2$-ounce can light tuna, packed in oil
2   cups long grain rice
4   cups water
3   tablespoons butter
1   teaspoon salt
fresh ground black pepper

1. In a heavy skillet, sauté the garlic in the olive oil until just golden brown. Discard the garlic cloves and turn off the heat. Add the tomatoes, basil and tuna fish. Simmer for 15 minutes, slightly mashing the tuna and tomatoes up with a fork. The sauce should be chunky. Season with salt and pepper to taste.

2. Put the rice, water, butter and salt in a medium saucepan, bring to a boil, cover, and reduce heat. Cook 10 to 15 minutes without stirring until rice has absorbed most liquid. Add the tuna sauce and continue stirring until rice is tender.

Sauce #2:

2   cups long grain rice
4   cups water
4   tablespoons butter
1   teaspoon salt
1   6^1/$_2$-ounce can light tuna, packed in oil (reserve oil)
6   tablespoons grated Parmesan cheese
2   tablespoons chopped parsley

1. Put the rice, water, half the butter and the salt in a medium pan and bring to a boil. Stir, cover, reduce the heat and simmer for 10 minutes.

2. Add the reserved oil, the last 2 tablespoons of butter and mix well with the Parmesan and parsley.

"How nice is rice!
How gentle, and how very free from vice
**   are those whose fodder is only rice!"**
                    – André Simon: "Food"

Lemon Penne with Shrimp and Artichoke Hearts   Serves 6

1   pound large shrimp, peeled and deveined
10 ounces penne pasta
1   9-ounce package frozen artichoke hearts
2   tablespoons olive oil
1   small onion, thinly sliced
2   cloves garlic, chopped
$1/_2$ teaspoon oregano
salt and freshly ground black pepper
$1/_3$ cup dry white wine
$1/_3$ cup fresh lemon juice
$1/_2$ cup ricotta cheese
1   tablespoon grated lemon zest

1. Blanch artichokes in lightly salted water for 1 minute. Drain and cut into wedges. In a large pot of boiling salted water, cook penne until al dente, 10 to 15 minutes.
2. While pasta is cooking, heat olive oil in a large skillet; add garlic and onion. Sauté over medium heat for 1 minute and add shrimp, oregano and salt and pepper. Sauté for 3 to 4 minutes until shrimp are pink.
3. Add wine, lemon juice, lemon zest and artichoke hearts. Simmer 1 minute until heated through and add the ricotta cheese and stir until creamy. When the pasta is ready, drain and add to the pan with the sauce. Toss well and serve immediately.

**"Off, off with my head – split
    me shell into three —
I'm a shrimp! I'm a shrimp —
    to be eaten with tea."**
                    – Robert Brough

Feta Fettucine Fullerton   Serves 6

1   pound medium shrimp, peeled
2   tablespoons olive oil
$1/_4$ cup pine nuts
1   small red pepper, sliced
4   cloves garlic, crushed
$3/_4$ cup chicken broth
$3/_4$ cup green or black olives (whole or sliced)
$3/_4$ cup crumbled Feta cheese (either plain or
    seasoned)
3   tablespoons chopped fresh basil
cooked fettucine

1. In a medium-size skillet, sauté garlic, red pepper and nuts in olive oil until vegetables are transparent and nuts have lightly toasted. Add the shrimp and sauté for 3 to 4 minutes until shrimp are pink.
2. Pour chicken broth into pan, add olives and basil. Cover and lightly simmer for 5 minutes. Crumble Feta over the shrimp and cover for one minute to melt the cheese. Spoon over cooked fettucine or other pasta of your choice.

**"Pray, does anybody here hate cheese?
I would be glad of a bit ...."**
                    – Jonathan Swift

Fidelis Garlicky Noodles and Clams Serves 4

A Collins Road favorite – you will love the broth.

Garlic mayonnaise:
$^2/_3$ cup mayonnaise
1 tablespoon fresh lemon juice
2 cloves garlic, crushed
$^1/_4$ cup olive oil
1 tablespoon fresh chopped parsley

4 cups bottled clam juice or fish stock
1 cup water
$^1/_2$ onion, thinly sliced
1 teaspoon whole black peppercorns

1 tablespoon olive oil
12 ounces vermicelli
20 cherrystone clams

1. In a small bowl, mix mayonnaise, lemon juice and garlic. Gradually whisk in olive oil, add parsley and season to taste with salt and pepper.
2. In a large pot, bring clam juice, onion, water and peppercorns to a boil. Simmer for 20 minutes, strain into another saucepan and discard the solids (mayonnaise and fish stock may be prepared 1 day ahead and refrigerated).
3. Heat 1 tablespoon olive oil in a large Dutch oven over medium heat. Break pasta into 3-inch lengths and add to the oil. Stir until noodles are golden brown, about 5 minutes. Add stock; cook over medium heat until pasta is almost tender but mixture is still soupy, about 3 minutes. Add clams and push down into broth. Cook until clams are open, about 8 minutes. Ladle into bowls and pass the garlic mayonnaise separately. Serve with crispy sliced Italian bread.

Key Largo Shrimp Alfredo Serves 4

We like these with our freshly caught Gulf shrimp right off the boats.

$1^1/_2$ pounds medium shrimp, peeled and deveined
4 tablespoons butter
2 shallots, finely minced
2 cloves garlic, minced
$^1/_4$ cup dry sherry
2 cups light cream
4 teaspoons cornstarch
$^3/_4$ cup grated Parmesan cheese
2 tablespoons chopped red pimento
salt and pepper to taste
4 cups cooked fettucine

1. Sauté shrimp in the butter with the shallots and garlic over medium-high heat for 2 minutes. Whisk the cornstarch into the sherry and add to the pan along with the cream.
2. Simmer the mixture, stirring occasionally for about 5 minutes until thickened. Add the Parmesan cheese, pimento and season with salt and pepper. Serve piping hot over the fettucine noodles.

Christmas Eve Seafood Sampler   Serves 8

Never even a morsel left for Santa.

3   tablespoons olive oil
1   large onion, minced
2   garlic cloves, minced
$1/4$ cup dry white wine
$1^1/_2$ teaspoons dry basil, or $1^1/_2$ tablespoons
     fresh
1   teaspoon dry marjoram or 1 tablespoon
     fresh
$1^1/_2$ cups canned stewed tomatoes, well drained
$1^1/_2$ pounds mussels, well scrubbed
2   pounds small clams in shell, well scrubbed
1   pound sea scallops, halved
1   pound shrimp, peeled and deveined
1   pound pasta (spaghettini, linguine, or
     whatever you prefer), cooked
salt and pepper to taste
dash of Tabasco sauce

1. Heat oil in a large saucepan. Add onion and garlic and sauté until soft. Stir in wine, basil and marjoram and cook for 1 minute. Increase heat, add tomatoes and simmer for another 5 minutes.
2. Reduce heat to medium, add mussels and clams and cook until shells open, about 5 minutes. Add scallops and shrimp, cover and cook 2 to 3 minutes until firm. Season with salt and pepper and Tabasco sauce to taste. Serve over pasta and finish off dinner by hanging up your stockings.

**"We'll dine and drink, and say if we think
    that anything better can be;
And when we have dined, wish all mankind
    may dine as well as we."**
                                    – Thomas Love Peacock

Fettucine Puttanesca with Shrimp and Scallops   Serves 4

Again appears "The lady of the night."

$3/4$ pound medium shrimp, peeled and
     deveined
$1/2$ pound sea scallops, cut in half into disks
6   tablespoons olive oil
2   pounds tomatoes, peeled, seeded and
     chopped or 1 28-ounce can plum tomatoes,
     lightly drained
2   tablespoons chopped Kalamata olives
$3/4$ pound fettucine, cooked
3   tablespoons capers
2   tablespoons chopped anchovies
1   tablespoon chopped garlic

1. Heat 4 tablespoons oil in a large skillet over high heat. Add tomatoes and cook for 10 minutes until the mixture begins to thicken, stirring occasionally.
2. Add the shrimp and scallops, sauté until just cooked through. Mix in Kalamata olives, capers, anchovies, and garlic.
3. Meanwhile, cook pasta in salted water and drain. Toss with the remaining 2 tablespoons of olive oil, add pasta to seafood mixture. Season with salt and pepper to taste and serve.

143

Musselman's Mussel Risotto   Serves 4

The smokey taste of the mussel paired with saffron .... outstanding!

$^1/_2$ cup dry white wine
$1^1/_2$ pounds mussels, scrubbed, beards
    removed
$^1/_4$ teaspoon saffron threads
1   tablespoon olive oil
1   onion, minced
2   cloves garlic, minced
$1^1/_3$ cups short grain Italian Arborio rice
2   tablespoons butter
$^1/_2$ teaspoon salt
black pepper
2   tablespoons chopped fresh parsley
freshly grated Parmesan cheese

1. Bring $2^1/_2$ cups water and wine to a boil in a large pot over high heat. Add the mussels and cook 2 to 3 minutes, or until the shells open. Drain in a colander and reserve broth. (Discard any that have not opened). Shell mussels and set aside.

2. Strain the cooking liquid through a cheesecloth or coffee filter into a small pan. Add 1 cup of warm water and saffron.

3. Heat oil over medium heat in a large saucepan. Add onion and garlic and sauté 3 to 4 minutes, or until golden. Add rice and stir well to coat with the oil. Cook for 1 minute and add the cooking liquid $^1/_2$ cup at a time, allowing the liquid to be absorbed between each addition. This should take about 20 minutes. When rice is tender but creamy, carefully stir in the butter and mussels. Add salt and parsley, season to taste with pepper. Serve with a bowl of freshly grated Parmesan cheese.

Angel Hair with Smoked Salmon and Lemon Thyme   Serves 4

All the flavors you love with salmon.

1   pound angel hair or other very thin pasta
    (spaghettini)
8   ounces smoked salmon
$^1/_4$ cup extra virgin olive oil
$^1/_4$ cup crème fraîche or heavy cream
2   tablespoons finely chopped lemon thyme
2   tablespoons finely chopped parsley
juice of 1 lemon
salt and pepper
sour cream
1   tablespoon capers

1. Cook pasta according to package directions. Meanwhile, slice salmon into bite-size pieces. Drain pasta, place in a large bowl.

2. Add the olive oil, crème fraîche, lemon thyme, parsley, lemon juice, salt and pepper to the pasta and toss well with salmon to thoroughly combine. Divide among 4 warmed plates, top with a spoonful of sour cream and sprinkle with capers.

Orzo Niçoise with Shrimp and Scallops   Serves 6 to 8

1   pound orzo
1   pound medium shrimp, peeled and
     deveined
1/2 pound sea scallops
2   tablespoons fresh chopped basil
2   tablespoons fresh chopped parsley
4   cloves garlic, minced
1/2 cup chicken broth
1/2 cup ripe green olives, drained and chopped
1   teaspoon freshly ground black pepper
2   teaspoons olive oil
1   cup Feta cheese
fresh salad greens

1. Cook orzo according to package directions, drain and place in a large mixing bowl.
2. Bring 4 cups of water to a boil in a medium saucepan, add a dash of salt. Add the scallops, then the shrimp, stir and cover; remove from the heat. (Cooking shrimp this way ensures that they taste nice and crisp). Let them rest several minutes until shrimp are pink, drain and rinse under cold water.
2. Add scallops, shrimp and remaining ingredients, except lettuce, to orzo in the bowl. Toss gently and add a little more chicken broth to moisten if you desire. Serve either chilled or at room temperature over lettuce leaves.

Fettucine with Squid Italian Style   Serves 8

The secret here is that final squeeze of lemon.

1   pound fettucine, cooked
1/3 cup olive oil
6   cloves garlic, peeled and minced
1/2 cup chopped onion
1/2 cup chopped green pepper
2   pounds squid, cleaned and cut into
     2-inch strips
4   medium tomatoes, seeded and chopped
1   cup dry white wine
2   8-ounce cans tomato sauce
dash of salt
Tabasco sauce
juice of 1 fresh lemon (2 tablespoons)
freshly chopped parsley

1. Cook pasta in boiling salted water according to package directions. Drain and set aside.
2. In medium saucepan, sauté garlic, onion and green pepper in olive oil for 3 minutes until soft. Add the squid, tomatoes, tomato sauce, white wine, salt and Tabasco sauce to taste. Simmer for 15 minutes. Squeeze the fresh lemon into the sauce right before serving and toss with the fettucine until well mixed. Sprinkle with parsley and serve with Parmesan cheese.

Seafood Stuffed Shells au Gratin   Serves 8

Bring these to your next pot luck dinner for rave reviews.

$^1/_2$ pound jumbo shells (24 shells)
4   tablespoons butter
1   carrot, diced
1   stalk celery, diced
1   onion, sliced
2   cloves garlic, minced
1   pound medium shrimp, peeled and coarsely
    chopped
1   pound cod or other white fish fillets, cut
    into $^3/_4$-inch chunks
$^3/_4$ teaspoon dried thyme
$1^1/_2$ teaspoon salt
$^1/_2$ teaspoon black pepper
2   tablespoons chopped parsley
3   cups milk
3   tablespoons flour
2   ounces Gruyere cheese, shredded,
    about $^2/_3$ cup
paprika

1. In a large pot of boiling, salted water, cook shells until almost done. Drain and set aside. Heat oven to 350°. Butter a 3 quart baking dish. In a large frying pan, over medium-low heat, melt 1 tablespoon of butter. Add carrot, celery, onion, and garlic. Cover and cook, stirring occasionally, until vegetables are soft, about 7 minutes. Add shrimp, cod, thyme, $^3/_4$ teaspoon salt and $^1/_4$ teaspoon pepper. Raise heat to medium and cook, until shrimp are pink and cod looks white, about 5 minutes more. Stir in parsley and set aside.

2. In small saucepan, bring $2^1/_2$ cups of milk just to a boil. In a saucepan over medium heat, melt remaining 3 tablespoons butter. Whisk in the flour and cook, whisking, until it foams, 1 to 2 minutes. Add hot milk, whisking constantly. Return mixture to a slow boil and cook until thickened, about 3 minutes. Whisk in the remaining salt and pepper. Stir $^3/_4$ cup of white sauce into fish mixture. Thin remaining white sauce with $^1/_2$ cup milk.

3. Stuff shells with fish mixture and arrange in baking dish. Pour remaining white sauce over shells. Sprinkle cheese and paprika over shells, cover with foil and bake $^1/_2$ hour. Uncover the dish and bake 15 minutes longer.

Fettucine with Peppered Scallops   Serves 4 to 6

You can vary the peppercorns – try a mix of pink, white and black.

1¹/₂ pounds scallops
2 teaspoons black peppercorns, crushed
3 cloves garlic, minced
3 tablespoons olive oil
1 cup fish stock or clam juice
¹/₂ cup dry white wine
1 tablespoon fresh lemon juice
2 tablespoons chopped fresh parsley
4 tablespoons butter
salt to taste
1 pound fettucine or other ribbon noodle
   cooked according to package directions
¹/₂ cup freshly grated Parmesan cheese

1. Cut scallops in half if they are large and place in a bowl. Toss with the crushed peppercorns, garlic and 1 tablespoon of the olive oil. Marinate, covered, for an hour or overnight. When ready to serve, have pasta water boiling.
2. Heat the remaining 2 tablespoons of olive oil in a sauté pan over medium-high heat. Add the scallops and brown on both sides, about 3 minutes. Add the fish stock or clam juice, wine, lemon juice, chopped parsley and a few pinches of salt. Simmer the sauce for 5 minutes, turn off heat and swirl in the butter until melted.
3. Drain the pasta and toss with the scallops. Serve the dish hot and pass the Parmesan.

Shrimp Penne with Herb Sauce   Serves 4

Spice this up to your taste with red pepper flakes.

1 pound medium shrimp, peeled and deveined
2 tablespoons olive oil
4 garlic cloves, minced
1 28-ounce can crushed tomatoes with purée
¹/₂ cup dry white wine
¹/₂ cup chopped fresh parsley
¹/₂ cup chopped fresh basil
1 tablespoon chopped fresh oregano
salt and crushed red pepper flakes
12 ounces penne, cooked
freshly grated Parmesan cheese

1. Heat olive oil in a large saucepan and sauté garlic until tender, about 3 minutes. Add shrimp and sauté until just pink.
2. Add crushed tomatoes, white wine, parsley, basil and oregano. Simmer over medium-low heat for 15 minutes until thickened. Season to taste with salt and red pepper flakes.
3. Toss the penne with the shrimp-herb sauce and serve with freshly grated Parmesan cheese.

Spaghetti with Mussels, Scallops and Shrimp   Serves 4 to 6

A remembrance from our past Stonington Warden C. H. Maxson, III.

3   tablespoons olive oil
1   large onion, minced
4   cloves garlic, minced
1/2 cup dry white wine
2   tablespoons fresh chopped basil, or 1
    tablespoon dried
1   tablespoon fresh oregano or 2 teaspoons
    dried
2   tablespoons fresh flat-leaf parsley, chopped
1 1/2 cups canned plum tomatoes
1 1/2 pounds mussels, washed and beards
    removed (you may substitute clams)
1   pound sea scallops, cut in half
1   pound large shrimp, peeled, deveined and
    butterflied
salt and freshly ground black pepper
red pepper flakes
1   pound thin spaghetti, cooked according to
    package directions, al dente
fresh grated Romano or Parmesan cheese

1. Heat olive oil in a 4 or 5-quart saucepan over medium-high heat. Add onion and sauté until lightly golden. Add garlic and cook for an additional 30 seconds. Stir in wine, basil, oregano and parsley. Add tomatoes, increase heat and simmer for 5 minutes.

2. Reduce heat to medium. Add mussels or clams, cover and cook for 5 minutes, until shells open about 1/2 inch. Add scallops and shrimp. Season to taste with salt, pepper and red pepper flakes. Cover and cook an additional 3 to 4 minutes until scallops and shrimp are just firm. Adjust seasoning, add spaghetti and toss gently to mix.

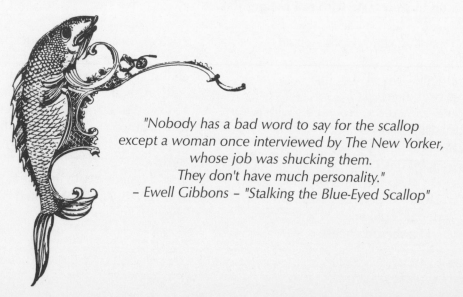

"Nobody has a bad word to say for the scallop
except a woman once interviewed by The New Yorker,
whose job was shucking them.
They don't have much personality."
– Ewell Gibbons – "Stalking the Blue-Eyed Scallop"

Starr Pasta with Mussels, Clams, Scallops and Shrimp   Serves 8-10

This has been our traditional Christmas Eve family dinner for years. You can increase or decrease all of the amounts depending on how many you are serving or the price of seafood.

3   tablespoons olive oil
1   large onion, minced
2   cloves garlic, minced
$1/4$ cup dry white wine
$1^1/_2$ teaspoons dry basil or $1^1/_2$ tablespoons
    fresh chopped
1   teaspoon dry marjoram
$1^1/_2$ cup plum tomatoes, well drained
$1^1/_2$ pounds mussels, beards removed
2   pounds cherrystone clams
1   pound sea scallops, cut in half if large
1   pound medium shrimp, peeled and
    deveined
1   pound spaghetti, cooked
Tabasco sauce (optional)
salt and pepper

1. Heat olive oil in large saucepan. Add onion and garlic, sauté until just soft. Add wine, basil and marjoram, simmer for 1 minute. Add tomatoes, increase heat to boiling and cook for 5 minutes.
2. Reduce heat, add mussels and clams, cook until shells open, about 5 more minutes. Add scallops and shrimp, cover and cook for 2 to 3 minutes until just firm. Season with salt and pepper to taste, and a few dashes of Tabasco sauce. Spoon over freshly cooked pasta.

Thai Noodles with Shrimp and Artichokes   Serves 4

A Golden Phoenix specialty.

$3/4$ cup rice vinegar
2   tablespoons sesame oil
$1/2$ teaspoon red pepper flakes
2   tablespoons soy sauce
$1^1/_2$ tablespoons chopped peeled fresh ginger
1   tablespoon Dijon mustard
1 12-ounce package fresh Chinese or Japanese
    water noodles or linguine pasta
$3/4$ pound peeled, cooked shrimp
2   6-ounce jars marinated artichoke hearts,
    drained
1   cup chopped scallions
$1/4$ cup chopped fresh cilantro
$1/4$ cup chopped fresh mint
$1/4$ cup chopped roasted peanuts

1. Combine first 5 ingredients in a blender or food processor and mix well. Can be prepared 1 day ahead and refrigerated.
2. If using Chinese noodles, drop into a pot of boiling water for 1 minute, rinse and drain. For linguine, cook according to package directions and drain. Combine noodles with remaining ingredients and toss with enough dressing to coat. Pass extra dressing separately and sprinkle with a few more chopped roasted peanuts.

Sea Shell Tagliatelle with Garlic Cream   Serves 6

2   pounds cherrystone clams, scrubbed
2   pounds mussels, scrubbed, beards removed
$^1/_2$ cup dry white wine
freshly ground black pepper
2   shallots, peeled and chopped
2   cloves garlic, minced
$^1/_4$ cup butter
4   tablespoons flour
$^1/_2$ cup heavy cream
$^1/_2$ cup grated Parmesan cheese
2   tablespoons chopped fresh parsley
1   pound tagliatelle, cooked (or other flat pasta or egg noodle)

1. Place the clams and mussels in a large saucepan with the wine, pepper to taste, shallots and garlic. Cook over high heat until the shells open. Remove with a slotted spoon. Shuck the clams and mussel meats from the shell. Strain the broth and reserve.
2. Melt the butter in a pan and add the flour; cook, stirring for 1 minute. Gradually whisk in the strained mussel and clam juice. Add the cream, Parmesan and parsley and simmer until smooth, blending well. Lightly mix in the clams and mussels.
3. Meanwhile, cook the tagliatelle in boiling salted water until tender, according to package directions, about 6 to 8 minutes. Drain and place in a warmed serving bowl. Spoon the sauce over the pasta and lightly toss. Serve with additional grated Parmesan.

Pasta Stone   Serves 6

Any other seafood, or even chicken, may be substituted for the scallops. A Canterbury favorite.

1   pound sea scallops
1   pound sweet or hot Italian sausage, sliced
2   tablespoons olive oil
2   teaspoons minced garlic
1   large red pepper, julienned
1   large green pepper, julienned
1   8-ounce package mushrooms, sliced
$^1/_2$ cup sliced red onion
2   tablespoons chopped fresh basil
2   tablespoons chopped fresh parsley
$^1/_2$ cup sun-dried tomatoes, diced
salt and pepper to taste
1   pound package pasta twists, cooked and drained
mesclun greens

1. If scallops are large, cut into bite-size pieces. Cook sausage in a large pan until browned, drain and set aside. In the same pan, heat olive oil, garlic, peppers, onions and mushrooms. Sauté for 5 minutes, scraping any sausage bits from the bottom of the pan. Add scallops and cook over high heat for another 5 minutes until just firm.
2. Reduce heat, add reserved sausage, basil, parsley, and sun-dried tomatoes. Toss with cooked pasta, season with salt and pepper and just before serving, add a few generous handfuls or more of mesclun greens. Drizzle with a little more olive oil and mix well.

Golden Gate Linguine with Shrimp, Asparagus, and Basil   Serves 4

We love to enjoy this on our porch overlooking San Francisco Bay.

1   8-ounce package linguine
1   cup packed fresh basil leaves
2   garlic cloves
$1/4$ cup lemon juice
1   tablespoon olive oil
salt
olive oil or nonstick cooking spray
1   pound asparagus, cut into 2-inch pieces
$3/4$ pound large shrimp, peeled and deveined
$1/8$ teaspoon crushed red pepper

About 45 minutes before serving:

1. Prepare linguine as label directs; drain.
2. Meanwhile, in food processor with knife attached or in a blender at high speed, process basil, garlic, lemon juice, olive oil, and $1/2$ teaspoon salt until smooth.
3. Spray nonstick 10-inch skillet with cooking spray. Over medium-high heat, cook asparagus, stirring frequently, until almost tender-crisp, about 5 minutes. Add shrimp, red pepper, and $1/4$ teaspoon salt. Cook, stirring frequently, until shrimp turn pink, about 4 minutes.
4. In large serving bowl, toss pasta with basil mixture, then stir in shrimp and asparagus. This can be served hot, cold or best at room temperature.

Linguine with White Clam "Sauce"   Serves 6

Encore - Encore from Seafood Secrets I

1 pound package linguine or other thin pasta
4 dozen hard shell clams (cherrystones or littlenecks)
6 large garlic cloves, crushed
$1/4$ cup olive oil
chopped fresh parsley for garnish
crushed hot red pepper flakes

1. Cook pasta in boiling salted water according to package directions. Drain and cover to keep warm. Wash clams under cold water and place in a large saucepan with $1/2$ inch of water. Cover and steam for 3 to 4 minutes until clams are barely open, being careful not to overcook. Discard any clams that do not open.

2. Working over the saucepan, insert a sharp knife in shell and carefully remove clam meat, reserving all clam juice (liquid) in the pan. Coarsely chop clam meat into large chunks, about $1/3$ the size of each clam, and set aside.

3. Heat olive oil in a large skillet over medium heat and add crushed garlic. Cook for one minute, being careful not to brown. Stir clam juice into oil and simmer for several minutes to reduce. Add clams to the sauce, gently heat and spoon clams over cooked pasta. Serve hot, sprinkled with chopped parsley and pass the hot pepper flakes to taste.

What is a clam?
According to Webster, "any of various equivalve edible
marine mollusks that live partly buried in sand or mud.
A clam is a shellfish that shuts up tightly."
"Clam," like clamp, comes from the Old English
clamm, to grasp tightly in one hand.
Despite its power, the clam has a very slow heartbeat,
two to twenty beats per minute, making it
a slow and sluggish creature.

Mama's Mussels with Linguine   Serves 4

From Mama's Mama in Sicily.

4   quarts mussels
3   tablespoons olive oil
3   tablespoons butter or margarine
4   cloves garlic, minced
6   scallions, thinly sliced
1   28-ounce can crushed plum tomatoes
1/2 teaspoon oregano
1   teaspoon basil
1/2 cup chopped parsley
1/2 cup dry white wine
3/4 pound linguine, cooked and drained
salt and pepper to taste
additional chopped parsley for garnish
grated Parmesan cheese

1. Scrub mussels under cold water and remove any beards. Do not use any mussels that are already opened.
2. In a large saucepan, heat butter and oil, sauté garlic and scallions for 2 minutes. Do not brown. Add tomatoes, oregano, basil, parsley and white wine. Bring to a vigorous simmer and add mussels. Cover and simmer over medium heat for 6 to 8 minutes until mussels open. Taste and season with salt and pepper.
3. Spoon mussels and sauce over cooked pasta and sprinkle with chopped parsley and pass the cheese. Some Italians do not serve cheese with any seafood pasta – Mama did!

Linguine with Clams Primavera   Serves 4

2   10-ounce cans whole clams
1   medium onion, chopped
6   cloves garlic, minced
4   tablespoons olive oil
1   small bunch of broccoli (about 1 1/2 pounds), cut into bite-size pieces
2   carrots, julienned
1/4 cup fresh grated Parmesan cheese plus additional for garnish
1/2 cup fresh parsley
freshly ground black pepper
3/4 pound linguine

1. Bring a large pot of salted water to a boil, add pasta and cook for 6 to 8 minutes until just al dente. Do not overcook.
2. Meanwhile, sauté onion and garlic in a large skillet until tender. Add clams and their juice, broccoli and carrots. Cover and simmer over medium low heat.
3. Drain pasta, reserving 1/2 cup of pasta water. When clams are cooked and vegetables still crunchy, add to the pasta. Mix well and cook until heated through. Add parsley, cheese, and season with black pepper. Toss and enjoy.

Tasty Thai Shrimp and Sesame Noodles   Serves 4

A terrific East-West combination.

1   pound medium shrimp, shelled and deveined
1   8-ounce bottle light Italian dressing
2   tablespoons chunky peanut butter
1   tablespoon soy sauce
1   tablespoon honey
1   teaspoon grated peeled ginger root
$^1/_2$ teaspoon crushed red pepper
8   ounces capellini or angel hair pasta
2   tablespoons vegetable oil
1   tablespoon sesame oil
1   medium carrot, peeled and shredded
1   cup chopped scallions
$^1/_4$ cup chopped fresh cilantro for garnish

1. In medium bowl, mix shrimp with $^1/_3$ cup dressing; cover and refrigerate 1 hour. In small bowl, mix peanut butter, soy sauce, honey, ginger, crushed red pepper and remaining dressing. Set aside. When shrimp have marinated for an hour, prepare pasta according to package directions. Drain.

2. In a 4-quart saucepan over high heat, heat vegetable oil and sesame oil until very hot. Cook carrot 1 minute. Drain off dressing from shrimp. Add shrimp and scallions to oil, cook, stirring constantly, about 3 minutes, or until shrimp turn opaque. In large bowl, toss hot capellini with peanut butter, soy mixture and add shrimp mixture. Sprinkle with chopped cilantro.

Baked Shrimp Pilaf   Serves 4 to 6

Serve this with chilled artichokes and crusty bread.

2   tablespoons butter
$^1/_2$ cup chopped green pepper
1   cup chopped celery
6   ounces mushrooms, sliced (about 10) or 1 8-ounce can mushrooms, drained
1   pound medium shrimp, peeled and deveined
$1^1/_2$ cups cooked white rice
$^1/_2$ cup ripe green olives, sliced
$^1/_2$ cup slivered almonds, toasted
1   10-ounce can cream of shrimp soup
1   tablespoon freshly squeezed lemon juice
2   teaspoons Worcestershire sauce
$^1/_2$ cup sherry
salt and pepper
paprika

1. Melt butter in a skillet and sauté green pepper, celery and onions for 3 to 4 minutes until tender-crisp. Combine with remaining ingredients, seasoning with salt and pepper. Pour into a lightly-greased 2-quart casserole, sprinkle generously with paprika and bake 30 minutes in a 350° oven until bubbling and browned.

"What will this sister of mine do with rice?"
                          – William Shakespeare

Penne with Stir Fried Shrimp and Asparagus   Serves 2

An unusual dish for the asparagus season. The pasta should be the individual piece type: penne, penne rigate, ziti, or the like.

$^1/_4$ cup olive oil
red pepper flakes
1   dozen baby asparagus, broken in 1-inch
    pieces
3   scallions, cut in 1-inch pieces
8   black kalamata olives, cut in half, pits
    removed
2   cloves garlic, finely chopped
1   tablespoon lemon juice
2   tablespoons sherry
$^1/_2$ teaspoon chili powder
1   teaspoon dried basil
white wine
1   dozen medium shrimp, cleaned, peeled,
    and deveined
salt and black pepper
pasta for 2

1. Bring water for pasta to boil, add a little oil
   and 1 tablespoon salt. Time cooking so
   pasta and sauce are done together. Cooking
   time for sauce is about 3 minutes.
2. Heat oil in sauté pan, add red pepper flakes
   to taste ($^1/_4$ teaspoon up), asparagus,
   scallions, and olives. Stir fry for about 1
   minute, then add garlic, lemon juice, sherry,
   chili powder and basil. Cook until liquid is
   reduced, but do not let the garlic brown.
3. Add a little white wine and shrimp. Sauté
   until shrimp is pink and just curled into
   circles, about 1 minute or so. At this point,
   the pasta should be done. Drain pasta and
   toss with sauce, add salt and pepper to
   taste, and serve.

Dancing Spirit Linguine and Clam Sauce

Serves 4

My boat, *Dancing Spirit*, has only a two-burner stove which runs on alcohol. About 10 years ago, my mother, Helen, suggested this dish for a special dinner aboard with a special date. Over the years, I have changed Mom's recipe to make it easier to do on the boat and changed the seasonings a bit. Oh, and I got married to that special date!

$^2/_3$ pound linguine
2   teaspoons chopped garlic
8   tablespoons butter (1 stick)
7   large clams in the shell (quahogs)
$^1/_2$ teaspoon dill
$^1/_2$ teaspoon Italian seasoning (or mixed basil and oregano)
$^1/_2$ teaspoon coarse ground black pepper

1. Boil the linguine in 2 quarts of lightly salted water until al dente, about 10 minutes. While the pasta cooks, melt butter in a large skillet and add garlic. Sauté on low heat for 2 minutes, then add Italian seasoning, simmer, stirring every 2 minutes. Meanwhile, open clams, drain, and chop the meat fine. You can add the clam juice to the boiling linguine water if you prefer stronger flavor.

2. When the linguine is done, drain it, add the clams to the butter and turn heat up until the clams sizzle. Stir continuously until the clams turn white - no more than 2 minutes, then add the linguine, pepper, and dill. Turn off the heat, toss well, and serve immediately.

Thin Spaghetti with Red Clam Sauce   Serves 8

A true Italian pasta with clams – spaghetti, not linguine.

1   pound vermicelli
2   pounds fresh cherrystone clams, or 2
    10-ounce cans baby clams
4   tablespoons olive oil
4   cloves garlic
2   cups peeled plum tomatoes
1   teaspoon salt
freshly ground pepper to taste
$^1/_2$ teaspoon oregano
$^1/_2$ teaspoon basil
1   tablespoon fresh chopped parsley

If you use the canned clams:

1. Sauté the garlic in 4 tablespoons of olive oil for 3 minutes. Drain the clams, saving half of the juice they are packed in, chop coarsely.
2. Add the tomatoes, $^1/_2$ cup of clam juice and the remaining ingredients and cook over medium heat for 15 minutes.

1. If using fresh clams, wash them thoroughly and sauté them in a wide skillet with 1 tablespoon of the oil over high heat. Stir the clams around until the shells open. Remove from heat and cool. Shuck the clams from the shells, reserving a few for garnish. Chop the clams coarsely and drain off the clam juice and oil in the skillet.
2. Add the remaining 3 tablespoons of oil to the skillet and sauté the garlic for 3 minutes, being careful not to brown. Add the clams, tomatoes, reserved clam juices, salt, pepper, basil and oregano. Simmer for 15 minutes until sauce has thickened. Add the parsley and pour over the cooked pasta. Garnish platter with whole clams.

Italian Cold Tuna and Risotto Salad   Serves 8

$1^1/_2$ cups white rice
1   teaspoon salt
2   carrots grated
2   large tomatoes, seeded and chopped
1   small zucchini, grated
$^1/_2$ cup chopped scallions
$^1/_4$ cup chopped capers
2   6-ounce cans tuna, packed in oil, drained and flaked
$^1/_4$ cup chopped fresh Italian parsley
2   tablespoons white wine vinegar
2   tablespoons olive oil
2   tablespoons water
2   teaspoons whole grain mustard
4   anchovies, chopped (optional)
freshly ground black pepper to taste

1. Bring 3 cups of water to a boil in a saucepan, add rice and salt, lower heat, cover and simmer for 15 to 18 minutes until water has been absorbed and rice is tender. Cool.
2. In a large bowl, combine rice, carrots, tomatoes, zucchini, scallions, capers, tuna and parsley; toss gently.
3. In a small bowl, whisk together vinegar, olive oil, water and mustard. Pour over the rice salad and toss to blend. Season with lots of ground pepper. Do not serve too cold. This is best when it is made ahead of time.

Fettucine al Salmone Affumicato
(Fettucine with Smoked Salmon)   Serves 2 (easily doubled for 4)

The salmon for this dish should be the type which is smoked in fillets and can be broken into flakes.

3   to 4 ounces smoked salmon, flaked
3   scallions, sliced short
1   small hot green pepper, diced (seeds discarded)
1   teaspoon capers
$^1/_2$ teaspoon green peppercorns
2   tablespoons green stuffed (salad) olives
hot red pepper flakes
pepper and salt
1   medium tomato, seeded and diced
1   teaspoon dried basil
2   teaspoons dried parsley flakes
1   tablespoon garlic mustard sauce*
$^1/_2$ teaspoons dried lemon grass
2   teaspoons soy sauce
2   tablespoons vodka
$^1/_4$ cup olive oil
fettucine for 2

1. Bring water for pasta to boil, add a little oil and 1 tablespoon salt. Add pasta to water, and begin cooking other ingredients when pasta is 2 to 3 minutes from being cooked.

2. Heat oil on medium heat in sauté pan while pasta is cooking and add all ingredients except soy sauce, vodka and salt and pepper. Sauté ingredients, stirring, until they are hot through, then add vodka and soy sauce to sauté, bringing to a boil. At this point, the pasta should be just cooked to the "al dente" stage. Drain pasta and add to sauté. Toss the pasta with the sauce, add salt and pepper to taste, and serve.

* The "garlic mustard sauce" is a commercial product. If not available, use two cloves garlic, minced, $1^1/_2$ teaspoon Dijon mustard, and 1 tablespoon lemon juice.

LiGHT THE FiRE

Swordfish with Warm Tomato Vinaigrette   Serves 8

Excellent served with a chilled rice salad.

8   8-ounce swordfish steaks
2   tablespoons plus $^1/_2$ cup olive oil
$^1/_4$ cup chopped shallots
1   tablespoon chopped garlic
1   28-ounce can diced tomatoes with the
     juices
$^1/_4$ cup chopped fresh basil
$^1/_4$ cup chopped fresh parsley
2   tablespoons red wine vinegar
2   tablespoons Balsamic vinegar
2   tablespoons Dijon mustard
dash of Worcestershire sauce
dash of Tabasco sauce
1   tablespoon capers, drained

1. Heat 2 tablespoons of olive oil in a large saucepan over medium heat. Add shallots and garlic and sauté until tender, about 3 minutes.
2. Add the tomatoes and simmer for 10 minutes until slightly thickened. Remove from the heat and add basil, parsley, vinegars, mustard, Worcestershire sauce, and Tabasco sauce and stir to blend. Gradually whisk in the remaining $^1/_2$ cup olive oil and season to taste with salt and pepper. Add capers and either refrigerate for later or let stand at room temperature if using now.
3. Grill swordfish steaks over a hot fire for 8 minutes per side, brushing with additional olive oil as needed. Bring vinaigrette to a low simmer, whisking constantly and spoon over swordfish.

Picnic Grilled Shrimp "Anyway You Want"

Select raw jumbo shrimp
    (4 to 6 per person)
If serving at an outdoor party, simply split shells up the back and devein. If serving indoors, peel first and then devein. Marinate in any of the following combinations:
* Equal parts of soy sauce, peanut oil and sherry, adding 2 cloves crushed garlic and a few drops of sesame oil.
* Equal parts of olive oil and vermouth or white wine and butter seasoned with tarragon or parsley. Squeeze in the juice of a fresh lemon and some freshly ground black pepper.

Drain shrimp from marinade and grill over charcoal or in oven for 4 or 5 minutes on each side. For a picnic, have lots of finger bowls and hot towels.

Throw a few leaves of bay on the charcoal when grilling fish or meat – it will give it a lovely flavor.

Bangkok Shrimp Sate Skewers   Serves 4

From a transported Chinatown gourmet.

3   tablespoons soy sauce
3   tablespoons water
2   tablespoons brown sugar
2   teaspoons lemon juice
1   teaspoon sesame oil
2   garlic cloves, crushed
2   red or green chilies, seeded and chopped
dash of hot pepper sauce to taste
1$^1/_2$ pounds large shrimp

Chi-Chi's Peanut sauce:
1   tablespoon peanut oil
3   garlic cloves, crushed
2   teaspoons dried chilies (or to taste)
1   teaspoon brown sugar
1$^1/_2$ cups coconut milk
$^1/_2$ cup peanut butter
2   tablespoons fresh lemon juice

1. Combine all of the above ingredients except shrimp in a large shallow dish.
2. Devein shrimp and split down the back but do not peel. Add to the marinade and refrigerate for at least 4 hours, turning occasionally.
3. Remove shrimp from marinade and thread on skewers. If you are using wooden skewers rather than metal ones, be sure to soak for 15 minutes in water so they will not burn. Grill over hot coals, basting occasionally with the marinade for 4 to 5 minutes on each side until shrimp are pink and crispy. Serve with peanut sauce.

Peanut sauce preparation:
Heat oil in a small saucepan. Add garlic and chilies, stirring over heat for 1 minute. Add brown sugar and peanut butter, cooking slowly, stirring until smooth. Gradually add coconut milk and bring to a boil, stirring constantly. Remove from heat and stir in lemon juice.

Grilled Fish Sandwiches   Serves 4

A fish lover's hamburger solution, a surprise at any picnic.

4   4-ounce pieces swordfish, tuna or salmon
$^1/_2$ cup mayonnaise
lemon pepper seasoning
paprika
4   kaiser rolls, buttered
2   tomatoes, sliced
sliced red onions
tartar sauce

1. Spread both sides of fish with mayonnaise and sprinkle generously with lemon pepper and paprika. Place fish on oiled grill over medium heat and cook 5 to 6 minutes per side until fish is just cooked through.
2. Grill rolls lightly over fire and serve sandwiches with red onion, slices of tomato, shredded lettuce and top with tartar sauce.

Whole Broiled Bass with Fennel

Serves 4-6

For this recipe it is best to use a double wire gridiron or basket so that it is easy to turn the fish. If you do not have one, you can turn the fish over with 2 large spatulas.

1   sea bass, 3 to 4 pounds, whole and split
salt and pepper
1   lemon, sliced
2   fennel bulbs, sliced
2   tablespoons olive oil
dried fennel sticks

1. Clean the fish and season with salt and pepper. Place lemon and fennel bulb in cavity and secure with several pieces of string.
2. Have a medium-hot fire prepared and sprinkle the dried fennel sticks on the coals. Rub the fish with the olive oil and place in fish rack or grill. Cook for 10 minutes per side, and check fish with a small fork to be sure it is done and flakes nicely. Remove fish to a large platter and surround with Hot Coleslaw and additional fresh fennel sprigs.

Hot Coleslaw:
1   small cabbage
$^1/_2$ teaspoon salt
3   tablespoons malt or cider vinegar
1   teaspoon coarse mustard
6   tablespoons oil
1   tablespoon chopped parsley
1   teaspoon fennel seeds
fresh ground black pepper

Hot Coleslaw preparation:
1. Shred cabbage finely and cook in boiling salted water for 4 to 5 minutes or until just tender. Drain well and set aside.
2. While the cabbage is cooking, whisk together the remaining ingredients until well mixed. Toss with the cabbage and serve with the grilled bass.

Swordfish with Mediterranean Bay Butter   Serves 4

Makes 2 cups of butter, enough to serve later with any other fish.

4   8-ounce swordfish steaks
6   large fresh bay leaves - use only fresh leaves,
    do not substitute dry
6   cloves garlic
1/2 teaspoon salt
1/2 pound softened butter
1   tablespoon chopped fresh parsley
1   tablespoon chopped fresh chives
2   teaspoons chopped oregano
1   teaspoon chopped thyme
1   tablespoon finely minced orange peel
pinch of white pepper
olive oil for basting fish

1. Cut the stem and center rib from the bay leaves and chop finely. Place the garlic in a small bowl and add the salt, mash to a smooth paste.
2. Combine all of the ingredients and mix well, adding more salt and pepper if needed. Refrigerate at least overnight to marry the flavors. This can keep up to 2 weeks in the refrigerator.
3. Brush swordfish with a little olive oil and grill over a hot fire for 6 to 8 minutes, depending on the thickness. Right before serving, put pats of the butter on the swordfish (be generous) and let it melt.

Orange-Glazed Swordfish Kebabs   Serves 4

grated zest and juice of 1 orange
1/4 cup orange marmalade
1   tablespoon olive oil
1   tablespoon prepared horseradish
1   tablespoon balsamic vinegar
1   teaspoon salt
1/4 teaspoon crushed red pepper flakes
1 1/2 pound swordfish, cut into 2-inch pieces
1   16-ounce can pineapple chunks
2   red and green peppers, cut into 2-inch pieces
3   scallions, white and green parts, cut into 2-inch lengths

1. In shallow dish, mix orange zest and juice with next six ingredients. Add swordfish, pineapple, peppers and scallions, turn to coat. Cover and refrigerate 40 minutes.
2. Position oven rack about 6 inches from heat source; preheat broiler, or have a hot charcoal fire ready. Thread swordfish, pineapple, pepper and scallions onto skewers on rack set in broiler pan. Broil, turning once, until pineapple is lightly browned and fish flakes easily, 15 to 18 minutes. In skillet over high heat, bring reserved marinade to a boil. Cook until slightly thickened, about 5 minutes. Drizzle over skewers, and serve with white rice.

"I with compassion, once may overlook
    A skewer sent to table by my cook:
But think no therefore tamely I'll permit
    That he should daily the same fault commit,
For fear the rascal send me up the pit!"
    – William King

Grilled Swordfish with Spicy Gazpacho Salsa   Serves 4

4   6-ounce swordfish slices
2   tablespoons olive oil
2   tablespoons Worcestershire sauce
Tabasco sauce to taste

Gazpacho salsa:
2   tablespoons olive oil
1   onion, diced
1   red pepper, diced
2   cloves garlic, minced
4   tomatoes, seeded, peeled and chopped
1   tablespoon red wine
2   teaspoons Balsamic vinegar
2   tablespoons chili sauce
1   small cucumber, peeled, seeded and chopped
2   scallions, chopped
1   stalk celery, chopped
salt and cayenne pepper

1. Mix olive oil, Worcestershire sauce and Tabasco sauce in a small bowl. Brush swordfish on both sides with mixture and set aside.
2. Make salsa: In a medium-size saucepan, cook onion, pepper and garlic for 2 minutes. Stir in the tomatoes, red wine, Balsamic vinegar and chili sauce. Cook for a few minutes until tomatoes have softened. Remove from heat and cool. Add the cucumber, scallions and celery. Season with a little salt and pepper.
3. Grill the swordfish for 5 minutes on each side over a hot fire, basting a few times. Spoon gazpacho salsa on each plate and top with the swordfish.

Exotic Grilled Swordfish   Serves 4

Keep this marinade in your refrigerator for any summer grilling.

1¹/₂ pounds swordfish steaks
¹/₂ cup light soy sauce
¹/₃ cup catsup
4   cloves chopped garlic
¹/₄ cup chopped parsley
¹/₄ cup chopped scallions
¹/₂ cup orange juice
2   tablespoons fresh lemon juice
1   tablespoon fresh lime juice
¹/₄ teaspoon black pepper
¹/₄ teaspoon oregano

1. In a large bowl, mix marinade ingredients (all ingredients except swordfish) together. Add swordfish steaks and marinate in the refrigerator for at least 3 hours, turning several times.
2. Cook swordfish over a hot grill for 8 to 10 minutes on each side or until fish is firm to the touch. Serve with wedges of fresh lime and lemon.

"I'll be with you in the squeezing of a lemon."
– Oliver Goldsmith

Society Salmon with Chive Blossom Butter   Serves 4

4   6-ounce salmon fillets
$^1/_2$ pound butter
4   cloves garlic, minced
4   tablespoons fresh chopped chives
$^1/_4$ cup purple chive blossoms, chopped
freshly ground black pepper

"Chibals, or chives, have their roots parted, as a garlick: a good pot herb, opening, but evil for the eyes."
                    – Gervase Markham: 1684

1. Combine butter, garlic, chives, blossoms and pepper. While butter is soft, lightly spread some on the flesh side of the salmon. Roll rest of butter in a fat cylinder, wrap in plastic wrap and chill until solid. It is best if refrigerated for at least 3 hours.
2. Have a nice medium-hot grill ready. Place the fish, skin side up, on the grill. Cook for 5 minutes, turn gently and grill for another 3 to 4 minutes, depending on the thickness of the fish. Serve the salmon with a nice slice of the chive butter, melting on the top. There will be herb butter left which can be frozen or refrigerated for up to a week. It is also wonderful for making industrial-strength garlic French bread.

Thai Swordfish with Lemongrass   Serves 4

A delicate marriage on the grill.

4   6-ounce swordfish steaks
2   tablespoons oil
1   tablespoon Oriental sesame oil
2   tablespoons soy sauce
4   tablespoons finely chopped lemongrass (discard outer leaves before chopping), or $^1/_2$ cup chopped scallions and 1 tablespoon lemon zest
few hot red pepper flakes
2   tablespoons dry sherry (optional)
1   tablespoon sesame seeds, toasted in an ungreased frying pan for 3 to 4 minutes until light brown
lemon and lime wedges

1. Place the swordfish in a single layer in a shallow dish or in a ziplock bag. Combine the oils, soy sauce, lemongrass, red pepper flakes and sherry. Rub the marinade into the fish and refrigerate, covered for 1 hour.
2. Heat the grill. Remove the swordfish from the marinade and cook for 4 to 5 minutes on each side, depending on the thickness. Before serving, sprinkle each steak with sesame seeds and serve each with a wedge of lemon and lime.

Beach-Grilled Shellfish with Basil Aioli

per person (at least):
3   clams in the shell
3   mussels in the shell
3   oysters in the shell
wire-hinged grill

Basil aioli:
1   cup mayonnaise
8   cloves garlic, minced
4   tablespoons finely chopped basil
3   tablespoons minced sun-dried tomatoes, in
    oil, drained

Combine all ingredients, refrigerating if made
ahead. Serve at room temperature.

1. Scrub the shellfish with a stiff brush and
    rinse under cold water. Discard any that are
    not firmly closed.
2. Heat the coals and brush the grill with a
    little oil. Arrange the shellfish, rounded side
    down (to preserve the juices) on the hot
    grill. Cook about 6 to 8 minutes for clams
    and mussels, 10 to 12 minutes for oysters,
    depending on the size. They are done when
    they pop open. Loosen the meat from the
    shell and top with a spoonful of aioli.

**It is known that any clambake has its own
bakemaster – in charge from start to finish. He
lays the fire, tends the coals and gets all the credit
at the end.**

Kon Tiki Shrimp Kebabs

Serves 6

Mix up the Mai Tai and Scorpion bowls.

2   pounds large shrimp, peeled and deveined
1   green pepper, seeded and quartered
1   red pepper, seeded and quartered
$^1/_2$ onion, separated and halved
12 medium mushrooms
12 cherry tomatoes
$^1/_2$ cup pineapple juice
3   tablespoons soy sauce
1   tablespoon honey
1   teaspoon sesame oil
1   teaspoon minced fresh ginger
2   teaspoons cornstarch
2   tablespoons fresh lime juice
1   tablespoon toasted sesame seeds

**"Here, sweetheart, here's some green ginger for
thee."**   **–Beaumont J. Fletcher**

1. Combine the pineapple juice, soy sauce,
    honey, sesame oil and ginger in a small pan.
    Dissolve cornstarch in 2 tablespoons of lime
    juice and add to the pan. Cook, stirring
    often until thickened, about 5 minutes.
    Cool. Add shrimp to marinade, toss well to
    coat and marinate for at least 1 hour.
2. Have ready a nice hot charcoal fire or
    preheat broiler or grill. Arrange shrimp on
    skewers, alternating with pieces of peppers,
    onion, mushrooms and tomatoes. Cook
    kebabs for 5 minutes, basting with the
    remaining marinade. When shrimp are pink,
    remove from fire and serve on a bed of your
    favorite rice, sprinkle with toasted sesame
    seeds.

Skewered Shrimp with Apricot-Curry Glaze   Serves 6

A quick and easy dinner, can also be prepared as an appetizer and served with toothpicks.

1¹/₂ pounds large uncooked shrimp, peeled, deveined and tail left on
3   tablespoons olive oil
3   tablespoons apricot preserves
1¹/₂ tablespoons white wine vinegar or rice vinegar
3   teaspoons Dijon mustard
3   teaspoons curry powder
4   cloves garlic, minced

12 10-inch bamboo skewers
shredded bok choy or iceberg lettuce
lemon wedges

1. Whisk together olive oil, preserves, vinegar, mustard, curry and garlic in a large bowl. Add shrimp, toss to coat, cover and refrigerate at least 2 hours. Meanwhile, soak bamboo skewers in water to cover for 30 minutes. This will prevent them from burning.
2. Thread shrimp on skewers, dividing evenly. Grill shrimp 6 inches from the heat until just cooked through, about 3 minutes per side. Place shredded bok choy or lettuce on platter, arrange shrimp skewers on top and garnish with lemon wedges.

Grilled Salmon Steaks with Lime Ginger Butter   Serves 6

6   1-inch thick salmon steaks, each about 8 ounces
8   tablespoons butter (1 stick), softened
grated zest and juice of 2 limes, plus wedges for garnish
2   tablespoons fresh chopped parsley
ground black pepper

1. In a small bowl, combine the softened butter, lime zest and juice, parsley and black pepper to taste. Reserving 2 tablespoons of the butter in a small saucepan, form butter into a cylinder. Wrap in plastic wrap and chill until firm. This may be made up to a week ahead, or may also be frozen.
2. Melt butter in saucepan and brush salmon on both sides. Grill over a hot fire for 4 minutes, turn, brush with butter and cook for 4 more minutes, until fish flakes.
3. Cut lime ginger butter into 6 pieces and top each piece of salmon with a pat. Garnish with additional lime wedges.

Szechuan Sea-babs

Serves 4

1¹/₂ pound swordfish, tuna or shark, cut into
    2-inch cubes
¹/₂ pound large sea scallops
2 green peppers, cut into 1¹/₂ -inch pieces
3 tablespoons fresh lime juice
3 tablespoons soy sauce
2 tablespoons Oriental sesame oil
1 teaspoon sugar
2 tablespoons chopped fresh parsley
2 cloves garlic, minced
toasted sesame seeds (optional)

1. Trim all skin from fish and place in a shallow glass or ceramic bowl.
2. Mix the lime juice, soy sauce, sesame oil, sugar, parsley, and garlic. Pour the mixture over the fish, season with black pepper and toss lightly to coat all sides. Allow to marinate for 30 minutes, but no longer than 2 hours.
3. Arrange fish on skewers, alternating with pieces of green pepper. Grill, turning skewers, about 15 minutes until fish is cooked and browned. Baste with remaining marinade and serve, sprinkled with sesame seeds.

"Real" Barbecued Crabs

Serves 4

Not just boiled and doused, a true crab lover's delight.

1 dozen large crabs, live if possible
¹/₂ cup white wine
¹/₂ cup (8 tablespoons) butter
2 tablespoons soy sauce
2 cloves garlic, minced
¹/₂ teaspoon marjoram
salt and pepper

1. Clean the crabs and crack the claws. Melt the butter in a saucepan and add remaining ingredients. Brush the crabs with the butter and grill them, top side down, over a hot fire. Turn after 8 minutes, baste and grill for another 5 minutes until bright red. Serve in deep dishes with any remaining sauce poured over.

**"These mortal wits to call them crabs agree,
The Gods have other names for things than we."
Thomas Parnell**

Peppered Tuna with Avocado Butter

Serves 4

This may alternately be prepared with swordfish.

4   6- to 8-ounce tuna steaks
olive oil
1   tablespoon coarsely cracked peppercorns
    (a mixed blend of pink, green, white and
    black is nice)
$^1/_4$ teaspoon cayenne pepper (optional)
salt
4   lemon or lime wedges
parsley sprigs

Rub tuna steaks generously with olive oil and roll in peppercorns, patting to coat. Dust lightly with cayenne pepper and sprinkle with salt. Grill over a hot fire, turning once, for 4 minutes per side. Transfer to a platter and top each piece with a spoonful of Avocado Butter. Garnish with lemon and parsley.

Avocado butter:
1   ripe avocado, mashed
4   tablespoons ($^1/_4$ cup) butter, room
    temperature
2   tablespoons fresh lemon or lime juice
1   tablespoon chopped fresh parsley
1   tablespoon chopped fresh cilantro
1   clove garlic, minced
salt to taste

Beat butter in a small bowl until soft and creamy. Mix in avocado, lemon juice, parsley, cilantro and garlic. Season with salt, cover and chill until ready to serve.

Seafood Swords

Serves 4 to 6

$^1/_4$ cup soy sauce
$^1/_4$ cup salad oil
$^1/_4$ cup lemon juice
$^1/_4$ cup minced fresh parsley or 1 tablespoon
    dried
$^1/_2$ teaspoon salt, dash pepper
1   pound fresh large shrimp, peeled, deveined,
    leaving tail intact
1   pound fresh scallops
large stuffed green olives
lemon wedges

Combine first 6 ingredients for basting sauce. Add shrimp and scallops to basting sauce and let stand one hour, stirring occasionally. On skewers alternate shrimp, olives, scallops and end with a lemon wedge. Broil over hot coals, turning and brushing seafood frequently with the sauce. Do not overcook.

"You must stay the cooling, too, or you may chance to burn your lips."
                                    – William Shakespeare

Grilled Shrimp and Bread Salad

Serves 4

Based on the traditional Tuscan Panzanella - be sure to use the best tomatoes you can find and serve right away, while the bread cubes are crisp.

4 $^3/_4$-inch thick slices Italian bread, cubed
2 tablespoons olive oil, preferably extra-virgin
1 teaspoon salt
2 teaspoons minced garlic
$^1/_2$ teaspoon chopped fresh rosemary
$^1/_4$ teaspoon freshly ground black pepper
$1^1/_2$ pounds large shrimp, peeled and deveined (tails left on)
2 tomatoes, seeded and diced
$^1/_2$ large cucumber, diced
2 stalks celery, sliced $^1/_2$-inch thick
12 imported black olives, pitted and coarsely chopped
2 tablespoons chopped fresh parsley
2 tablespoons chopped fresh basil
2 tablespoons chopped scallion greens
2 tablespoons Balsamic vinegar

" 'Man cannot live by bread alone'
    'tis well and wisely spoken,
But make that bad, he'll die unknown
    and give the world no token."
        – Andrew Boorde: 1536

1. Preheat oven to 375°. Spread bread cubes on a baking sheet and toast for 15 to 20 minutes, or until golden and crisp. Reserve.

2. In a shallow dish, combine 2 teaspoons olive oil, $^1/_2$ teaspoon of the salt, 1 teaspoon of the garlic, rosemary and pepper. Add shrimp and turn to coat well. Cover with plastic wrap and refrigerate for 15 minutes.

3. Meanwhile, combine tomatoes, the remaining 1 teaspoon garlic and $^1/_2$ teaspoon salt in a large serving bowl; set aside at room temperature for 20 minutes. Arrange the shrimp on a wire-hinged grill and broil, turning midway, until the shrimp are pink, about 3 minutes per side.

4. Add cucumbers, celery, olives, parsley, basil, scallions, vinegar, 1 tablespoon oil and reserved bread cubes to the tomatoes and toss gently to combine. Arrange shrimp over the bread salad. Serve immediately.

Grilled Softshell Crabs with Basil Butter   Serves 4 to 6

A spring ritual at any Maryland table.

12 softshell crabs
8   tablespoons butter or margarine (1 stick), melted
2   tablespoons olive oil
4   tablespoons fresh basil leaves, minced
2   tablespoons fresh parsley, minced
$1/8$ teaspoon cayenne pepper
juice of $1/2$ lemon
$1/2$ cup toasted sliced almonds
lemon wedges

1. Mix butter, olive oil, basil, parsley, lemon and cayenne pepper. Brush crabs with butter sauce and place in a hinged grill rack. Grill for about 3 minutes on a medium-hot fire or until the crabs turn red and are thoroughly cooked, basting several times. If a leg pulls off easily, they are done. Sprinkle with almonds and serve with remaining basil butter, warmed.

Herb's Herb Grilled Shrimp   Serves 6

Real picnic fare... peel and eat.

2   pounds jumbo shrimp, deveined, but not peeled
$1/2$ cup vegetable oil
$1/2$ cup freshly squeezed lemon juice
$1/4$ cup soy sauce
2   tablespoons minced parsley
2   teaspoons tarragon leaves
6   cloves garlic, minced
$1/2$ teaspoon salt
freshly ground black pepper

1. Mix all marinade ingredients and pour over the shrimp in a non-metallic bowl. Marinate for 2 to 3 hours.
2. Arrange shrimp in a hinged wire grill and cook over charcoal for 3 to 4 minutes on each side, basting several times. Serve with fluffy white rice and plenty of napkins.

**"Listen, in ashes first your onions roast
    till they are brown as toast,
Then with sauce and gravy cover
    eat them, you'll be strong all over."
                                  – Athanaeus**

Fresh Salmon on the Grill

Serves 4

Place a 1^1/$_2$-2 pound piece of salmon on a large piece of tin foil and brush olive oil on both sides. Cover top side of salmon completely with black pepper and salt to taste. Fold up tin foil into a package and place on your grill with top down at medium heat for 20-25 minutes. The nice thing is you can prepare the salmon well in advance for company and your husband can take credit for cooking it!

"Salmon, lamb, peas, innocent young potatoes, a cool salad, sliced cucumber, a tender duckling — all there."

– Charles Dickens

Oriental Grill in a Bag

Serves 4

A quick, no mess way for cooking offshore.

4   large cloves of garlic
^{1}/$_4$ cup soy sauce
^{1}/$_4$ cup seasoned rice wine vinegar
4   fish steaks (tuna, sword, or salmon)

1. Place garlic cloves in a large ziplock bag and crush with the bottom of a pot or cutting board. Add the soy sauce and vinegar.
2. Place the fish in the bag, seal and marinate for at least an hour. Cook on a preheated grill until fish is flaky.

Quick Grilled Swordfish Caesar

Marinate fresh swordfish in any Caesar salad dressing for at least 5 minutes. Place on your grill at medium heat with top down for about 7 minutes. Turn fish over, pour on remaining Caesar marinade and grill until done, another 5 minutes.

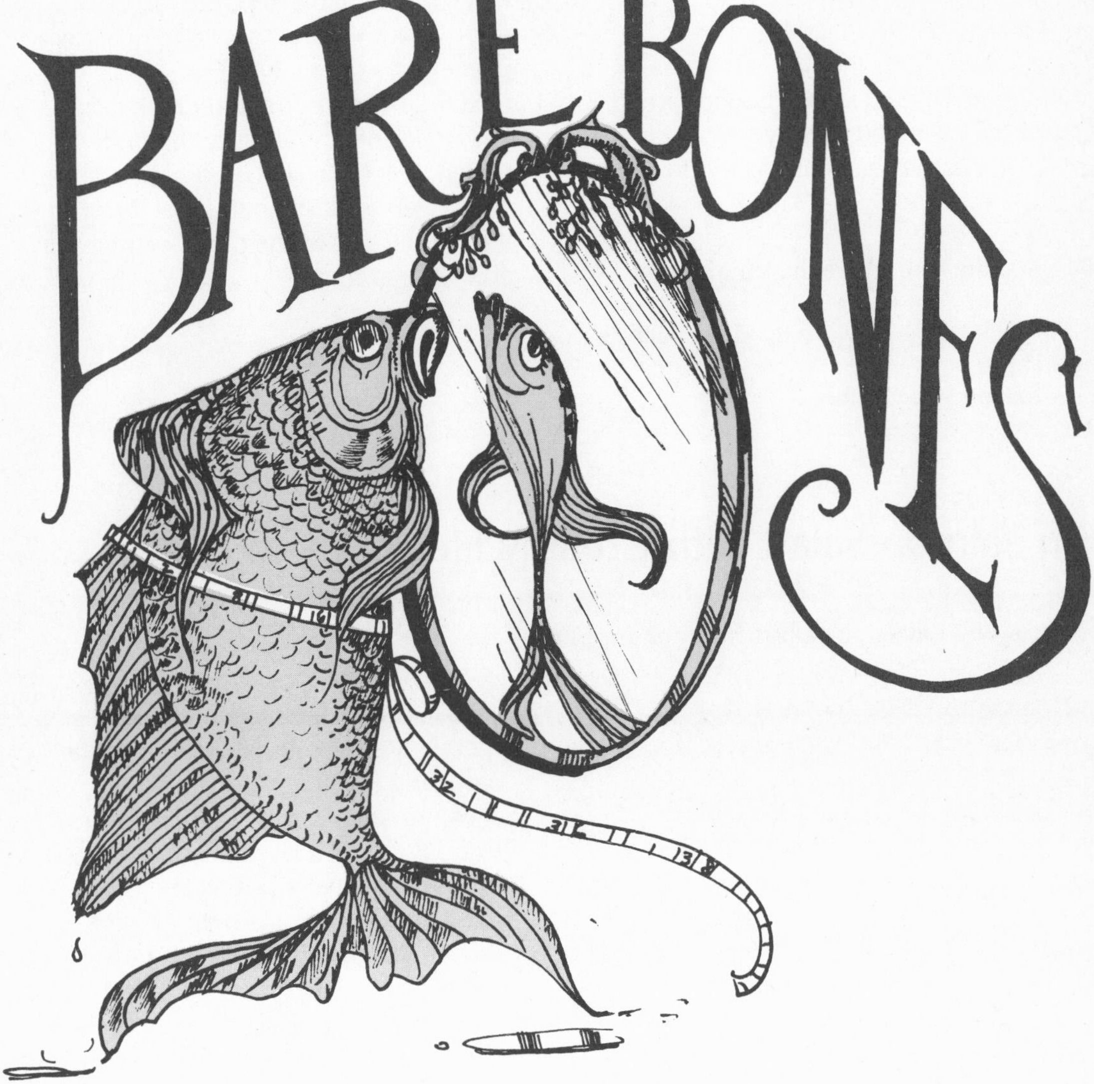
BARE BONES

Orange Baked Cod Bundles

Serves 4

4   8-ounce cod fillets, haddock or any other
    firm fish may be substituted
juice of ¹/₂ lemon
¹/₂ teaspoon fennel seeds
salt and freshly ground black pepper
1   medium onion, thinly sliced
1   orange, thinly sliced
2   tablespoons reduced-fat margarine spread
2   tablespoons chopped parsley
4   12-inch square pieces of aluminum foil
vegetable oil spray

**"Know'st thou the land where the lemon trees
    bloom,
Where the gold orange glows in the deep thickets
    gloom?"
        – Johann Von Goethe**

1. Spray half of sheets of foil with vegetable oil
   spray. Place the cod fillets on top, sprinkle
   with lemon juice, fennel seeds and season
   with salt and pepper.
2. Place some onion rings on each fish fillet
   and top with orange slices. Sprinkle with
   parsley and dot with butter.
3. Fold foil over the top and crimp edges from
   top to bottom, being sure the ends are
   sealed. Place packets on a baking sheet in a
   350° oven for 25 minutes. Let guests open
   the foil packets at the table so they can
   enjoy the aroma!

Warm Salmon Salad with Creamy Herb Vinaigrette

Serves 6

A show-stopping entrée for a luncheon or supper.

6   6-ounce salmon fillets, skinned
3   cups mixed salad greens (endive, leaf
    lettuce, radicchio)
2   cups fresh spinach, cut into thin strips
1   small zucchini, cut into matchstick pieces,
    about 2-inches long

Creamy herbed vinaigrette:
¹/₃ cup low fat or nonfat plain yogurt
¹/₃ cup low fat or nonfat mayonnaise
2   teaspoons fresh lemon juice
1   tablespoon Dijon mustard
2   teaspoons balsamic vinegar
4   tablespoons chopped fresh parsley
3   tablespoons chopped fresh chives
3   tablespoons chopped fresh dill
salt and black pepper

1. Toss salad greens, spinach and zucchini
   together. Refrigerate. Make vinaigrette by
   combining ingredients in a medium bowl.
   Season to taste with salt and pepper.
2. Place salmon in a large ovenproof casserole.
   Brush liberally with herb vinaigrette and
   broil 4 inches from the heat for 8 to 10
   minutes until fish flakes and is firm to the
   touch.
3. Toss remaining vinaigrette with salad greens,
   reserving ¹/₄ cup. Place salad on individual
   dishes and top each with a salmon fillet.
   Drizzle remaining vinaigrette over fish and
   serve.

Baked Bluefish au Poivre   Serves 4

4   6-ounce bluefish fillets, skinned
4   tablespoons fresh lemon juice
2   cloves garlic, finely minced
1   teaspoon olive oil
1   tablespoon cracked black peppercorns
salt to taste
1   lemon, thinly sliced
2   tablespoons chopped parsley plus sprigs for
    garnish

Bluefish Rule #1:
When dining out, never order bluefish except
at a seaside restaurant where freshness is
guaranteed.

Bluefish Rule #2:
Never freeze – the oily fish takes on a bitter
taste.

1. Place fillets in a 9-by-14-inch baking dish.
   Spoon 2 tablespoons lemon juice over the
   fish, rub with the garlic and $1/2$ teaspoon of
   oil. Press half of the crushed peppercorns
   into the fish. Season with salt.
2. Turn the fish over and repeat on the other
   side, using the remaining 2 tablespoons
   lemon juice, $1/2$ teaspoon oil and 2
   teaspoons peppercorns. Cover with the
   lemon slices, sprinkle with parsley. Bake at
   325° for 10 minutes per inch of thickness or
   until fish flakes with a fork. To serve, spoon
   pan juices over the fish and garnish with
   parsley.

Flounder Roll-Ups with Curried Yogurt Sauce   Serves 4

$1^1/2$ pounds flounder or 2 medium fillets per
    person
$1/2$ cup chopped scallions
1   cup plain low fat yogurt
$1/4$ cup fresh lime juice
2   teaspoons curry powder
2   teaspoons ground cumin
1   tablespoon chopped fresh parsley
salt and pepper

1. Lay flounder on countertop and sprinkle
   with chopped scallions. Roll up end to end
   and place in a baking dish which has been
   slightly coated with vegetable oil.
2. Combine yogurt, lime juice, curry powder,
   parsley and cumin in a small bowl. Whisk to
   blend and season with salt and pepper.
3. Bake flounder in a 325° oven for 20 minutes
   or until sauce is bubbly. Serve rolls over
   white rice with lots of sauce.

Cantonese Oven Steamed Flounder   Serves 4

4   6-ounce flounder fillets (snapper, sole, or sea bass are excellent also)
1   2-inch piece of ginger root, peeled and chopped
6   scallions, cut into 2-inch julienne strips
1   small carrot, peeled and cut into 2-inch julienne strips
2   tablespoons light or reduced-sodium soy sauce
1   teaspoon sesame oil
2   tablespoons dry sherry
1/2 teaspoon sugar
dash hot chili oil or hot red pepper flakes
chopped cilantro or parsley

1. Scatter half of the scallions, ginger root and carrot into a 9-by-13-inch baking dish. Place fillets in the dish, folding ends under slightly. Scatter the remaining scallions, ginger root and carrot on top.
2. In a small bowl, combine soy sauce, sherry, sesame oil, sugar and chili oil or pepper and pour the mixture over the fish and let marinate for 1/2 hour.
3. Completely seal the baking dish with aluminum foil and bake in a preheated 375° oven for 15 minutes, or until the fish is opaque. Serve with white rice and sprinkle generously with cilantro.

"With a friend in the cookhouse, you can expect something good to eat."
– Chinese Proverb

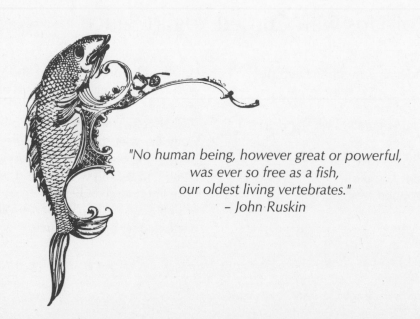

"No human being, however great or powerful, was ever so free as a fish, our oldest living vertebrates."
– John Ruskin

Celebrity Salmon

Serves 6

This is a delectable way of preparing salmon or any firm-fleshed, delicately flavored fish – ideal for people who like to eat lightly. If you like to serve a sauce with the salmon, try simple melted butter with lots of fresh lemon and a variety of herbs, parsley, dill or chives.

1   3-pound salmon, cut into 6 8-ounce steaks
salt and pepper
6   small carrots, peeled and julienned
1   pound mushrooms, sliced
3   stalks celery, julienned
2   leeks, split, washed and julienned
3   shallots, very finely chopped
6   bay leaves
white wine
lemon slices for garnish

1. Preheat oven to 450°. Butter 6 (8-by-12-inch) pieces of parchment paper.
2. Sprinkle the salmon steaks with salt and pepper. Divide $^1/_2$ the julienned vegetables and chopped shallots in the center of each piece of paper and set a piece of salmon on top. Cover with the remaining vegetables, top with bay leaves and sprinkle with white wine. Bring the edges of the paper together and pleat to form a seal. Fold over the ends to make a neat bundle. The fish should be tightly wrapped in paper.
3. Arrange the salmon bundles seam-side down on a baking sheet. Bake in preheated oven for 12 minutes or until the fish flakes easily. Do not overcook. Cut the paper in the center and remove the bay leaves. Serve the salmon right in the paper on hot dinner plates with lemon slices on the side.

Tijuana Roasted Shrimp and Scallops

Serves 6

1   cup lightly packed cilantro leaves
6   garlic cloves, thinly sliced and divided
$^1/_2$ cup each low fat yogurt and low fat sour
    cream
1   tablespoon lime juice
$^1/_2$ teaspoon ground cumin
$^1/_4$ teaspoon salt
$^3/_4$ pound sea scallops
$^3/_4$ pound large shrimp, peeled and deveined
1   tablespoon olive oil
1   bunch fresh spinach, trimmed and steamed

1. Heat oven to 450°. In food processor, blend cilantro, 3 cloves garlic, yogurt, lime juice, cumin and salt until smooth; cover and chill. In roasting pan, toss seafood with remaining 3 cloves garlic and oil.
2. Roast 10 minutes, turning once, until lightly browned. Serve over spinach and top with sauce.

Reynolds Hill Shrimp Bisque   Serves 10

3 cups of fresh corn or frozen whole kernel corn, thawed and divided
2 cups low fat chicken broth
1 tablespoon olive oil
1 cup chopped onion
1 cup chopped green pepper
1 cup skim milk
$^3/_4$ pound medium shrimp, peeled and deveined
$^1/_4$ cup fresh cilantro, chopped
$^1/_4$ cup fresh parsley, chopped
$^1/_4$ teaspoon salt
$^1/_8$ teaspoon pepper
Tabasco sauce

1. Combine 2 cups of corn and 1 cup of chicken broth in a blender. Process until smooth.
2. Heat oil in a medium saucepan, add onion and peppers, sauté 5 minutes. Stir in pureed corn, remaining 1 cup broth, and milk; bring to a boil and simmer for 5 minutes.
3. Stir in the remaining 1 cup corn, shrimp, cilantro, parsley, salt and pepper. Simmer for 5 more minutes until shrimp are cooked. Season with a little Tabasco sauce to taste.

"Pray let me, an American, inform the gentleman, who seems ignorant of the matter, that Indian corn is one of the most agreeable and wholesome grains in the world. Its green ears roasted are a delicacy beyond expression."
– Benjamin Franklin: 1765

Zesty Baked Lemon Pepper Salmon   Serves 4

1 $1^1/_4$ to $1^1/_2$-pound center-cut salmon fillet
$^1/_2$ cup chopped scallions
$^1/_4$ cup capers, drained
1 tablespoon chopped fresh dill
1 tablespoon lemon pepper seasoning
grated rind of one lemon
splash of white wine
lemon wedges

"Next came a great piece of salmon."
– William Makepeace Thackeray

1. Place a large sheet of aluminum foil on a baking sheet, spray foil with nonstick vegetable oil spray. Place salmon on foil.
2. Mix scallions, capers, dill, lemon pepper and lemon rind in a small bowl. Spread over salmon fillet, rubbing it into the flesh. Sprinkle a little white wine around the fish and fold up foil edges to enclose salmon. Seal.
3. Bake salmon in a preheated 400° oven for $^1/_2$ hour or until just opaque in the center. Garnish with lemon wedges and spoon any juices over top.

Fourth of July Salmon Loaf with Horseradish Cream   Serves 6

Even our vegetarian daughter devours this dish.

8   ounces salmon, cooked and flaked
$^3/_4$ cup uncooked bulgur wheat
1   cup evaporated skim milk
$^2/_3$ cup grated carrot
$^2/_3$ cup minced red pepper
$^2/_3$ cup chopped onion
2   cloves garlic, minced
1   tablespoon chopped fresh parsley
1   tablespoon chopped fresh dill
1   teaspoon salt
$^1/_4$ teaspoon pepper
1   egg and 2 egg whites
parsley sprigs for garnish

Horseradish cream:
4   ounces low-fat sour cream
4   ounces low-fat yogurt
1   tablespoon prepared horseradish
2   tablespoons finely chopped scallions
1   teaspoon lemon juice

Mix all ingredients and refrigerate for at least 2 hours before serving with salmon loaf.

1. Combine the bulgur and skim milk in a one-quart microwavable bowl. Cover with heavy-duty plastic wrap, vent one corner and microwave on high for $3^1/_2$ minutes. Let stand, covered, for 15 minutes.
2. In a medium skillet coated with cooking spray, sauté the carrots, red pepper, onion and garlic until tender, about 5 minutes. Combine with the bulgur and remaining ingredients and mix well.
3. Pack the mixture into a 5-cup ring mold that has been sprayed with cooking spray. Pack down with the back of a spoon. Cover with aluminum foil and bake in a 375° oven for 25 minutes. Uncover and bake for 15 more minutes until cooked through. Let rest for 10 minutes and unmold on a warm platter. Serve a slice of the salmon loaf with a dollop of horseradish cream.

Southport Broiled Best Swordfish   Serves 2

1   1 pound swordfish steak
1   teaspoon dried dillweed or 1 tablespoon of fresh, if available
$^1/_3$ cup orange juice
$^1/_3$ cup dry white wine or vermouth
1   tablespoon butter
2   tablespoons lemon juice
freshly ground black pepper

1. Sprinkle fish generously on both sides with dill and place in a broiling pan sized to be not much bigger than the swordfish.
2. Mix equal parts of orange juice and white wine (about $^1/_3$ cup) to just cover the bottom of the pan. Dot with butter chunks and sprinkle lemon juice on top. Broil 8 to 10 minutes, basting once or twice - comes out moist and yummy every time!

Slimmer Crab Cakes

Serves 4

A light version of your restaurant favorite.

1 pound crabmeat, fresh or frozen
1 teaspoon mustard
1 egg, beaten
2 tablespoons low-fat mayonnaise
$^1/_4$ cup finely chopped green pepper
1 tablespoon parsley, chopped
pinch salt
Tabasco sauce
$^1/_2$ cup cracker crumbs
vegetable oil

Chunky Cucumber sauce:
$^1/_2$ cup diced cucumber, seeded and chopped
$^1/_3$ cup chopped scallions
$^1/_2$ cup low fat sour cream
$^1/_2$ teaspoon salt
$^1/_4$ teaspoon paprika
1 teaspoon fresh lemon juice

1. Mix together mustard, egg, mayonnaise, green pepper, parsley, salt, Tabasco sauce and cracker crumbs. Add the crabmeat and mix lightly so as not to break up the crabmeat.
2. Form into 3-inch cakes, fry in a small amount of oil until brown; turn and brown on the other side. If you really don't want any oil, these can be lightly coated with a vegetable spray and broiled.

Pass cucumber sauce and serve with lemon wedges.

Combine and mix ingredients. Cover and refrigerate until ready to use.

Middle Eastern Swordfish

Serves 4

4 6-ounce swordfish steaks, about $^3/_4$-inch thick
2 tablespoons finely chopped parsley
1 minced jalapeño pepper
1 tablespoon vegetable oil
3 tablespoons fresh lemon juice
2 cloves garlic, minced
1 teaspoon ground turmeric
1 teaspoon ground cinnamon
1 teaspoon ground cumin
salt and freshly ground black pepper to taste
lime wedges

1. Place swordfish in a shallow nonmetallic dish. In a small bowl, combine remaining ingredients. Spread mixture over both sides of fish, cover and refrigerate for 1 hour
2. Prepare a charcoal fire or preheat a gas grill. Grill the steaks for 4 to 5 minutes and serve with lime wedges.

Swordfish with New-Wave Tartar Sauce

Serves 4

4   6 to 8-ounce swordfish steaks, $^3/_4$-inch thick
1   tablespoon olive oil
1   tablespoon fresh squeezed lemon juice
1   tablespoon fresh minced dill plus sprigs for
    garnish
salt and black pepper
lemon wedges

Tartar sauce:
$^2/_3$ cup reduced-calorie mayonnaise
$^1/_3$ cup plain low-fat yogurt
$^1/_3$ cup chopped cornichons or dill pickles
2   tablespoons fresh minced dill
2   teaspoons prepared horseradish
2   teaspoons Dijon mustard
1   tablespoon capers, drained

1. Prepare tartar sauce by combining all ingredients. Refrigerate covered for at least 3 hours.
2. Place olive oil, lemon juice and 1 tablespoon fresh dill in a small bowl, whisk until blended. Baste both sides of swordfish with the mixture and season with salt and freshly ground black pepper.
3. Broil fish for 5 to 6 minutes on each side or cook over a hot charcoal fire until just firm to the touch. Serve with tartar sauce on the side and garnish with dill sprigs and lemon wedges.

"The table is the only place where you do not get weary the first hour."
        – Brillat-Savin

Haddock Dilly

Serves 4

4   6 to 8-ounce haddock fillets
$^1/_2$ cup nonfat yogurt
$^1/_3$ cup low fat mayonnaise
$^1/_2$ cup cucumber, peeled, seeded and
    chopped, plus 8 thin slices for garnish
1   tablespoon chopped fresh dill
1   tablespoon chopped fresh parsley
3   cups water
$^1/_2$ cup dry white wine
1   bay leaf
salt and black pepper to taste

1. In a bowl, mix yogurt, mayonnaise, chopped cucumber, dill and parsley. Season to taste with salt and pepper. Chill for at least 2 hours.
2. In a large skillet, bring water, wine and bay leaf to a boil. Place fish in pan and poach for 10 to 12 minutes depending on thickness of fish. Gently remove fish to a serving platter. Spoon the sauce over the top and garnish with cucumber slices.

"Blest be those feasts with simple plenty crowned."
        – Oliver Goldsmith

Broiled Salmon with Horseradish-Ginger Crust   Serves 4

This crust can also be used for chicken or game birds.

4   3-ounce skinless salmon fillets
1¹/₂ cups fine fresh bread crumbs, preferably
       made from sourdough bread
1¹/₂ tablespoons grated fresh horseradish or
       ¹/₄ cup prepared horseradish, squeezed dry
1   tablespoon grated fresh ginger
1   tablespoon olive oil
1   tablespoon rice wine or sake
¹/₂ teaspoon salt, preferably kosher
¹/₄ teaspoon freshly ground white pepper

Sauce:
2   tablespoons reduced-sodium soy sauce
2   tablespoons rice wine or sake
2   tablespoons water
¹/₂ teaspoon sugar

1. Preheat the broiler. Lightly oil a baking sheet
   or coat it with nonstick spray. Set salmon
   fillets on the baking sheet.
2. In a food processor, combine bread crumbs,
   horseradish, ginger, oil, rice wine or sake,
   salt and pepper; process until evenly
   moistened. Lightly press ¹/₄ of the crumbs
   over the top of each fillet. Broil, about 4
   inches from the heat source, until the crust
   is golden brown and the salmon is opaque
   in the center, about 8 minutes.
3. To make sauce: While the salmon is
   broiling, stir sauce ingredients together in a
   small bowl until the sugar dissolves. Serve
   alongside the salmon.

Chinese Swordfish Baked in Paper   Serves 6

Open these packets at the table for a real show.

6   12-by-24-inch sheets parchment paper (or
     you may use aluminum foil)
6   6- to 8-ounce swordfish slices (or any other
     firm fish such as scrod or haddock)
¹/₄ cup soy sauce
3   tablespoons sesame oil
2   tablespoons sherry
6   scallions, julienned using greens
1   teaspoon minced garlic
2   tablespoons chopped fresh parsley
1   teaspoon minced ginger root
red pepper flakes

"Whatever will fill your belly is good food."
          – Chinese Proverb

1. Using a whole sheet of paper, fold in half
   and cut into a heart shape large enough for
   fish to fit on one side with extra room to
   crimp edges. Place a piece of fish on the
   right side of each heart.
2. In a bowl, combine remaining ingredients
   and spoon over fish. Fold paper over fish
   and twist pointed end together to seal
   tightly. Place packages on a baking sheet
   and cook in a 400° oven for 12 to 15
   minutes depending on thickness of fish.
   Paper or foil should be puffed. Remove to
   serving dishes, cut an X in the center of
   each packet and fold back the 4 points.

Sesame Chow Mein with Shrimp   Serves 6

A light, easily prepared one-dish meal with a zesty Oriental flavor. Have all of your ingredients on a tray, ready to stir fry.

1¹/₂ pounds fresh Chinese thin egg noodles or
    1 pound thin vermicelli
1   teaspoon vegetable oil
1   tablespoon minced peeled ginger root
3   cloves garlic, minced
1   pound fresh medium shrimp, peeled and
    deveined
48 snow peas, trimmed
1¹/₂ cups bean sprouts
8   large shitake mushrooms, stems removed,
    and sliced
1¹/₂ cups sliced bok choy
1   medium carrot, julienned
2   tablespoons soy sauce
1   tablespoon oyster sauce
4   tablespoons chicken broth
1   teaspoon sesame oil
freshly ground black pepper
2   tablespoons toasted sesame seeds
2   tablespoons chopped scallions

1. In a large pot of boiling salted water, cook noodles for 2 to 3 minutes or vermicelli for 6 to 8 minutes until tender but still firm. Drain, rinse under cold water and set aside.

2. In a wok or large nonstick skillet, heat oil over high heat until a haze appears. Add ginger and garlic and stir fry for 30 seconds. Add shrimp and stir fry for 20 seconds. Add snow peas, sprouts, mushrooms, bok choy and carrots. Stir fry for 3 more minutes until vegetables are tender-crisp.

3. Add the reserved noodles, oyster sauce, soy sauce and chicken stock and toss until well mixed and heated through. Remove from heat, add sesame oil, season with pepper and serve sprinkled with sesame seeds and scallions.

The Chinese eat a good deal of shrimp, but if you see "brushwood shrimp" on the restaurant menu, beware: it means grasshoppers!

Quick Bouillabaisse for Two   Serves 2

Ready to serve in only a half hour.

4   scallions, chopped fine
2   cloves garlic, minced
4   tablespoons olive oil
1   14$\frac{1}{2}$-ounce can Italian plum tomatoes,
     broken up
$\frac{1}{2}$ cup white wine
1   cup fish stock or clam juice (optional)
$\frac{1}{2}$ teaspoon saffron, crushed
$\frac{1}{2}$ teaspoon basil
8   medium shrimp, peeled and deveined
1   pound firm fleshed fish (cod, haddock,
     halibut) cut into 2-inch pieces
1   dozen mussels, beards removed
6   hard-shell clams
1   1-pound lobster, quartered
1   teaspoon grated lemon
salt and freshly ground black pepper
chopped parsley

1. Sauté scallions and garlic in olive oil for 3 to 4 minutes until lightly browned. Add tomatoes, wine, clam broth, saffron and basil. Simmer for 10 minutes.
2. Add shrimp, fish, mussels, clams and lobster, submerging everything in the tomato sauce. Add grated lemon, cover and cook for 10 to 15 minutes until lobster shells are bright red. Season to taste with salt and pepper and serve in deep bowls, sprinkled with parsley and garnished with buttered crusty toasts.

"This Bouillabaisse a noble dish is – A sort of soup or broth, or brew, or hotchpotch, of all sorts of fishes that Greenwich never could outdo; Green herbs, red peppers, mussels, saffron, soles, onions, garlic, roach, and dace; All these you eat at Terre's Tavern in that one dish of Bouillabaisse."
          – William Makepeace Thackeray

Lime Snapper with Pineapple Salsa   Serves 6

6   8-ounce red snapper fillets, skin on
juice of 3 limes
2   tablespoons vegetable oil
salt and freshly ground black pepper

Salsa:
1   green pepper, seeded and chopped
1   red pepper, seeded and chopped
$\frac{1}{2}$ medium red onion, minced
2   cups fresh pineapple, coarsely chopped
$\frac{1}{2}$ cup chopped fresh cilantro

1. Mix salsa ingredients in a medium bowl. Cover and chill.
2. Mix the lime juice, oil, salt and pepper. Brush the snapper fillets on both sides and grill for 5 to 8 minutes on each side, depending on the fire. Baste with the lime mixture until fish flakes when tested with a fork. Spoon a little salsa on individual plates, top with the snapper and more salsa and cilantro sprigs if desired.

"Better slight a guest than starve him."
          – Chinese Proverb

Mu Shu Shrimp

Serves 4

A light treatment for this Chinese restaurant classic.

1 pound medium shrimp, coarsely chopped
1 1/2 tablespoons vegetable oil
2 large eggs, lightly beaten
4 cups shredded green cabbage (1/3 small cabbage)
10 dried Chinese black mushrooms, soaked in hot water for 20 minutes, drained, stems removed, caps thinly sliced
8 scallions, green part only, cut into 1-inch lengths
1/2 cup hoisin sauce
8 Mandarin pancakes* or flour tortillas, steamed

Marinade:
2 1/2 tablespoons reduced-sodium soy sauce
1 1/2 tablespoons rice wine or sake
1 teaspoon sesame oil

Minced seasonings:
6 cloves garlic, minced
1 1/2 tablespoons minced fresh ginger

Sauce:
3 tablespoons chicken broth
2 tablespoons rice wine or sake
1 tablespoon reduced-sodium soy sauce
1 tablespoon cornstarch
1/2 teaspoon sugar
1/4 teaspoon freshly ground black pepper

* Mandarin pancakes are available in Oriental markets. In a pinch, flour tortillas make a good substitute. To steam pancakes (or spring roll wrappers or tortillas), separate and wrap in a clean cotton or linen towel. Place in a steamer tray set over boiling water. Cover and steam until heated through, about 10 minutes. Turn off the heat and let sit, covered, until serving time.

1. Marinate shrimp: In a medium bowl, combine marinade ingredients. Add shrimp and toss lightly to coat. Cover with plastic wrap and refrigerate for 30 minutes.
2. Mix minced seasonings: In a small bowl, combine garlic and ginger; set aside.
3. Make sauce: In a small bowl, combine sauce ingredients and blend well; set aside.
4. Stir-fry mu shu filling: Heat a wok or large skillet over high heat, add 1/2 tablespoon of the vegetable oil and heat until very hot. Add the marinated shrimp and stir-fry until pink, about 2 minutes. Remove with a slotted spoon and set aside. Cook down any remaining juices to a glaze and add to the shrimp. Add another 1/2 tablespoon oil to the wok and heat until very hot. Add eggs and stir-fry, scrambling them until just dry. Remove and set aside. Add the remaining 1/2 tablespoon oil and heat until very hot, add the reserved minced seasonings and stir-fry until fragrant, 10 to 15 seconds. Add cabbage and mushrooms and stir-fry until tender, about 2 minutes. Pour in the reserved sauce mixture and stir constantly until thickened, about 1 minute. Return shrimp and eggs to the pan and toss until heated through. Stir in scallions. Transfer to a platter.
5. To serve, spread some hoisin sauce over a steamed pancake or tortilla, spoon some of the stir-fried mixture on top, roll up and eat.

Scallop Salad with Orange-Ginger Vinaigrette

Serves 4

1¹/₂ pounds fresh sea scallops
³/₄ cup fresh orange juice
1 teaspoon Dijon mustard
6 tablespoons olive oil
3 teaspoons minced peeled fresh ginger
4 scallions, chopped
12 frozen baby artichoke hearts
8 ounces fresh spinach leaves, torn into bite-size pieces
1 tablespoon vegetable oil
2 oranges, peeled, cut into segments

1. Cook orange juice in heavy small saucepan over medium-high heat until reduced to ¹/₃ cup, about 8 minutes. Reduce heat to low. Whisk in mustard, then oil. Stir in ginger. Season with salt and pepper. Remove from heat and add scallions. (Can be made one day ahead. Cover and chill.)
2. Steam artichoke hearts until tender, about 6 minutes. Cool. Remove any chokes and slice artichoke hearts. Divide spinach among 4 serving plates, top with sliced artichoke hearts. Heat oil in heavy large skillet over medium-high heat. Add scallops and sauté until light brown and cooked through, about 1¹/₂ minutes per side. Place scallops atop spinach. Rewarm dressing in same skillet. Spoon dressing over salad and season with pepper. Garnish with orange segments and serve warm.

Middle Eastern Swordfish

Serves 4

4 6-ounce swordfish steaks, about ³/₄-inch thick
2 tablespoons finely chopped parsley
1 minced jalapeño pepper
1 tablespoon vegetable oil
3 tablespoons fresh lemon juice
2 cloves garlic, minced
1 teaspoon ground turmeric
1 teaspoon ground cinnamon
1 teaspoon ground cumin
salt and freshly ground black pepper to taste
lime wedges

1. Place swordfish in a shallow non-metallic dish. In a small bowl, combine remaining ingredients. Spread mixture over both sides of fish, cover and refrigerate for 1 hour.
2. Prepare a charcoal fire or preheat a gas grill. Grill the steaks for 4 to 5 minutes and serve with lime wedges.

"To take parsley away from the cook, would make it almost impossible for him to exercise his art."
–Louis Augustin Guillaum Bosc d'Antic

Lemony Stuffed Sole

Serves 4

1¼ pound sole fillets (2 pieces per person)
4   slices whole wheat bread, crumbled
2   teaspoons vegetable oil
¹/₃ cup chopped celery
¹/₄ cup chopped onion
2   tablespoons chopped fresh dill
2   tablespoons chopped fresh parsley
2   tablespoons fresh lemon juice
1   teaspoon grated lemon zest
¹/₄ teaspoon salt
¹/₄ teaspoon freshly ground black pepper
¹/₂ cup dry white wine
paprika

"My living in Yorkshire was so far out of the way, that it was actually twelve miles from a lemon!"
– Sydney Smith: 1771

1. Preheat oven to 350°. Spread bread crumbs on a baking sheet and bake for 6 to 8 minutes or until crisp, stirring occasionally. Transfer to a bowl and set aside.
2. In a small nonstick skillet, heat oil over medium heat. Add celery and onion and sauté for 3 to 5 minutes, or until softened. Add to the bread crumbs, along with 1 tablespoon dill, parsley, lemon juice, lemon zest, salt and pepper. Mix well.
3. Arrange half of the fish in a single layer in an ungreased 8-by-8-inch baking dish. Sprinkle the bread crumb mixture evenly over the fillets and place the remaining fillets over top. Pour wine over the fillets and cover the dish with foil. Bake for 15 to 20 minutes, or until the fish flesh is opaque. Garnish with the remaining 1 tablespoon dill and paprika.

"Zero" Shrimp Salad

Serves 4

No fat, no calories, lots of taste.

1   pound cooked and peeled medium shrimp
12 cherry tomatoes, cut in half
1   green pepper, julienned
¹/₂ cucumber, seeded and thinly sliced
12 radishes, sliced
¹/₄ cup chopped red onion
3   cups salad greens (use a variety leaf lettuce, spinach, romaine)
³/₄ cup tomato juice or V-8 juice
1   tablespoon olive oil
¹/₄ cup red wine vinegar
1   tablespoon chopped fresh parsley
1   tablespoon chopped fresh chives
2   cloves garlic, minced
¹/₂ teaspoon salt

¹/₂ teaspoon oregano, crushed
pinch of sugar
freshly ground black pepper

1. Combine shrimp, tomatoes, green pepper, cucumber, radishes, and red onion in a large bowl. Prepare dressing: whisk tomato juice with remaining ingredients, mixing well. Pour dressing over shrimp and toss to coat. May be prepared up to 2 hours ahead and refrigerated.
2. When ready to serve, add the salad greens, toss again and serve on chilled plates with warm crusty bread or pita pockets.

Sweet and Simple Salmon

Serves 4

With Basmati rice and fresh asparagus - a hit every time!

4   6- to 8-ounce salmon fillets
4   tablespoons butter
3   tablespoons honey
$^{1}/_{4}$ teaspoon vanilla
2   tablespoons chopped fresh parsley

"Bless the girls! A nice fresh salmon was frizzling on the gridiron for our supper."
– William Makepeace Thackeray

1. Place salmon, skin side down, in a 9-by-13-inch baking dish. Melt butter and add honey and vanilla. Spoon half the sauce over the fish, coating well. Bake in a 350° oven for 25 to 30 minutes until fish flakes with a fork; remove from oven.
2. Turn oven broiler on and when hot, brown salmon for 2 minutes. Remove to a hot platter, drizzle with remaining sauce and sprinkle with parsley.

A Duet of Sauces - One Hot, One Cold

Sauce #1:
1   cup low fat plain yogurt
3   tablespoons Dijon mustard
2   tablespoons chopped fresh herbs: chives, parsley, tarragon or thyme
2   tablespoons fresh lemon or lime juice
grated lemon or lime zest
salt and pepper to taste

Makes $1^{1}/_{2}$ cups
Put all ingredients into a small bowl and whisk until blended. Brush onto any skinless white fish fillets, flounder, haddock, or scrod, and bake in a 325° oven until done.

Sauce #2:
1   medium cucumber, peeled, seeded and chopped
1   cup low fat sour cream
2   tablespoons fresh dill
1   tablespoon chives, chopped
2   tablespoons scallions, chopped
1   tablespoon wine vinegar
salt and pepper to taste

Makes $1^{1}/_{2}$ cups
Put chopped cucumber into a strainer, sprinkle with salt and allow to drain for $^{1}/_{2}$ hour. Stir the drained cucumber into the sour cream and add dill, chives, scallions, and vinegar.

**"He who bears chives on his breath
Is safe from being kissed to death."**
– John Randolph: 1770

CAPTAINS
COURAGEOUS

Easton Fish Chowder in under an Hour

Serves 6

From the Maryland shore, so easy it almost makes itself.

1¹/₂ pounds white fish, cod or tautog, cut into 1-inch cubes
1   large onion, chopped
6   stalks celery, thinly sliced
6   potatoes, peeled and cubed
6   carrots, thinly sliced
6   strips bacon, coarsely chopped
1   8-ounce can mushrooms, drained
1   pint light cream
¹/₂ cup frozen peas or corn (optional)
salt and pepper

1. Place fish in large saucepan with 2 quarts of water, bring to a low boil.
2. Place bacon, celery, mushrooms and onions in frying pan and sauté until tender, about 5 minutes. Add to the soup pan with the fish, carrots and potatoes. Simmer for 10 minutes or so.
3. Remove from heat, add cream, season to taste and let cool for ¹/₂ hour.
4. Reheat gently with corn or peas before serving with big slices or French or Italian bread.

Tuna-Ghetti à la Parmesan

Serves 6 to 8

This captain stocks his ship's locker with the basics for this recipe, making it possible to whip it up at the last minute while guests are cocktailing.

2   tablespoons butter
³/₄ cup onion, minced
1   green pepper, thinly sliced
2   cloves garlic, minced
¹/₂ teaspoon salt
¹/₄ teaspoon pepper
1   teaspoon oregano
¹/₂ teaspoon basil
¹/₄ cup fresh chopped parsley, sprigs for garnish
1   1-pound can whole tomatoes
1   8-ounce can tomato sauce
2   6-ounce cans solid white tuna, drained
¹/₂ cup grated Parmesan cheese
1   1-pound package spaghetti, cooked and drained

1. In a 3-quart pot, melt butter, add onion, pepper and garlic and sauté until tender. Stir in remaining ingredients except the tuna and Parmesan, simmer for 15 minutes, stirring occasionally.
2. Flake tuna into large pieces, add to the sauce along with Parmesan. Cook gently for 10 minutes and spoon over cooked pasta.

Chili Con Salmon

Serves 4

This recipe is special to me - being of Spanish heritage and an avid salmon lover.

1   1-pound fillet of salmon, skinned
4   tablespoons butter
1   medium onion, finely chopped
2   cloves garlic, minced
1   green pepper, chopped
1   4-ounce can green chopped chilies, drained
1   12-ounce can stewed tomatoes
1   8-ounce can tomato sauce
$^1/_2$ teaspoon cumin
Tabasco sauce
salt and freshly ground black pepper
chopped scallions for garnish

1. Cook salmon in boiling water to cover for 5 to 8 minutes until firm, depending on the thickness of the fish. Remove from the water with a slotted spoon, drain, cool and flake.

2. Melt butter in a saucepan and add onion, garlic and green pepper, sauté until just tender crisp. Add green chilies, tomatoes, tomato sauce and cumin. Season with salt and pepper. Simmer for 15 minutes.

3. Add flaked salmon to the "chili sauce" and fold in gently. Add a few dashes of Tabasco sauce if you like and ladle into big bowls with white rice. Sprinkle with chopped scallions.

Grilled Orange Swordfish with Almond Butter

Serves 6

Prepare the marinade and butter ahead and grill on your boat.

6   $^3/_4$-inch thick swordfish steaks
$^1/_2$ cup soy sauce
2   cloves garlic, minced
2   teaspoons fresh lemon juice
$^1/_2$ cup orange juice
$^1/_2$ teaspoon each orange rind, lemon rind
$^1/_2$ cup softened butter
$^1/_3$ cup chopped almonds
whole almonds, lemon and orange slices

1. Combine soy sauce, garlic, lemon juice, orange juice, lemon and orange rind. Pour over fish in a glass dish and marinate for several hours, turning once.

2. While fish is marinating, combine butter and chopped almonds. Form into a log and wrap tightly in plastic wrap. Refrigerate.

3. Prepare grill or charcoal fire. Grill fish, turning once and basting often, about 10 minutes on each side. Slice butter into $^1/_2$-inch circles, top fish with butter and sprinkle with additional almonds. Garnish each plate with a lemon and orange slice, cut in half and twisted together.

Tuna Glazed with Ginger and Lime   Serves 6

Tuna has become more popular than swordfish in our house lately. This is our best preparation so far.

6   6-ounce tuna steaks
3   tablespoons fresh lime juice
2   tablespoons soy sauce
3   garlic cloves, crushed
3   teaspoons fresh ginger, grated
3   teaspoons sesame oil
1   teaspoon fresh hot chilies (such as jalapeño), minced and seeded, or pinch of dried red pepper flakes
1   teaspoon sugar

1. Arrange fish in a shallow glass baking dish. Whisk remaining ingredients together in a small bowl. Pour marinade over fish and turn to coat. Cover with plastic and let marinate for 30 minutes at room temperature or 1 hour in the refrigerator, turning fish once or twice and spooning marinade over.
2. Preheat broiler. Transfer fish to a broiler pan or ridged foil pan and spoon some marinade over. Broil 4 inches from heat until glazed and golden, basting twice, about 3 minutes. Carefully turn fish over and spoon remaining marinade over. Broil until glazed and just cooked through, basting once with juices in pan, about 3 more minutes.

Blue Crab Beer Steam   Serves 6

3   dozen blue crabs
2   tablespoons seafood seasoning (Old Bay preferred)
$^1/_4$ cup salt
3   cups white vinegar
3   bottles beer, domestic, homemade, lager or imported
melted butter

1. Mix seasonings, vinegar and 2 bottles beer in a medium bowl. Put half of the crabs in a very large pot with a rack and a tight fitting lid - a canning pot does the trick. Add the rack and remaining crabs, making 2 layers.
2. Pour the seasoning mixture in the pot, cover and steam for 20 to 30 minutes until the crabs turn bright red. Spread out on a picnic table with lots of newspaper, crackers and bowls of butter. Serve remaining beer to the chef.

**"These mortal wits to call them crabs agree;
The Gods have other names for things than we."**
            – Thomas Parnell

Crab Cakes by Mrs. Mose   Serves 4-6

Mrs. Mose is a pet name my best sailing friend and I call his mother. She lives in Essex, Maryland and has the luxury of getting fresh lump crab at her local grocery store. Although frozen or canned (pasteurized) blue crab meat works in this recipe, Maine crab and most other species do not.

Other than the arduous but important task of picking all of the shell fragments out of the crab meat, this is a quick and easy recipe to make on a boat. You can avoid much of the picking work by buying backfin crab meat, which is relatively shell free, but to a Chesapeake purist, not as flavorful as the natural mix of claw, backfin, and leg meat, known down there as "special".

1   pound Maryland crab meat, cleaned of all shell fragments.
1   medium onion, finely chopped
1   teaspoon butter
2   raw eggs
1   tablespoon parsley flakes
1   teaspoon celery seed
1   teaspoon Old Bay seasoning
$^1/_2$ teaspoon salt
1   tablespoon Worcestershire sauce, preferably white wine Worcestershire sauce
$^1/_4$ teaspoon pepper
1   teaspoon dry mustard
2   tablespoons mayonnaise
$^1/_2$ cup Italian bread crumbs

Sauté onions in butter until clear but not brown. Allow onions to cool. Mix all ingredients adding mayonnaise last to get proper consistency - stiff. Form into patties, 1 inch thick by 3 to 4 inches diameter. Fry without oil until brown on both sides.

Mrs. Mose serves these in a sandwich, on rye bread, with mayonnaise, lettuce, and tomato slices. I prefer them with caper tartar sauce, either in a sandwich or on a plate.

Caper tartar sauce:
$1^1/_2$ cups mayonnaise
$^1/_4$ cup capers
$^1/_4$ cup relish
$^1/_2$ tablespoon dry mustard
$^1/_4$ tablespoon Worcestershire sauce
$^1/_2$ teaspoon lemon juice
$^1/_4$ teaspoon Tabasco sauce

Blend all ingredients, keep chilled.

Cold Fish and Remains

The following 2 recipes are from *The Belgian Cook Book*, published in 1915 by E.P. Dutton for the benefit of Belgian war relief. The preface, written by a famous Belgian chef, concludes with the following statement: "And lastly, the good cook must learn about food what every sensible woman learns about love — how best to utilize the cold remains."

Cold fish:
"When there remains any cold fish, take away all skin and bones, mixing the flesh with salt, butter, pepper, and 1 or 2 raw eggs as you wish. Take some small fireproof cases and place in each some lemon juice with a little melted butter and grated bread crumbs. Bake the cases till the top of the fish is of a golden color."

Remains of fish:
"Make a good white sauce, add pepper, salt, and a little nutmeg and juice of a lemon. Add the remains of fish and a few pickled shrimps. Fill some shells with it and sprinkle over the top a good powdering of grated Gruyere cheese. Lay a pat of butter in the middle of each shell and put them in the oven. When they are colored a good golden brown, serve them decorated with parsley."

Really Good Seafood   Serves 6

This name was "dubbed" by the husband of the house.

For special occasions add clams or mussels.

1   tablespoon olive oil
1   cup chopped Vidalia onion (or other mild onion)
1   cup chopped celery
2   teaspoons minced garlic
Old Bay seasoning
1   14-ounce can pasta-ready tomatoes
1   pound medium shrimp, peeled and deveined
1   pound cod or haddock, cut into large chunks
1   pound sea scallops
2   tablespoons chopped fresh parsley

1. Sauté onion, celery and garlic in olive oil until translucent. Sprinkle generously with Old Bay seasoning and continue cooking, scraping pan to release any browned bits.
2. Add 2 tablespoons juice from canned tomatoes, shrimp and cod. Dust again with Old Bay seasoning and return to a simmer. When shrimp begin to turn pink, add scallops and tomatoes. Cook over medium heat for 2 minutes, cover and let steam for 5 minutes until all seafood is done. The fish should be flaky, the shrimp curled and pink, the scallops slightly firm. Serve over rice or linguine, sprinkled generously with parsley.

Two If By Sea

We were the owners of the *Hope* – a 56 foot Long Island Sound oyster sloop – built in Greenwich, Connecticut in 1943. (She was the last oyster sloop built on Long Island Sound and the only one still sailing.)

We participated in Op Sail 76, the Boston Harbor Festival, the East Coast Harbor Festival (Norfolk, Baltimore, Philadelphia and New York), several wooden boat shows in Newport, Rhode Island, several antique boat festivals at Mystic Seaport, and a couple of antique boat shows in Essex, Connecticut. In addition, we cruised Long Island Sound, Block Island, Fisher's Island, Cuttyhunk, and other Southern New England waters.

In the fall of 1981, finding ourselves no longer able to physically maintain her as we would wish, we donated the *Hope* to the Norwalk Seaport Association where she remains today as a living exhibit at the Maritime Center.

Living aboard a boat while cruising for a week or two, especially when it is necessary to carry a "crew," can put a strain on the "first mate" as far as food preparation is concerned. Our galley contained a ship mate wood burning stove, but in the summer it was simply too hot to use this wonderful old relic! We carried a two-burner Coleman propane stove which we used on deck in good weather, and placed on top of our cast iron friend when the weather was inclement. With the number of cooking "surfaces" limited, we were challenged to find menus which could be easily and quickly prepared using only two burners.

The following two recipes were some which we used when cruising on the *Hope*. Both chowders were excellent when we had run out of "fresh" foods. Each recipe can be prepared easily in only one saucepan with simple emergency canned ingredients from your pantry.

On Board Salmon Chowder   Serves 4 to 6
1 pound can salmon, drained
1 15-ounce can petite peas, with liquid
1 15-ounce can cream of celery soup
1 15-ounce can of milk or 2 cups fresh, or reconstituted powdered milk
1 teaspoon thyme
1 tablespoon dill weed
salt and pepper

Open cans - drain salmon, but not peas. Flake the salmon into a medium saucepan, carefully removing small bones and skin. Add peas, soup, milk and seasonings. Heat gradually just to a simmer, do not boil. Cook for 5 minutes and ladle into bowls. Serve with oyster crackers or breadsticks.

"Canned" Clam Chowder   Serves 4 to 6
8 strips bacon, diced
2 15-ounce cans cream of potato soup
2 cans milk (rinse out the soup cans)
1 medium onion, chopped
3 stalks celery, chopped
2 6-ounce cans chopped clams
1 1/2 teaspoons thyme
salt and pepper

Sauté bacon bits until light brown. Add onion and celery and cook until translucent, drain off any excess bacon grease. Add potato soup, milk, and clams, bring to a low simmer. Cook for 5 minutes, season to taste and serve with thyme sprinkled on the top. Serve with crusty bread for dunking.

Blow Me Down Bluefish

Serves 6

1 bluefish (preferably caught by you)
1 cup olive oil
1 tablespoon Liquid Smoke
1 to 2 tablespoons Old Bay Seasoning

The bluefish has often been likened to an animated chopping machine, the business of which is to cut to pieces and otherwise destroy as many fish as possible in his wake in as short a period of time as possible.

1. Clean and fillet bluefish in your favorite fashion – some folks like the skin on, some like it off. Some folks want the dark meat (where the real flavor is – any bluefish eater worth his salt knows this!) and of course some folks don't. Cut fillets into serving sizes. Start the grill.

2. Mix together the olive oil, Liquid Smoke and Old Bay Seasoning — mix vigorously so it all blends. Brush the bluefish with the mixture. If you're shipboard, make sure the sails are furled and away from the grilling arena.

3. Let the show begin — with a grand gesture of the spatula place the bluefish over the coals, the oil hitting the grill will cause a burst of flame and sizzle and attract the attention of all the other boats moored around you (this is why style is important because you are now the center of attention). As the bluefish cooks continue to baste with the olive oil causing the flames to burst and sizzle as the fish cooks. The bursting and sizzling of the fire is an important flavor fixative as much as a show by the Captain's "Cookrageous." Bluefish is done when the meat is opaque clear through, probably within 5 to 10 minutes, depending on how dramatic we were with the fire show. Assuming your fellow mariners did not call the fire boats out on you, serve your bluefish with pride along with your favorite side dishes.

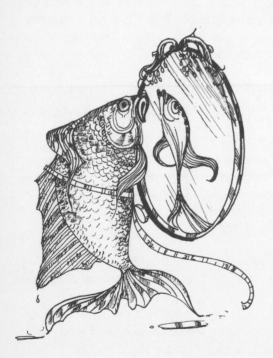

Cuttyhunk Smothered Cod   Serves 4

We like to row ashore and pick up a fresh piece of fish at the dock, return for cocktails and prepare this favorite dish at anchor.

4 6 to 8-ounce cod (scrod or haddock fillets)
4 tablespoons butter
2 large onions, thinly sliced
8 strips of bacon, cut into 1/2-inch pieces
1/2 cup fresh bread crumbs
1 lemon or lime, whichever is on board

1. Melt 2 tablespoons of butter in a skillet and sauté onions until tender and lightly browned. Place in a 9-by-12-inch casserole and top with fish fillets.
2. In the same pan, cook bacon for 3 to 4 minutes, until medium crisp. Add bread crumbs to pan and mix well. Top fish with bacon crumbs, dot with remaining 2 tablespoons of butter and bake for 30 minutes in a 350° oven. Squeeze lemon or lime on top before serving and garnish with additional wedges.

World Trophy Swordfish   Serves 4

Original every time - just change your spice combinations.

4 8-ounce swordfish steaks
1 teaspoon olive oil
1/4 cup milk
1/4 cup white wine
garlic powder, to taste
powdered ginger, to taste
salt
freshly ground black pepper

Alternate spices: sage, mustard, cumin, clover, and cinnamon.

1. Select an oven-proof broiling dish that will fit the swordfish easily. Lightly spread olive oil on bottom and place fish in the pan.
2. Combine milk and wine, pour over fish. Starting with the garlic powder, sprinkle spices on top of the steaks, seasoning with salt and black pepper. Chill for at least 1 hour.
3. Under a preheated broiler, broil fish for 10 to 15 minutes, depending on the thickness. Do not turn or let the liquid completely boil away. When done, fish will be nicely charred on the top and poached on the bottom - that's the world trophy secret. Pour any remaining sauce over fish and sprinkle with chopped parsley and paprika.

Camden Crab Potatoes

Makes 8 servings

You may substitute lobster if feeling really indulgent.

4   large baking potatoes
4   tablespoons butter
$^1/_2$ cup chopped onion
$^1/_2$ cup sliced mushrooms
$^1/_2$ cup lump crabmeat
freshly ground black pepper to taste
$^1/_2$ cup dry vermouth
2   tablespoons lowfat plain yogurt
2   tablespoons sour cream
$^1/_2$ cup half-and-half
$^3/_4$ cup Gruyère cheese
paprika

"A fat kitchen, a lean will."
– Chaucer

1. Bake potatoes in a 350° oven for 1 hour. Cool slightly and cut in half lengthwise. Scoop out pulp into a bowl, leaving about $^1/_4$-inch shell and mash with a fork, breaking up any lumps.
2. Melt butter in skillet and sauté onion until it takes on a light coloring, about 5 to 6 minutes. Add mushrooms and sauté another 5 minutes. Add the crabmeat and pepper. Add vermouth and bring to a boil, stirring frequently. Cook mixture until liquid is absorbed.
3. Remove from heat, add yogurt, sour cream, and then half-and-half. Combine crabmeat mixture, pulp from potato and $^1/_2$ cup Gruyère. Add additional ground black pepper and a bit more half-and-half, if desired. Place the mixture into the potato skins. Sprinkle with remaining $^1/_4$ cup cheese and paprika. Bake at 400° until cheese bubbles.

Cream of the Sea

Serves 4

1   can tuna, drained
1   can mushroom soup
1   small tin petite peas, drained
1   cup milk
3   potatoes, peeled and sliced
few dots of butter

Open cans. Mix tuna, soup, peas and milk in a casserole dish. Top with potatoes and butter and bake for 45 minutes in a 350° oven until potatoes are crisp and brown. If you don't have an oven on your boat, heat everything in a saucepan and skip the potatoes, finishing off with crushed potato chips.

"And we must glorify a mushroom!"
– Ben Johnson

Great Salt Pond Scallop Skewers   Serves 2

Easy to prepare on your boat— especially watching the sunset at anchor at Block Island.

1   pound sea scallops
4   cloves garlic, minced
juice of 3 lemons (use <u>only</u> fresh juice)
$^1/_2$ cup olive oil
$^1/_2$ teaspoon Worcestershire sauce
freshly ground black pepper
wooden skewers

1. Mix garlic, lemon juice, olive oil and Worcestershire sauce in a small bowl (if dining offshore, prepare this at home).
2. Soak skewers in water for $^1/_2$ hour and thread scallops on skewers. Brush with marinade and grind some black pepper over all; refrigerate for several hours.
3. Grill over medium-hot coals, basting often with extra marinade, for 6 minutes on each side until scallops are browned.

Frank's Tuna Franks   Serves 6-8

From a notorious Stonington skipper.

1   $6^1/_2$ ounce can tuna, drained
3   hard-boiled eggs, chopped
1   cup shredded Cheddar cheese
$^1/_2$ cup mayonnaise
2   teaspoons chopped sweet pickle
2   teaspoons chopped green pepper
1   tablespoon chopped red onion
2   tablespoons stuffed olives, chopped
$^1/_2$ teaspoon salt
$^1/_2$ teaspoon black pepper
Frankfurter rolls

Combine all ingredients. Split rolls and fill with tuna mixture; wrap each in foil. Bake in a 375° oven for 20 minutes. Serve in foil with chips and pickles.

Jensen Beach Crispy Almond Fish Fingers

Serves 4

From a famous Hutchinson Island surf fisherman.

4 light-colored fish fillets, each 6-8 ounces
   (whiting, grouper, snapper or flounder)
1 1/2 cups corn flakes
1/2 cup sliced almonds
2 eggs
1/3 cup half-and-half
3/4 cup flour, seasoned with salt, pepper and
   garlic powder
oil (Canola or vegetable)
lemon wedges

Mazur Mustard-Dill sauce:
2 tablespoons Nance's Hot Mustard, available
   in most supermarkets
4 tablespoons mayonnaise
4 fresh dill sprigs, chopped, plus a few sprigs
   for garnish
1 teaspoon freshly squeezed lemon juice
paprika

In a small bowl mix mustard, mayonnaise,
chopped dill and lemon juice. Place in a
serving dish for dipping, sprinkle with paprika
and garnish with remaining dill sprigs.

1. Rinse fish, pat dry and cut into 1 1/2- or
   2-inch strips. Dust each piece of fish with
   seasoned flour.
2. Beat eggs and half-and-half in a medium
   bowl. Crush corn flakes in a plastic bag and
   add almonds. (If you are preparing a large
   batch, use approximately 1 part almonds to
   3 parts corn flakes.)
3. Dip floured fish fingers into egg mixture and
   coat each piece with corn flake/almond
   mixture.
4. Use either a deep fryer or, if not available, a
   frying pan. If a frying pan is used, heat
   enough oil to cover 1/4-inch in the pan. Heat
   oil to 400°.
5. Place several fish fingers in hot oil and cook
   1 1/2 to 2 minutes until crispy, depending on
   the thickness. Continue to cook in small
   batches. Place on paper towels and pat dry
   to remove oil. Keep warm in a low oven
   until all the fingers are cooked. Serve with
   lemon wedges and Mazur Mustard-Dill
   sauce.

Soy Spiced Bluefish

Serves 6

This is even better if marinated ahead before baking.

2 pounds bluefish fillets
1/4 teaspoon salt
1/8 teaspoon black pepper
1 clove garlic, minced
1/2 cup butter or margarine, melted
3 tablespoons soy sauce
1 tablespoon fresh lime juice
1/4 teaspoon crushed red pepper flakes

1. Place fish in a 13-by-9-by-2-inch baking dish.
   Combine butter, soy sauce, lime juice, and
   red pepper flakes, pour over fish.
2. Mix salt, black pepper and garlic in a small
   bowl. Sprinkle mixture over fish and bake
   for 30 minutes in a 400° oven.

Bristol Baked Shrimp Newburg

Serves 6 to 8

Can be made ahead, or even frozen, and just popped in the oven on your boat.

1 pound cooked medium shrimp
1 16-ounce package egg noodles, cooked and drained
1 11-ounce can cream of shrimp soup
$^2/_3$ cup evaporated milk (the small can), plus enough milk to make 1 cup
$^1/_2$ cup mayonnaise
1 6-ounce can French fried onions
4 ounces sharp cheddar cheese, grated
2 tablespoons chopped parsley
$^1/_3$ cup sherry
salt and pepper
paprika

1. Heat shrimp, soup and milk in a large saucepan. Add mayonnaise, cheese, salt and pepper to taste, parsley and sherry. Stir until cheese has melted and gently fold in the shrimp.
2. Mix with the cooked noodles and pour into a lightly-greased 9-by-13-inch baking dish, sprinkle with paprika and cover, then bake in a 350° oven for 20 minutes. Uncover, top with onions and bake for 8 to 10 minutes until nicely browned.

Exxon Valdez Halibut

Serves 2-3

This was invented in an Exxon trailer in Valdez, Alaska. The kitchen was equipped with a skillet, a saucepan, a coffee pot, and a toaster. My mission - cook a 1-pound chunk of halibut. Available spices: salt and pepper and a few little squeeze packets of mayonnaise and a jar of Dijon mustard, thus...

1 pound halibut steak
salt and pepper
mayonnaise
Dijon mustard

Place halibut in a skillet and top with a mixture of mayonnaise and Dijon mustard. Sprinkle with salt and pepper and bake until topping is brown and bubbling and fish flakes.

Cliff's Bluefish Pelorus

Serves 4

Can also be used for other strong flavored fish or chicken.

1 $^1/_2$-pound bluefish fillet
1 tablespoon Oriental black bean sauce
2 teaspoons fresh grated ginger
2 cloves garlic, minced
juice of one lemon
4 tablespoons mayonnaise

1. Place bluefish in a shallow baking or broiler pan, baste with fresh lemon juice.
2. Mix remaining ingredients in a small bowl and spread over fish. Broil for 10 to 12 minutes, depending on the thickness of the fish or until it flakes in the middle.

Crispy Catch of the Day

Serves 6

6 firm white fish fillet (flounder, small cod or haddock)
$^1/_3$ cup vegetable oil
2 cups crushed cornflake crumbs
1 tablespoon Creole seasoning (optional)
chopped parsley for garnish
lemon wedges for garnish

1. Pat the fillets dry and cut in half. Brush the fillets with oil. Mix the cornflake crumbs and the Creole seasoning (lemon pepper is also great). Dip the fillets into the crumbs and shake off any excess.
2. Place the fish on a baking sheet (use foil if on the boat) and bake for 15 minutes in a 425° oven until crisp and browned. Serve with a little chopped parsley and garnish with lemon wedges.

Quick Seafood from the Shelf

Serves 4

An easy "at sea" supper or emergency fare.

1 can cream of mushroom Soup
1 cup shredded cheddar cheese
2 6-ounce cans shrimp, drained
1 8-ounce can mushrooms in butter sauce
$^1/_4$ cup pimento, chopped
dash of Worcestershire sauce

Combine soup, cheese and juice from the can of mushrooms. Heat until the cheese melts and add shrimp, mushrooms, pimento and Worcestershire sauce. Heat thoroughly and serve over toast points, English muffins, or hot rice.

Thai Chili-Tomato Dip

Makes 1³/₄ cups

Great with a cold fish plate or crispy vegetables.

2 large banana chilies or New Mexican or
   yellow wax hot chilies
3 large shallots (3 ounces), peeled and halved
4 to 5 cloves garlic, peeled
2 medium-size ripe tomatoes (¹/₂ pound)
1 tablespoon chopped fresh cilantro
1¹/₂ to 2 tablespoons fish sauce*
1 tablespoon fresh lime juice

*available in the Oriental section of most
 supermarkets.

This may be prepared 3 days ahead and stored,
covered in the refrigerator.

1. Heat a large, heavy skillet over high heat. Add whole chilies and dry-fry for about 4 minutes, pressing down with a wooden spoon and turning occasionally. Add shallots and garlic to the skillet and continue to dry-fry, turning occasionally, for about 5 minutes, or until the chili skins are blackened. Transfer the mixture to a bowl and cool. Add tomatoes to the skillet and dry-fry for about 5 minutes, turning occasionally, or until the skins are blackened. Let cool.

2. Remove stems from the chilies and cut in half lengthwise (do not remove skins). Remove seeds if you prefer less heat. Core the tomatoes and cut into quarters. (Do not remove skins). Place chilies, tomatoes, shallots and garlic in a food processor and, pulsing, process until the mixture is coarsely chopped and salsa-like in texture (not pureed). Alternatively, chop vegetables finely with a knife. Transfer the mixture to a small bowl and stir in cilantro, fish sauce and lime juice.

Sambuca Romano Butter

Makes 1 cup

8 tablespoons butter
2 cloves garlic, minced
2 tablespoons olive oil
2 ounces Sambuca Romano liqueur
2 tablespoons fresh parsley, chopped
dash of salt

Melt butter in a small saucepan, add garlic and sauté for 1 minute. Remove from heat, whisk in the olive oil and Sambuca. Add the parsley, season to taste with salt and serve as a dipping sauce with cooked shrimp.

Philadelphia Oyster Sauce

Makes 2 cups

Spoon over freshly poached fish or as a side dish with your holiday turkey.

1   pint fresh oysters
2   tablespoons butter
2   tablespoons flour
1   cup cream or milk
2   tablespoons chopped pimento
1   hard-boiled egg, chopped
1   cup sliced mushrooms
2   teaspoons chopped parsley
dash nutmeg
salt and cayenne pepper

**"As without flattery there were no society,
so, without sauces there were no gastronomy."
        – G. H. Ellwanger**

1. Cook oysters in their juice in a small pan until edges begin to curl and they are heated through. Set aside.
2. Melt butter in pan, add flour and whisk in milk slowly. Cook until thickened, adding some of the oyster liquor to thin the sauce to the desired consistency. Add mushrooms and simmer, stirring, for 5 minutes.
3. Gently fold in the hard-boiled egg, pimento, mushrooms and parsley. Season with nutmeg, salt and cayenne pepper. Serve hot in a sauce boat.

Roasted Tomato Relish

Makes 2 cups

Make a batch of this when your summer tomatoes are at their peak.

4   large ripe tomatoes, peeled, seeded and cut
    in half
1   tablespoon olive oil
salt and pepper
1   tablespoon butter
1   small red onion, diced
2   shallots, diced
1   small jalapeño pepper, seeded and diced
1   teaspoon brown sugar
1   teaspoon Balsamic vinegar
1   tablespoon chopped fresh cilantro
1   tablespoon chopped fresh parsley
salt and freshly ground black pepper

1. Place tomatoes in a nonstick pan, drizzle with olive oil and season with salt and pepper. Roast in a preheated 450° oven for $1/2$ hour. Cool and coarsely chop.
2. In a large skillet melt butter and add onion, shallots and jalapeño pepper. Sauté 5 minutes, add brown sugar and vinegar. Reduce heat and simmer gently for 15 minutes. Remove from heat and cool. Add roasted tomatoes, cilantro and parsley; season to taste. Serve at any temperature with cooked or cold seafood.

Pickled Nasturtium Seeds

Makes 2 cups

Make your own capers from the garden.

2 cups green nasturtium seeds
1 cup white wine
2 to 3 chopped shallots
1 teaspoon fresh horseradish
$^1/_2$ teaspoon salt
pepper to taste
6 whole cloves ($^1/_2$ teaspoon ground cloves may be used)
$^1/_2$ teaspoon mace
$^1/_2$ teaspoon coarsely ground nutmeg

1. Pick 2 cups nasturtium seed while green. Soak 3 days in cold salted water in ceramic or glass dish.
2. Meanwhile, make pickle juice. Combine white wine, shallots, horseradish, salt, pepper, cloves, mace and nutmeg. Drain seeds, add to pickle juice. Put mixture into bottle and cork tightly. (White vinegar may be added to cover.) Refrigerate and let sit for 2 weeks.

Uses: in potato salad, green salads, tuna salad, sandwiches, or wherever capers are called for.

Mexican Sauce Verde

Makes 1 cup

Especially pretty over grilled pink salmon.

1 small green pepper
2 jalapeño peppers
2 teaspoons chopped scallions, including green tops
2 teaspoons vegetable oil
3 tablespoons green peppercorns in brine, drained
2 teaspoons all-purpose white flour
$^1/_2$ cup dry white wine
$^1/_4$ cup milk
1 tablespoon Tabasco sauce
1 tablespoon chopped fresh dill

1. Preheat broiler. On a foil-lined baking sheet, broil peppers for 7 to 8 minutes, or until blackened, turning once. Place in a paper bag and set aside until cooled. Remove skin, stems and seeds. Chop finely.
2. In a medium-size saucepan over medium heat, sauté scallions in oil for 2 minutes until softened. Add green peppercorns and sauté for 2 minutes more. Add flour and cook for 2 minutes, stirring constantly. Stir in wine and milk and blend well. Add chilies, Tabasco sauce and dill. Bring to a boil, reduce the heat and simmer about 5 minutes, or until the sauce has been reduced and thickened. Serve hot or at room temperature.

Broccoli Pesto

Makes 1¹/₂ cups

Toss this with your favorite pasta or seafood salad.

1   pound broccoli, cut into large flowerets and
    stems reserved for another use
¹/₂ cup pine nuts
2   garlic cloves, chopped
¹/₂ cup fresh basil leaves
¹/₂ cup freshly grated Parmesan cheese
¹/₃ cup extra virgin olive oil
black pepper

Extra pesto may be frozen in small ziplock bags
so you may break pieces off for adding to
soups, sauces and pasta dishes.

1. In a large saucepan of boiling salted water,
   cook broccoli until very tender, about 5
   minutes, and reserve about ¹/₄ cup cooking
   water. Drain broccoli well.
2. In a small nonstick dry skillet, cook pine
   nuts and garlic over moderate heat, stirring,
   until pale golden. In a blender or food
   processor, blend together broccoli, basil,
   Parmesan cheese, olive oil, and reserved
   cooking water. Add garlic and pine nuts and
   process until well blended but still a bit
   chunky.

Island Rum Butter

Makes 1¹/₂ cups

**A quick and easy topping for fish that can be made ahead and even frozen. Just slice the butter
into small pats and serve on swordfish, sole, snapper or catfish.**

¹/₂ pound butter
¹/₂ cup finely chopped pineapple, well drained
2   tablespoons dark rum
1   jalapeño or ¹/₂ poblano chile, seeded and
    finely chopped
1   clove garlic, minced or pressed
2   tablespoons chopped fresh parsley
pinch ground allspice (optional)
freshly ground black pepper

To make the rum butter, soften the butter in a
food processor or with an electric mixer. Stir in
the pineapple, rum, chile, garlic, parsley and
allspice and keep blending until well mixed.
Spread the butter in a thin strip onto plastic
wrap or parchment paper, dust with black
pepper, and roll up like a sausage about 1 inch
in diameter, twisting the ends of the roll to
secure it. Refrigerate the butter until firm (at
least 1 hour).

**"Then pour more rum, the bottles stopping.
Stir it again and say its topping."**
                    – Old New England Rhyme

Chapin Favorite Fish Topping   Makes ³/₄ cup

1   cucumber, finely chopped
¹/₄ cup chopped red onion
¹/₄ cup capers (drained)
¹/₄ cup fresh lemon juice
1   large tomato, finely chopped
2   tablespoons fresh chopped parsley
Tabasco sauce
salt and pepper

Combine all ingredients and season to taste with Tabasco sauce, salt and pepper. Refrigerate for several hours for flavors to blend. Serve with your favorite fresh fish.

Fourth of July Red Pepper Parsley Sauce   Makes 3 cups

4   large red peppers
4   tablespoons olive oil
¹/₂ cup water
freshly ground pepper
2   shallots, finely minced
2   teaspoons of Balsamic vinegar
3   tablespoons freshly chopped parsley

1. Core and seed peppers. Remove white membrane, and cut peppers in slices. Sauté in a large frying pan with olive oil for 3 to 4 minutes. Add the water, pepper and shallots, and gently cook with a lid on for 10 minutes, or until the peppers are soft.
2. Puree the peppers in a food processor until smooth, and add Balsamic vinegar. Refrigerate or serve warm. Before serving, sprinkle puree with chopped parsley.

Mango and Lime Salsa   Makes 1 cup

2   teaspoons cumin
1   teaspoon minced garlic
¹/₄ cup thinly sliced scallions
1   teaspoon cracked pepper
1¹/₂ teaspoon coarse salt
1   small mango, peeled, pitted and chopped
1¹/₂ tablespoon minced jalapeño peppers
¹/₃ cup extra virgin olive oil
2   limes

Combine all ingredients, squeezing the lime juice into the salsa. Mix gently and allow to blend for 2 hours. Serve with any fish. Especially good with swordfish or tuna.

"A cheerful look makes a dish a feast."
— Seneca

Claudia's Killer Pesto

Makes about 1^1/$_2$ cups

From a friend's fabulous herbal garden.

1^2/$_3$ cups Genovese basil
^{1}/$_3$ cup young arugula leaves
3   tablespoons pine nuts
2   large garlic cloves
pinch of salt
^{1}/$_2$ cup olive oil
1   tablespoon unsalted butter
3   heaping tablespoons of ricotta cheese
^{1}/$_3$ cup asiago cheese
^{1}/$_8$ cup pecorino romano cheese
^{1}/$_8$ cup parmigiano-reggiano cheese

Combine all ingredients in a food processor except cheese. Grate cheese and fold in.

Warm Watercress Cream

Makes 3 cups

Spoon over your best baked-stuffed fish.

6   tablespoons butter
6   tablespoons flour
3   cups chicken broth
1   bunch watercress
1   cup heavy cream
^{1}/$_4$ teaspoon grated <u>fresh</u> nutmeg
salt and freshly ground black pepper

1. Melt 4 tablespoons butter in a saucepan and add the flour, stirring with a wire whisk. When blended, add the broth, stirring rapidly. Cook for 10 minutes until thickened.
2. Meanwhile, cut off and discard the tough bottom stems of the watercress. Drop the cress into a small saucepan of boiling water and simmer for 30 seconds. Drain in a colander under cold running water and squeeze out any excess liquid.
3. Add the cream to the sauce along with salt, pepper, nutmeg and watercress. Swirl in the remaining 2 tablespoons of butter and serve.

Two Shrimp Dipping Sauces

Both of these sauces keep nicely for up to 2 days, but don't cook your shrimp until the day you plan to serve them.

Southwestern Sauce-Olé! Makes 1¹/₄ cups

1   cup prepared seafood cocktail sauce or 1 cup chili sauce and 1 teaspoon horseradish
1   tablespoon fresh lime juice
1   jalapeño pepper, seeded and minced
2   tablespoons minced fresh cilantro

Combine and dip!

Zesty Dijon Sauce Makes 1¹/₂ cups

1   cup sour cream, regular or lowfat
¹/₄ cup Dijon mustard with seeds (country-style)
3   tablespoons fresh chopped parsley
¹/₄ teaspoon grated fresh lemon peel
¹/₄ teaspoon salt
¹/₈ teaspoon freshly ground black pepper

Combine and dip!

Guilt-Free Dressing

Makes 1¹/₂ cups

Keep a batch of this in the refrigerator for those summer potato and pasta salads.

1   clove garlic, peeled
1   anchovy fillet, rinsed and patted dry
¹/₂ teaspoon salt
¹/₂ cup chopped fresh parsley
¹/₃ cup nonfat plain yogurt
¹/₄ cup reduced-fat mayonnaise
12 imported green olives, pitted and finely chopped
1   tablespoon drained capers, rinsed and chopped
1   tablespoon Balsamic vinegar
2   teaspoons Dijon mustard
¹/₂ teaspoon freshly ground black pepper

Place garlic, anchovy, salt and parsley in a medium bowl. Mash with the back of a fork until garlic is well minced. Combine with remaining ingredients and mix well. Refrigerate several hours or, best, overnight before using.

Sun Dried Tomato Tapenade

Makes 3^1/$_2$ cups

1 cup pitted black olives in brine, drained and rinsed
1 bunch basil leaves, stems removed
1 cup sun-dried tomatoes, drained, but reserve the oil
1 heaping teaspoon green peppercorns in brine, rinsed and drained
2 large cloves garlic
1 2-ounce tin anchovies including the oil
4 ounce jar capers, drained and pressed between double layers of paper towels
3 tablespoons oil from the tomatoes
freshly ground black pepper

Place the olives, basil leaves, drained sun-dried tomatoes, green peppercorns, garlic, anchovies, capers, tomato oil and black pepper in a food processor and pulse to form a coarse paste. It's important not to over-process; the ingredients should retain some of their identity.

The tapenade can be made 2 to 3 days ahead and kept in the refrigerator.

Saybrook Shrimp Butter

Makes 1^1/$_2$ cups

Take-along on your boat or RV, top off grilled fish, serve as a dip or toss with hot pasta.

1 7-ounce can tiny shrimp, drained
8 tablespoons (1 stick) butter, softened
1 8-ounce container whipped cream cheese
2 tablespoons mayonnaise
^{1}/$_2$ cup finely chopped red pepper
^{1}/$_2$ cup finely chopped green pepper
1 stalk celery, chopped
1 tablespoon finely chopped onion
1 tablespoon finely chopped parsley
salt
dash of Tabasco sauce

In a medium bowl, mix all ingredients, seasoning with salt and Tabasco sauce to taste. Chill at least overnight before using.

Victor Hugo Salad Dressing

Makes 1 cup

An old family recipe, great on greens or cold seafood.

1 tablespoon grated onion
$^1/_2$ cup olive or vegetable oil
$^1/_3$ cup catsup
1 teaspoon salt
$^1/_4$ cup sugar
$^1/_4$ cup vinegar
juice of 1 fresh lemon or 2 tablespoons lemon
juice

Combine all ingredients and refrigerate. Whisk again well before serving.

"The sauce is costly for it far exceeds the cakes."
– Greene

Anchovy Caper Salad Dressing

Makes 1 cup

1 teaspoon dried tarragon
$^1/_3$ cup white wine
1 cup mayonnaise
1 tablespoon anchovy paste
2 tablespoons capers, drained
2 tablespoons chopped parsley
1 tablespoon chopped onion
2 garlic cloves, minced
salt
Tabasco sauce

Soak tarragon in wine for $^1/_2$ hour. Combine with remaining ingredients, seasoning with salt and Tabasco sauce to taste. Let chill for at least 4 hours before serving with seafood or chicken salad, or pour over crisp salad greens.

"A cook is quite as useful as a poet,
And quite as wise, and those anchovies show it."
– Euphron

Cucumber Salsa

Makes about $2^1/_2$ cups

2 cups finely chopped seeded, peeled
cucumber
1 cup chopped radishes
$^1/_3$ cup chopped fresh cilantro
$1^1/_2$ tablespoons white wine vinegar
1 tablespoon sugar
salt and pepper to taste

Mix all ingredients in medium bowl. Season with salt and pepper. (Can be prepared 6 hours ahead. Refrigerate.)

Class Muffalata Spread

Makes 1 cup

Great on burgers, sandwiches or crackers.

$1/2$ cup Spanish olives
$1/2$ cup black olives, oil cured
1 tablespoon capers
$1/2$ teaspoon dried thyme
3 cloves garlic, crushed
$1/2$ cup olive oil
$1/2$ cup fresh chopped parsley
1 tablespoon fresh lemon juice
1 tablespoon Parmesan cheese

1. Coarsely chop olives and capers either on a cutting board or in a food processor. Place in a small bowl.
2. Add remaining ingredients and whisk until well mixed. Refrigerate for several hours for flavors to blend well.

"Spreads and sweets in puff'd prosperity."
– Alexander Pope

Neptune's Dip

Makes 1 cup

An unusual twist for shrimp cocktail or any cold seafood salad.

2 cloves garlic, minced
1 8-ounce container sour cream
2 tablespoons mayonnaise
1 cup chopped fresh parsley
2 tablespoons lemon juice
$1^1/2$ teaspoons anchovy paste
2 scallions, minced
1 teaspoon dried tarragon leaves
black pepper

Mix garlic, sour cream and mayonnaise. Add remaining ingredients and season with black pepper. Cover and refrigerate for up to 3 days.

Key West Lime Marinade

Makes $3/4$ cup

Perfect for any white fish, shrimp or scallops.

$1/4$ cup fresh lime juice
2 teaspoons honey
2 teaspoons grated lime zest
1 teaspoon minced garlic
salt and pepper to taste
$1/2$ cup olive oil

Place all the ingredients in a bowl and whisk until blended. Store covered in the refrigerator for up to one week. If using on a seafood salad, serve at room temperature for best flavor.

Your Own Old Bay Seafood Spice   Makes ²/₃ cup

Try this for a shrimp or crab boil - a terrific no-salt seasoning.

2   tablespoons whole black peppercorns
3   tablespoons whole yellow mustard seeds
1   tablespoon whole celery seed
1   tablespoon dried thyme
12 whole dried hot red peppers (1 tablespoon)
1   teaspoon coriander seed
1   teaspoon fennel seed
24 cloves
6   allspice berries

Combine all ingredients and transfer to an airtight container. You will need about a tablespoon for each gallon of water you use, depending on your taste. You may leave them whole, or for a spicier flavor, grind in a blender or spice mill before using.

Zucchini-Basil Dressing   Makes 1 cup

This thick, tangy dressing clings well to salad greens.

1   small zucchini, coarsely chopped
¹/₂ cup mayonnaise
¹/₄ cup sour cream
2   tablespoons buttermilk
1   tablespoon snipped fresh basil
2   cloves garlic, finely minced
2   tablespoons finely minced onion
¹/₄ teaspoon freshly ground black pepper
dash salt

In a blender or food processor, blend all the ingredients until the mixture is nearly smooth. Store, covered, in the refrigerator for as long as a week.

"To proceed then to this knowledge of cookery, you shall understand, that the first step thereunto is, to have knowledge of all sorts of herbs belonging unto the kitchen."
– Gervase Markham: 1683

Mexican Chili Marinade

Makes 1¹/₄ cup

Equally good with seafood, chicken or beef.

1 cup fresh orange juice
¹/₄ cup fresh lime juice
1 to 2 small jalapeño peppers, chopped
4 cloves garlic, minced
2 scallions, finely chopped
2 tablespoons wine vinegar
2 teaspoons dried oregano
1 teaspoon cumin
1 teaspoon grated orange zest
1 teaspoon grated lime zest
¹/₂ teaspoon salt
¹/₂ teaspoon freshly ground black pepper

Combine orange juice and lime juice in a small pan and boil until reduced by half; cool. Pour juice mixture into a blender and add remaining ingredients. Purée until smooth.

Fennel Saffron Marmalade

Makes 3 cups

4 tablespoons olive oil
2 large fennel bulbs, chopped (about 4 cups)
3 cups chopped onion
1 tablespoon crushed fennel seeds
6 cloves garlic, minced
1¹/₂ cups dry white wine
1¹/₂ cups chicken broth
³/₄ teaspoon crushed saffron threads
2 tablespoons chopped fresh parsley
black pepper

Heat oil in a large saucepan and add fennel, onions and fennel seeds; cook until fennel and onions are tender, about 20 minutes. Add remaining ingredients and simmer until thickened, stirring occasionally, about another 20 minutes. Serve warm or at room temperature over your favorite grilled fish.

**"Crabs, salmon, lobsters, are with fennel spread
Who never touched that herb till they were dead."
– William King**

215

Fresh Tomato Herb Salsa

Makes 1¹/₂ cups

Best made in the morning with your "just picked" crop.

6   large plum tomatoes
¹/₄ cup chopped fresh basil
¹/₄ cup chopped fresh parsley
2   shallots, minced
1   garlic clove, minced
2   tablespoons Balsamic vinegar
2   tablespoons olive oil
salt and pepper to taste

Bring a medium-size pan of water to a boil. Add tomatoes and blanch for 30 seconds. Transfer to a bowl and peel. Cut the tomatoes in half, squeeze and discard the juices and seeds. Coarsely chop the tomatoes and return to the bowl. Add remaining ingredients and season with salt and pepper.

Six Spice Grilling Rub

Makes ³/₄ cup

This develops its flavor during cooking.

2   tablespoons chili powder
2   tablespoons paprika
1   tablespoon freshly ground black pepper
1   tablespoon dried basil
¹/₂ teaspoon cayenne pepper
¹/₄ cup brown sugar
1   tablespoon salt

Combine all ingredients in a blender and spin for 20 seconds. Transfer to a jar and refrigerate for up to 2 weeks before using.

"Sinament and ginger
**   Nutmeg and cloves**
And they gave me
**   This jolly red nose."**
**   – Beaumont & Fletcher**

Spicy Peanut Dipping Sauce

Makes ³/₄ cup

For your skewered shrimp and scallops.

¹/₂ cup peanut butter
2   tablespoons water
4   tablespoons soy sauce
3   tablespoons sesame oil
2   tablespoons sherry
1   tablespoon rice wine vinegar
4   cloves garlic, minced

¹/₄ cup honey
¹/₄ teaspoon hot red pepper flakes
1   tablespoon minced fresh ginger root

Combine all ingredients in a blender or food processor and purée until mixture is smooth. This is also good with Oriental salads.

Southwest Orange Salsa

Makes 2 cups

3 oranges, peeled, seeded and diced (be sure to remove the white pith)
1 1/2 cups chopped, seeded tomatoes
1/4 cup minced red onion
1/4 cup chopped fresh parsley
2 tablespoons fresh orange juice
1 tablespoon Balsamic vinegar
1 teaspoon minced fresh ginger

3 cloves garlic, minced
1/2 teaspoon cumin
1/8 teaspoon cayenne pepper
pinch of salt

Toss all ingredients in a large bowl and season to taste with salt and pepper. Let stand at least 1 hour before serving.

Quick Parsley Sauce

Makes 1 1/2 cups

Nice with any smoked fish.

3 tablespoons butter, softened
2 tablespoons flour
1 cup milk or half-and-half
1/2 cup chopped fresh parsley
salt and freshly ground pepper
1 tablespoon capers, drained (optional)

1. In a small bowl, mix softened butter and flour together to make a thick paste.
2. Heat milk until just below the boiling point. Add the butter mixture in small batches, whisking constantly until the sauce is smooth and thick. Stir in the parsley, seasonings and capers if you wish. Pour over your favorite fish fillets.

"Epicurean cooks sharpen with cloyless sauce his appetite." – **William Shakespeare**

Green Pea Vinaigrette

Makes 1 1/2 cups

A perfect combination for that Fourth of July cold poached salmon.

1 cup cooked peas
1/3 cup white wine vinegar
3/4 cup olive oil
1 tablespoon Dijon mustard
2 tablespoons chopped fresh dill
2 tablespoons chopped fresh chives
white pepper

In a blender, purée peas until just chunky. Add remaining ingredients and chill. May also be used as a salad vinaigrette by adding a few tablespoons grated Parmesan cheese.

"Everything I look on, seemeth greene." – **William Shakespeare**

Rosemary Walnut Pesto

Makes 1 cup

This pesto makes a delightful accompaniment to grilled or broiled fish or chicken.

$^1/_2$ cup fresh rosemary leaves, stripped from their stems and loosely packed in a measuring cup

3 to 5 large cloves of garlic

$^1/_2$ cup walnut pieces

$^1/_4$ cup olive oil

2 tablespoons grated Pecorino or other sharp cheese

$^1/_4$ cup water

In a blender, combine all ingredients and blend to a smooth paste. Store covered in the refrigerator.

Caviar Caesar

Makes 1$^3/_4$ cups

$^1/_2$ cup white wine vinegar

$^3/_4$ cup olive oil

$^1/_2$ cup vegetable oil

2 tablespoons Dijon mustard

juice of 2 lemons (about 4 tablespoons)

4 garlic cloves, minced

dash Worcestershire sauce

salt and white pepper

3 to 4 ounces caviar

In blender at low speed, slowly mix vinegar and oil until well blended. Add mustard, lemon, garlic, Worcestershire sauce, and seasonings, mixing until smooth. Pour into a bowl and gently stir in the caviar. Toss with fresh Romaine leaves and sprinkle generously with freshly grated Parmesan cheese.

"He doth learn to make strange sauces, to eat anchovies, macaroni, buoli, fagioli and caviar."
– Ben Johnson

GO WITH

Lighthouse Inn Potato Bake

Serves 6 to 8

From the landmark New London restaurant.

2$^1/_2$ pounds potatoes, peeled, russet or Idaho
$^1/_2$ cup melted butter
2   cups light cream
salt and pepper to taste
$^1/_2$ cup bread crumbs
$^1/_3$ cup grated Parmesan cheese
$^1/_3$ cup melted butter

1. Put potatoes in a medium saucepan, cover with water and boil until tender. Remove to a bowl and chill, covered, overnight.
2. Coarsely chop the potatoes. Melt $^1/_2$ cup of butter in a large pan, add the potatoes and cream. Mix well. Cook until thickened, about 10 minutes, stirring several times. Season with salt and pepper.
3. Spoon into a 2-quart baking dish, sprinkle with bread crumbs and cheese. Drizzle with $^1/_4$ cup melted butter and bake in a 375° oven for 45 minutes until brown and bubbly.

Nealy's Niçoise Mushrooms

Serves 4

1   pound mushrooms, a variety if you have them available
2   tablespoons olive oil
1   large onion, chopped
2   cloves garlic, minced
2   large tomatoes, peeled, seeded and chopped
$^2/_3$ cup dry white wine
$^2/_3$ cup chicken stock
juice of 1 fresh lemon
1   tablespoon chopped fresh tarragon
salt and pepper

1. Clean mushrooms. Heat oil in a large skillet, add onion and cook for 3 to 4 minutes until soft. Add garlic, mushrooms and tomatoes. Cook over high heat until the liquid from the tomatoes evaporates.
2. Pour in the white wine, chicken stock, and lemon juice. Cook over high heat to reduce liquid, about 5 minutes. Remove from heat, add tarragon and season with salt and pepper. Serve chilled or best at room temperature.

**"Mushrooms are the gift of nature
a good cook is the gift of God."
– Cooke**

Hillandale Herbed Lentils and Rice   Serves 8

A Farmington favorite.

$^3/_4$ cup dry lentils
$2^2/_3$ cups chicken or vegetable broth
$^3/_4$ cup chopped onion
$^1/_2$ cup brown rice
$^1/_4$ cup dry white wine
$^1/_2$ teaspoon dried basil
$^1/_4$ teaspoon salt
$^1/_4$ teaspoon dried oregano
$^1/_4$ teaspoon garlic powder
$^1/_8$ teaspoon pepper
$^1/_2$ cup shredded Swiss cheese (2 ounces)
8   thin strips Swiss cheese (2 ounces)

1. Combine lentils, broth, onion, rice, wine, seasonings and shredded Swiss cheese. Pour into an ungreased $1^1/_2$ quart casserole dish with a tight-fitting lid.
2. Bake, covered, in a 350° oven for $1^1/_2$ to 2 hours until lentils and rice are tender. Uncover, top with Swiss cheese strips and return to oven. Cook until cheese is melted. Garnish with watercress or parsley sprigs and serve hot.

Rustic Roasted Eggplant and Potatoes   Serves 4

2   large eggplants
2   large peeled potatoes, Idaho or russet
2   medium onions, peeled and cut into segments
4   tablespoons olive oil
3   cloves garlic, chopped
4   bay leaves
$1^1/_2$ teaspoons thyme
salt and freshly ground black pepper

Tomato vinaigrette:
3   tablespoons olive oil
2   teaspoons red wine or Balsamic vinegar
1   tablespoon fresh lemon juice
1   small tomato, seeded and chopped
1   tablespoon chopped fresh parsley
1   tablespoon chopped fresh basil

1. Place the eggplants, whole, into a roasting pan. Cut the potatoes into large wedges and add to the pan along with the onions, garlic and seasoning. Drizzle with the olive oil and bake in a 400° oven for one hour, basting several times and stirring vegetables around in the pan.
2. Make the vinaigrette while eggplants are roasting. Whisk oil, vinegar and lemon juice together in a small bowl. Stir in tomato, parsley and basil. Season to taste.
3. When ready to serve, split the eggplants as you would a baked potato, pour over the vinaigrette. Return to the oven for 5 minutes. Serve with the pan juices and lots of crusty bread.

Warm Cherry Tomato Surprise   Serves 6

Just the right way to treat the "love apple."

1¹/₂ pounds ripe cherry tomatoes
2   mild hot green chilies (New Mexican
     poblano or jalapeño)
2   cloves garlic, minced
4   tablespoons olive oil
2   tablespoons fresh sage, chopped
¹/₂ cup crumbled feta cheese
crusty French or Italian bread, sliced and
     brushed on both sides with olive oil
salt and freshly ground black pepper to taste
Italian parsley and whole sage leaves for
     garnish

1. Place tomatoes in a bowl with chilies and garlic. Pour olive oil on top and toss with sage and cheese, season with salt and pepper.
2. Place tomato mixture in a shallow pan and bake in a 300° oven for 20 minutes until just warmed. While tomatoes are baking, toast or grill bread on both sides until golden. Serve with warm tomatoes piled on toasted bread, garnish with chopped parsley and sage leaves.

Brownfield Farms Noodle Casserole   Serves 6-8

Also known as a kugel, a traditional favorite among Jewish families.

1   tablespoon unsalted butter
1   tablespoon olive oil
3   medium onions, thinly sliced
8   ounces wide egg noodles
2   eggs, lightly beaten
¹/₄ cup golden raisins
¹/₄ teaspoon salt
¹/₂ teaspoon freshly ground pepper

1. Preheat the oven to 425°. Butter a 9- or 10-inch pie plate.
2. In a large heavy skillet, melt the butter in the oil until foamy. Add the onions and cook over moderately high heat, stirring frequently, until golden brown, about 15 minutes.
3. Cook the noodles in a large pot of boiling salted water until al dente, about 7 minutes. Drain. Wipe out the pot, return the noodles to it and stir in the onions. Add the eggs, raisins, salt and pepper and toss gently.
4. Transfer the noodle mixture to the prepared pie plate and bake for about 30 minutes, or until set and golden brown. Cut into large wedges and serve.

Spinach Stuffed Eggplant Rollatini Serves 4 as an entrée or 6 as an appetizer

When the Tabor crowd arrived for the weekend – a double batch.

1   eggplant (1 to 1$^1/_4$ pounds)
1   tablespoon olive oil
$^1/_2$ teaspoon salt
$^1/_2$ teaspoon basil
2   tablespoons seasoned bread crumbs
2   cups tomato sauce, preferably a well-
    seasoned Italian one
$^1/_2$ cup shredded mozzarella cheese
$^1/_4$ cup grated Parmesan cheese

Filling:
$^1/_2$ pound fresh spinach, blanched, drained and
    chopped or $^1/_2$ of a 10-ounce box
    frozen chopped spinach, well drained
1   cup ricotta cheese (the skim milk variety is
    fine)
$^1/_4$ cup shredded mozzarella cheese
$^1/_4$ cup grated Parmesan cheese
salt and freshly ground black pepper
$^1/_2$ teaspoon oregano

1. Coat a baking sheet with nonstick vegetable oil cooking spray. Preheat broiler.
2. Cut eggplant lengthwise into $^3/_8$-inch thick slices. Arrange in a single layer on baking sheet. Brush lightly with oil and sprinkle with salt and basil. Broil for 3 minutes, turn and broil on other side for 3 more minutes until lightly browned. Reduce oven heat to 425°.
3. In a small bowl, mix spinach filling ingredients until well blended. Spread each eggplant slice with filling and roll up. Dip in bread crumbs.
4. Spread $^1/_2$ cup tomato sauce on bottom of a shallow baking dish and arrange rolls in dish. Spoon over the remaining sauce and sprinkle with Parmesan and mozzarella cheeses. Bake for 25 minutes at 425° until heated through and bubbling.

Oxford House Russian Potatoes   Serves 8 to 10

A 4-star Fryeburg restaurant favorite - great fuschia color.

6   medium Russet potatoes
1   14-ounce can sliced beets, drained
6   tablespoons low-fat mayonnaise
6   tablespoons plain non-fat yogurt
2   tablespoons Dijon mustard
2   tablespoons cider vinegar
2   tablespoons horseradish
1   teaspoon chopped fresh tarragon
salt and freshly ground black pepper to taste

1. Peel, cube and boil potatoes in a medium saucepan until tender, about 10 minutes. Drain potatoes and return to pan. Add beets and mash coarsely with a hand masher or fork.
2. Add remaining ingredients and mix until well encorporated. Reheat either on stove, in the oven, or in a microwave.

Ten Layer Salad

Serves 10-12

Even better than potato salad for a picnic or lunch on the boat.

first layer: 2 cups chopped lettuce
second layer: 1 cup chopped celery
third layer: 4 large chopped tomatoes
fourth layer: $^1/_2$ cup chopped red onion
fifth layer: one package frozen petite peas
sixth layer: completely blanket the layer of peas and seal the edges with a blanket of mayonnaise mixed with a little sour cream
seventh layer: 3 chopped hard-boiled eggs, seasoned with salt and pepper
eighth layer: 6 strips crispy bacon, cooked and crumbled
ninth layer: 1 cup shredded sharp cheddar cheese
tenth layer: sprinkle with $^1/_2$ cup chopped scallions

Arrange layers in a large bowl, cover and refrigerate at least 6 hours or overnight. The peas somehow miraculously keep the greens crisp. Make according to how many people you plan to serve. If there's any leftover (not usually) toss in a can of drained white tuna and serve for lunch the next day.

Chinese Sesame Eggplant Salad

Serves 6

A lighter version of the traditional wok-fried eggplant.

2 pounds eggplant, peeled and cut into 2-inch cubes
$^1/_2$ cup sesame seeds
4 scallions, chopped
1 tablespoon fresh ginger root, grated and peeled
1 clove garlic, minced
3 tablespoons vegetable oil
2 teaspoons sesame oil
1 tablespoon soy sauce
2 teaspoons lime juice

1. Cook eggplant in a large pot of boiling water for 3 minutes until barely tender. Drain well.
2. Spread sesame seeds on a baking sheet and toast them in a 350° oven until lightly browned.
3. In a large skillet, sauté scallions, ginger and garlic in vegetable oil for 2 minutes. Add eggplant and sauté for 2 to 3 more minutes until mixture is heated through. Add sesame seeds, sesame oil, soy sauce and lime juice. Toss to mix well and serve hot or cold.

Gnocchi with Gorgonzola Sauce   Serves 8

A welcome addition from a memory of Venice.

2¼ pounds potatoes, peeled and chopped
1 egg yolk
freshly grated nutmeg
salt and pepper
1⅓ cups flour
1 stick butter
1 cup heavy cream
¼ pound gorgonzola cheese, crumbled
¼ cup chopped fresh parsley

1. In a large pot, cook potatoes in boiling salted water to cover for 40 minutes, or until they are tender. Drain well and place in a bowl.
2. Beat the potatoes until smooth, add the egg yolk, nutmeg, salt and pepper, and mix well. Add the flour ⅓ cup at a time, to make a smooth soft dough. Form the dough into ¾-inch balls, drop the balls into boiling salted water, and cook for 20 seconds after they rise to the surface. Transfer the gnocchi with a slotted spoon to a warm dish as they are cooked.
3. Melt butter in a large skillet over moderately low heat. Add the cream and crumbled gorgonzola cheese, cook the mixture, stirring until the cheese is melted and the sauce is smooth. Add the gnocchi, toss gently and heat in the sauce for 5 minutes. Sprinkle with the chopped parsley before serving.

Marty's Georgia Hushpuppies   Serves 6 to 8

A great side dish with any seafood.

2 cups corn meal
2 rounded tablespoons flour
2 rounded tablespoons baking powder
1½ teaspoons sugar
1 teaspoon salt
¼ teaspoon black pepper
5 scallions, finely chopped
2 eggs
1 cup of fresh cooked corn
buttermilk
vegetable oil for frying

1. Stir the dry ingredients into a bowl. Add slightly beaten eggs, scallions, corn, and enough buttermilk to make a drop batter (about the same consistency as sour cream).
2. Heat oil in a deep, heavy skillet and drop batter by the spoonful, fry until golden brown and crisp on the outside. Only cook a few at a time or the oil will cool too fast and the hushpuppies will not brown well.

East Neck Chilled Carrot Salad   Serves 8

2   pounds carrots, peeled and thinly sliced
1   green pepper, diced
1   medium onion, diced
$^1/_4$ cup vinegar
$^1/_2$ cup vegetable oil
$^3/_4$ cup sugar
2   tablespoons chopped fresh parsley
$^1/_4$ teaspoon allspice
freshly ground black pepper

1. Cook carrots in boiling salted water until just tender crisp. Drain well and place in a large bowl. Cool.
2. Mix together remaining ingredients and pour over cooked carrots. Toss lightly and chill for several hours or overnight. Sprinkle with more chopped parsley before serving.

Breezy's Golden Waldorf Coleslaw   Serves 6

A take along for a kayaking weekend.

3   Golden Delicious apples
2   tablespoons lemon juice
2   cups shredded cabbage
1   cup diced celery
$^1/_2$ cup golden raisins
$^1/_2$ cup chopped walnuts
$^2/_3$ cup mayonnaise
$^1/_2$ cup sour cream
1   teaspoon sugar
dash of salt and pepper

1. Wash and core apples, cut into $^1/_2$-inch chunks. Toss with the lemon juice, cabbage, celery, raisins and walnuts.
2. Combine the mayonnaise, sour cream, sugar and dash of salt with the apple mixture. Serve immediately while everything is nice and crisp.

Fluffy Chevre Mashed Potatoes   Serves 6

$2^1/_2$ pounds potatoes, preferably Yukon Gold, peeled and cut into chunks
1   tablespoon salt
4   ounces goat cheese (chevre), cut into small pieces
2   tablespoons chopped fresh herbs, chives or parsley
$^1/_2$ to $^2/_3$ cup milk, heated
salt and freshly ground black pepper to taste

1. Cook potatoes in a large saucepan with salt until tender, about 10 minutes. Drain and return the potatoes to the pan.
2. Using a potato masher or beater, mash potatoes. Stir in goat cheese and enough hot milk to make a smooth mixture. Add herbs and season to taste. These can be made ahead and reheated nicely in the microwave.

Tarragon Summer Rice Salad

Serves 6 to 8

5   cups cooked rice, a combination of white,
    Italian or brown rice is best
6   scallions, finely sliced
3   celery stalks, diced
2   tablespoons chopped fresh tarragon
2   tablespoons chopped fresh flat-leaf parsley
3   tablespoons capers, drained
3   tablespoons white wine vinegar
3   tablespoons olive oil
salt and freshly ground black pepper
1   cup cooked and chopped fresh asparagus
    or $\frac{1}{2}$ cup frozen peas, defrosted
3   hard-boiled eggs, coarsely diced
tarragon sprigs for garnish

1. Place the rice in a large bowl and fluff with a fork. Add the scallions, celery, tarragon, parsley and capers, toss well.
2. Drizzle the salad with the olive oil and vinegar; season with salt and pepper. Gently mix in the chopped eggs, asparagus or peas and refrigerate for at least an hour or up to 24 hours. If you let it sit overnight you may have to add a little extra oil and vinegar before serving. Garnish with extra tarragon sprigs.

Roasted Potatoes with Caramelized Garlic

Serves 4 to 6

6   to 8 red new potatoes, unpeeled, cut into
    1-inch chunks
4   tablespoons olive oil
12 cloves garlic, sliced
1   tablespoon sugar
$\frac{1}{4}$ cup Balsamic vinegar
2   tablespoons white wine
$\frac{1}{3}$ cup freshly chopped basil
freshly ground black pepper
1   tablespoon freshly chopped parsley

1. Preheat oven to 425°. Put 2 tablespoons olive oil in the bottom of a 9-by-13-inch baking dish. Heat the dish in the oven for 5 minutes. Add the potatoes, stir around in the oil and roast for 30 to 35 minutes until crisp and tender.
2. While the potatoes are baking, prepare the garlic. In a small skillet, heat remaining 2 tablespoons olive oil. Add the garlic, cover pan and cook over very low heat for 5 minutes until garlic is tender. Sprinkle with sugar and sauté until garlic is golden. Add vinegar, wine and basil; simmer 2 minutes. Spoon the garlic mixture over the roasted potatoes, sprinkle with pepper and parsley.

Tomato Tart - Two Ways   Serves 8 as an appetizer, or 6 as an entrée

That Barbara, always famous for her tarts.

1   refrigerated ready-to-use pie crust or your
    own pastry for a single crust 9-inch pie.
4   ounces crumbled goat cheese or 4 ounces
    Italian fontina cheese, thinly sliced
2   tablespoons chopped fresh basil
2   tablespoons toasted pignoli nuts
10 medium plum tomatoes or 4 regular
    tomatoes, thinly sliced
2   teaspoons olive oil, preferably extra virgin
coarse salt
freshly ground black pepper

1. Preheat oven to 450°. Unfold pie crust, if
    using a ready to use crust and center in a
    9-inch tart pan with a removable bottom.
    Gently press into pan over bottom and up
    the sides. Trim off any excess and prick
    pastry all over with a fork. Bake 9 to 11
    minutes until crust is lightly browned and
    remove pan to stove top or rack to cool.
2. Place cheese of choice evenly over bottom
    of tart shell. Top with tomato slices,
    overlapping in concentric circles, from edge
    of the tart to the middle. Put tart back in the
    oven for 5 minutes to just soften cheese.
    Remove from oven, drizzle with olive oil
    and season with salt and pepper. Sprinkle
    tart with basil, fontina or goat cheese, and
    pignoli nuts. Cut into wedges.

"Toms" and "Chokes" on the Side   Serves 6

1   2-pound 3-ounce can whole tomatoes, well
    drained
1   14-ounce can artichoke hearts, well drained
    and quartered
1/2 cup onion, sliced
1   to 2 tablespoons chopped fresh basil
4   tablespoons butter
1   teaspoon sugar
salt and pepper
basil sprigs for garnish

1. Lightly butter a shallow 1½ quart casserole.
    Melt butter in a skillet and sauté onion and
    garlic until just soft, add the basil.
2. Rinse and drain "chokes" - cut "toms" up a
    little and add to the pan with the onions.
    Heat gently and season with salt and
    pepper. Pour into casserole and bake for 15
    minutes at 350°. Garnish with basil sprigs
    before serving.

Tina's Mediterranean Rice Salad   Serves 6

A Moose Pond favorite - from Denmark, Maine

3   cups cooked long-grain rice
1   cup cooked wild rice
1   cup (4 ounces) crumbled feta cheese
$^1/_2$ cup chopped red onion
$^1/_3$ cup chopped green bell pepper
$^1/_3$ cup chopped red pepper
$^1/_3$ cup chopped yellow bell pepper
$^1/_4$ cup chopped fresh parsley
$^1/_4$ cup sliced ripe olives
$^1/_4$ cup sliced green olives
2   tablespoons capers
1   15-ounce can cannellini beans or other white beans, rinsed and drained
3   tablespoons white wine vinegar
2   tablespoons water
1   tablespoon extra-virgin olive oil
1   teaspoon Dijon mustard
$^1/_2$ teaspoon salt
$^1/_4$ teaspoon pepper
1   garlic clove, minced

1. Combine first 12 ingredients in a large bowl; toss well.
2. Combine vinegar and next 6 ingredients (vinegar through garlic) in a bowl; stir well with a whisk. Pour over rice mixture; toss well. Cover and chill. Serve with pita chips, if desired.

"The gambler would quickly abandon his dice;
**   The criminal classes be quiet and nice,**
If carefully fed upon nothing but rice.
**   Yes; Rice! Rice! Beautiful rice!"**
**   – Marquis de Cussy**

Zucchini Madeleines   Makes 35

Wonderful in place of rolls for lunch with salad/soup or any dinner.

$4^1/_2$ cups shredded zucchini, salted and drained at least $^1/_2$ hour
$^1/_2$ large onion, finely chopped
$^1/_2$ clove garlic, finely chopped
5   eggs, well beaten
$^3/_8$ cup oil ($^1/_2$ olive oil, $^1/_2$ vegetable oil)
1   cup grated Parmesan cheese
$^3/_4$ teaspoon black pepper
1   cup Bisquick

1. Squeeze zucchini and pat dry. Mix all ingredients together (Bisquick should be added last).
2. Grease and flour madeleine pans and fill molds with mixture. Bake at 350° for 20 to 25 minutes until puffed and brown. Serve warm. (Freezes well).

Spicy Stove Top Black Beans

Serves 8-10

It can be made on a boat without an oven, if you do not mind taking the time. A better idea is to make it ahead at home and reheat it on the boat. This is one of those dishes that is even better the next day.

The East meets West spice combination of cumin and curry were suggested by my friend, Scot Michelson, who is now one of the top chefs at Foxwoods Casino.

4   cups dried black beans
5   cups chicken stock (approximately - see below)
4   slices bacon
1   small red onion
1   teaspoon salt
$^1/_2$ teaspoon pepper
1   tablespoon cumin
1   teaspoon curry powder
dash Tabasco sauce

1. Pick through beans and rinse them. Soak beans overnight in enough water to cover by at least an inch. Use bottled water for soaking if you do not have good tasting tap water because the flavor will go into the beans. Rinse and drain the beans when you are ready to start cooking.
2. Separately dice the onion and bacon fine. Make the stock from concentrate or use canned. Put the bacon in a 5-quart pot over medium heat. After 3 minutes, add onion.When the onions are clear, add beans. Add enough stock to cover and bring to a boil.
3. Add salt, pepper, curry powder, and cumin, and reduce to simmer and cover. Stir well and check the stock level every half hour - add only enough to cover the beans. Cook for 2 hours in this way, add Tabasco sauce in the last half hour. The beans will be tender but not mushy when done. Allow the pot to cool a half hour before serving.

Cool Corn Amandine

Serves 6

A one-step picnic addition.

3   cups cooked corn (about 6 ears) or same amount frozen, cooked and drained
$^1/_2$ cup chopped red onion
1   small red pepper, diced
$^1/_3$ cup slivered almonds, toasted
2   tablespoons olive oil
salt and freshly ground black pepper

Combine all ingredients in a medium bowl, season to taste and refrigerate for at least 1 hour.

"Corne, which is the staffe of life."
– Edward Winslow: 1595

Root Family Coleslaw

Serves 8

An old family recipe - always a hit.

1 medium cabbage
1 medium onion
1 large green pepper
3 carrots
salt and pepper
$^1/_2$ teaspoon sugar
$^1/_4$ cup white vinegar
$^1/_3$ cup vegetable oil
$1^1/_2$ cups mayonnaise

1. Quarter and core cabbage. Coarsely grate by hand or in a food processor fitted with a grating blade. Place in a large bowl and sprinkle generously with salt as you do each batch. Place a plate on top at room temperature for an hour.

2. Meanwhile, grate onion and carrots and finely chop green pepper. Drain off any excess liquid from the cabbage and add the vegetables, sugar, vinegar and oil. Mix well, season with black pepper, and fold in just enough mayonnaise to moisten. Refrigerate for at least 2 hours before serving. If you are not planning to serve the same day or are "traveling" with it, add cold mayonnaise at the last minute.

Rick's Famous Pickled Tomatoes

Serves 10-12

Try a combination of some of the heirloom varieties: red, orange and yellow.

3 pounds tomatoes, quartered (about 12 to 14)
2 bunches scallions, sliced on the bias
3 jalapeño peppers, sliced, with seeds
$1^1/_2$ cup white wine vinegar
$^1/_2$ cup brown sugar
2 tablespoons kosher or sea salt
$^1/_4$ cup fresh grated ginger
2 tablespoons yellow mustard seeds
1 tablespoon cracked black pepper
2 tablespoons cumin
$^1/_2$ teaspoon cayenne pepper
1 teaspoon turmeric
1 cup olive oil

Toss tomatoes, scallions and jalapeño peppers in a large bowl. Heat remaining ingredients in a medium saucepan just to a simmer. Cool slightly, about $^1/_2$ hour. Pour over tomato mixture, mix and refrigerate for at least 2 hours before serving.

"Them" Goring Potatoes

Just vary the amounts depending on number of guests.

potatoes
margarine or butter
salt and pepper
garlic powder
milk or cream
cream cheese
grated cheese
sour cream
paprika

Boil, drain and mash potatoes with salt, pepper, garlic powder, margarine or butter, a little milk or cream (mixture should be rather stiff) and 1 small package of cream cheese if doing small amount of potato - or 1 large package if preparing a large amount.

Place $^1/_2$ mixture in buttered casserole, cover with good amount of grated cheese, and cover with remaining potato. Top with lots of sour cream, poke holes through so sour cream can dribble down through, and sprinkle with paprika. Bake at 350° for about $^1/_2$ hour. This can be prepared a couple of days previously - just bring to room temperature before baking.

Elegant Eggplant Bake

Serves 8

1   eggplant
1   teaspoon salt
$^1/_2$ teaspoon pepper
3   tablespoons butter
3   tablespoons oil
1   cup chopped onion
2   cloves garlic, minced
2   cups peeled and chopped tomatoes
$^1/_8$ teaspoon thyme
$^1/_4$ cup chopped parsley
$^1/_2$ cup bread crumbs
1   cup grated Gruyere cheese

1. Peel eggplant. Cut into 8 slices. Place eggplant slices in oiled 9-by-13-inch ovenproof dish. Sprinkle with salt and pepper. Broil until soft, about 5 minutes.
2. In medium saucepan, melt butter with oil. Sauté onion and garlic until golden. Add tomatoes and cook until thick. Stir in thyme, parsley and crumbs. Pour over eggplant slices. Cover with cheese. Bake at 350° until cheese melts, about 7 minutes.

The Vegetarian's Sirloin

Serves 4

a.k.a. Grilled Portabello Mushrooms

4   large portabello mushroom caps
$^1/_2$ cup extra virgin olive oil
$^1/_2$ cup Balsamic vinegar
3   cloves garlic, minced
2   teaspoons oregano
cayenne pepper
salt and freshly ground black pepper

1. Brush mushrooms with a damp towel and mix remaining ingredients for marinade and season to taste with cayenne pepper, salt and pepper.
2. Place mushroom caps on a large platter and brush generously on both sides with marinade. Let rest at room temperature for 1 hour.
3. Grill mushrooms over a medium barbecue or under a preheated broiler for 4 minutes on each side, basting several times. The secret is to keep the mushrooms moist while cooking. Makes an excellent side dish to other grilled seafood - sword, shrimp or scallops. They may be served whole or thickly sliced.

Andover Beet Red Eggs and Onions

Makes 16 servings

A festive platter for any summer buffet.

1   1-pound can sliced beets
1   cup vinegar
$^3/_4$ cup sugar
1   tablespoon salt
1   tablespoon mixed pickling spices
2   tablespoons chopped fresh parsley
8   hard-boiled eggs
1   small red onion, thinly sliced and separated into rings
salad greens
parsley sprigs

1. Drain beets, reserving liquid. Pour liquid into a glass jar or bowl; add vinegar, sugar, salt, spices and parsley. Stir until sugar dissolves.
2. Add beets, eggs and onion slices. Cover and chill at least 2 hours before serving to allow flavors to blend. When ready to serve, arrange greens on a platter. Slice eggs in half lengthwise and arrange around edges of platter. Pile beets and onions in the center and garnish with fresh parsley sprigs.

Salsa Cornbread

Serves 8 to 10

The true gold of the Americas, corn endows us with an endless variety of tasty, nutritious preparations. This recipe is as good with game stews and chilies as it is breakfast eggs, or it can be sliced cold and served with smoked trout, salmon, or catfish pâté. It is also wonderful grilled and topped with onions and caviar.

2   tablespoons melted butter
$^1/_2$ cup yellow cornmeal
$^3/_4$ cup flour
$1^1/_2$ teaspoons baking powder
$^1/_2$ teaspoon salt
pepper to taste
1   tablespoon honey
3   eggs, beaten until light and foamy
$^1/_2$ cup milk or buttermilk
$^1/_2$ cup whole kernel corn
1   small onion, diced
1   clove garlic, diced
1   small jalapeño pepper, diced
$^1/_2$ cup chopped tomato
$^1/_2$ cup cheddar cheese, grated

1. Generously coat an 8- or 9-inch cast-iron skillet with the butter and place it in oven while the oven preheats to 425°. Blending well, combine all of the remaining ingredients except for the cheese; reserve it to sprinkle over the top of the prepared batter.
2. When the butter has melted and the skillet is thoroughly heated, remove the hot skillet from the oven and carefully pour the batter into it, spreading it out evenly. Sprinkle the cheese over the batter. Return skillet to oven and bake for 20 to 30 minutes or until a knife inserted in the center comes out clean. Remove and cool for 5 minutes. Serve warm and enjoy!

Marinated Goat Cheese

Serves 6

1   garlic clove, minced
2   tablespoons minced fresh parsley
2   tablespoons finely chopped onion
1   tablespoon minced fresh basil or
     $^1/_2$ teaspoon dried, crumbled
$^1/_2$ teaspoon dried thyme, crumbled
$^1/_2$ teaspoon freshly ground black pepper
1   bay leaf
1   cup olive oil
1   8-ounce piece goat cheese, rolled in a
     cylinder

Warm seasonings with oil in a small pan until barely at a simmer, about 2 to 3 minutes. Remove from heat and cool $^1/_2$ hour. Place cheese in a glass jar or bowl and pour marinade over top. Refrigerate for at least 3 days or up to 2 weeks. Before serving, remove cheese with a slotted spoon and serve at room temperature with Melba toast or French bread.

Taylor Cold Bean Salad

Serves 10 to 12

This is a quick and easy recipe that originated with a great aunt. It is very good on a hot summer day.

1   14- to 15-ounce can cut green beans
1   14- to 15-ounce can wax beans
1   14- to 15-ounce can red kidney beans
1   14- to 15-ounce can garbanzo beans
1   small green pepper, thinly sliced
1   small onion, sliced thin
1   cup apple cider vinegar
$^1/_2$ cup granulated sugar
$^1/_4$ cup oil
salt and pepper to taste

Drain vegetables. Combine vinegar, sugar, oil, salt and pepper. Pour over vegetables. Mix well. Store in glass jar or airtight container in refrigerator. Will keep for 2 to 3 weeks.

"They tempt me, your beans there; spare a plate."
– Robert Browning

Pineapple Noodle Salad

Serves 6

A "go-with" for any dish.

4   ounces cellophane (bean-thread) noodles
$1^1/_2$ teaspoons cornstarch
$^1/_2$ cup pineapple juice
1   teaspoon sesame oil
1   clove garlic, minced
$^2/_3$ cup fresh or drained canned crushed
     pineapple
$^1/_4$ cup light or regular soy sauce
$^1/_2$ cup julienne red pepper
$^1/_4$ cup chopped fresh parsley
2   tablespoons chopped fresh basil leaves
2   to 4 tablespoons chicken stock (or water)
1   5-ounce can sliced water chestnuts, drained
1   cup fried Chinese noodles (available
     canned, in the Oriental section of your
     supermarket)

1. In a large bowl, soak cellophane noodles for $^1/_2$ hour in hot water. Drain and cut into 3-inch lengths.
2. Stir cornstarch and juice together in a small dish until dissolved. Heat sesame oil in a saucepan and sauté garlic for 1 minute. Add juice mixture to garlic with pineapple, soy sauce, parsley and basil. Bring to a boil, add red pepper, and simmer, stirring for 2 minutes.
3. Add noodles and water chestnuts to the pan and cook, stirring and tossing until noodles are transparent and tender, 1 to 2 minutes. Moisten with chicken stock as needed and serve, sprinkled with crispy fried noodles.

ek Spinach Spanikopita Loaf   Serves 6

2   eggs
1   package (10 ounces) frozen chopped
    spinach, thawed, drained and pressed
³/₄ cup cottage cheese
2   tablespoons grated Parmesan cheese
¹/₂ teaspoon grated lemon peel
2   teaspoons lemon juice
1   teaspoon garlic powder
4   hard-boiled eggs, chopped
1   11-ounce can refrigerated French bread
    dough
lemon slices
tarragon sprigs

1. In medium bowl, beat 2 eggs until well blended. Reserve 2 teaspoons of the beaten eggs for glazing the bread. Stir spinach, cheeses, lemon peel, lemon juice and garlic powder into remaining beaten eggs until well combined. Gently stir in hard-boiled eggs.
2. Evenly coat baking sheet with pan spray. Set aside. Unroll dough. (Dough should measure about 12 by 15 inches.) Spread spinach mixture evenly across dough up to ¹/₂ inch from edges. Starting with long end, roll up dough. Pinch edge against rolled portion to seal. Pinch short edges together to seal. Place on reserved baking sheet. Brush with reserved beaten egg.
3. Bake in preheated 350° oven until golden brown and heated throughout, about 35 to 40 minutes. To serve, cut into 2- to 3-inch slices. Garnish with lemon slices, if desired.

End of the Summer-Squash Casserole   Serves 6 to 8

It goes over very well at family dinners on Sundays and it is a great way to use up all that squash.

2   pounds yellow and/or zucchini squash
¹/₂ cup chopped onion
1   15-ounce can cream of chicken soup
1   cup sour cream
1   cup shredded carrot
1   8-ounce package herb stuffing mix
¹/₂ cup butter, melted

1. Wash and cut squash into bite-size pieces, combine with chopped onion and ¹/₂ cup water. Bring to a boil and cook covered for 5 minutes; drain.
2. Combine soup, sour cream and shredded carrots, fold in squash and onion mixture. Combine stuffing mix and melted butter.
3. Spread ³/₄ of stuffing mix into a lightly buttered 1¹/₂-quart casserole. Spoon in vegetable mixture and sprinkle remaining stuffing mixture over the top. Bake at 350° for 30 minutes.

Sally's Cabbage Crunch

Serves 8

small head of cabbage
1   bunch scallions
package of ramen noodles (any flavor)
1   cup sunflower seeds
small package of sliced almonds (3 or 4
    ounces)
2   tablespoons butter or margarine
$^1/_2$ cup oil
$^1/_2$ cup white vinegar

Slice cabbage and onions and mix together. Sauté noodles (crunch up into small pieces), sunflower seeds and almonds in butter or margarine until lightly browned. Add to cabbage and onion mixture. Mix oil and vinegar together, then add noodle seasoning package and pour over cabbage mixture.

Can add cooked chicken for a complete meal, or try shrimp-flavored noodles with cooked shrimp.

If not using immediately, toss noodles and nuts in just before serving.

Crusty Baked Eggplant

Serves 4

$1^1/_4$ pounds firm eggplant
1   teaspoon salt
2   eggs
4   tablespoons grated Parmesan cheese
$^1/_2$ cup fine dry bread crumbs
1   tablespoon finely chopped parsley
$^1/_3$ cup flour
2   tablespoons melted butter or olive oil
your favorite tomato sauce

1. Peel eggplant, if desired, and cut into $^1/_2$-inch slices. Sprinkle salt on both sides of slices. Let stand 30 minutes, rinse with water and pat dry.
2. In a pie pan, beat eggs slightly. In another pan, combine cheese, bread crumbs and parsley. Dust each eggplant slice with flour, dip in egg to coat all over, and dredge in crumb mixture. Brush butter (or oil) over bottom of a shallow, rimmed baking pan. Arrange eggplant slices in a single layer. Bake, uncovered, in a 400° oven for 25 minutes, turning once to brown on both sides. Serve with tomato sauce, if desired.

Double Onions

Serves 6

Any sweet Bermuda or Texas onion works fine.

Vidalia onion custard:
2   pounds Vidalia onions, sliced thin (about 6 cups)
3   tablespoons unsalted butter
1   cup milk
2   large whole eggs
1   large egg yolk
1   teaspoon salt
$1/4$ teaspoon nutmeg
pepper

1. In a large skillet, cook onions in butter over moderate heat, stirring occasionally, for 10 minutes, or until they are golden and soft, and let cool. In a large bowl whisk together remaining ingredients and beat the mixture until it is well combined.
2. Stir in the onions, transfer the mixture to a well-buttered 1-quart baking dish, and bake the custard in a preheated moderately slow oven (325°) for 40 minutes, or until it is lightly golden and a skewer inserted in the center comes out clean. Serve the custard hot or at room temperature as a side dish.

Vermont Onion and Apple Gratin:
$1^1/2$ pounds onions, chopped
$1^1/2$ pounds tart apples, cored, peeled, and sliced thin
$1/2$ cup firmly packed light brown sugar
$1/4$ cup heavy cream
$1/4$ cup (4 tablespoons) unsalted butter, melted and cooled
1   tablespoon lemon juice
salt and cayenne pepper

1. In a bowl, combine onions, apples, brown sugar, cream, butter, lemon juice, and salt and cayenne pepper to taste.
2. Transfer the mixture to a well-buttered 2-quart shallow baking dish and bake it in a preheated moderate oven (350°) for 1 hour. Sprinkle the top with $1/2$ cup fresh bread crumbs and bake the mixture for 1 hour and 30 minutes more, or until the apples are tender and the bread crumbs are golden brown. Serve the gratin with pork.

**"If you of onyons would the smell expell
Eat garlicke that should drown the onyons' smell."
– Old Rhyme**

Loretta's Scalloped Corn

Serves 4 to 6

This is one of the family's favorites. People whisper trying to find out who made it at pot luck suppers.

2 slices stale bread, broken into small pieces
1 large egg, beaten
$^1/_2$ cup sugar
$^1/_2$ cup milk
salt and pepper to taste
1 15$^1/_2$-ounce can whole corn, drained
1 15$^1/_2$-ounce can creamed corn
$^1/_3$ stick butter (5$^1/_3$ tablespoons)
24 crushed Ritz-style crackers

1. Mix together bread, egg, sugar, milk, salt and pepper. Add the drained whole corn and the creamed corn, and mix well. Place in a greased 1$^1/_2$-quart casserole, dot with butter then sprinkle with crushed Ritz crackers.
2. Bake at 375° for 30 minutes or until knife inserted in middle comes out clean.

Chadwick Biscuits

Makes about 1 dozen

A family recipe from Chadwick, Missouri, in the Ozark Mountains.

1 packet active dry yeast ($^1/_4$-ounce)
1 cup warm water
1 tablespoon sugar
2 tablespoons olive oil, plus additional to grease pan
2 teaspoons salt
2 cups flour

1. In a large bowl combine water, yeast, and sugar. Stir until dissolved. Add remaining ingredients and mix thoroughly.
2. Sprinkle a little flour on cutting board to prevent sticking and spread dough out on board. Put a liberal amount (about 2 tablespoons) of oil in 9-inch round or square baking dish. Using a glass or 2-inch biscuit cutter, cut out biscuits, coat each side with oil in pan and arrange, sides touching in pan. Cover with a towel and place in a warm place and let rise for $^1/_2$ hour. Bake in a 400° oven for 15 to 20 minutes until golden on top.

West Indies Glazed Tomatoes   Serves 12

This makes an excellent vegetarian dish served over rice.

6   large tomatoes, split and seeded (or 10
    plum tomatoes)
$^1/_2$ cup butter
1   onion, finely diced
$^1/_4$ cup of brown sugar
$^2/_3$ cup orange marmalade
1   tablespoon curry powder
$^1/_4$ cup chopped fresh mint
$^1/_2$ cup toasted slivered almonds

1. Arrange tomato halves in an ovenproof casserole dish.
2. In a medium saucepan, melt butter, add onion and sauté for several minutes until translucent, but not brown. Stir in brown sugar, marmalade, curry, and mint. Spoon over tomatoes and sprinkle with almonds. Bake 20 minutes at 325°.

Piedmont Peppers

combination of colored peppers (red, orange,
    purple, green), at least $^1/_2$ per person
tomato
1   anchovy per pepper
4   slices of garlic
few sprigs of fresh basil
virgin olive oil
salt
pepper
French bread

1. Arrange split and seeded peppers, face up in an ovenproof baking dish.
2. Stuff with wedges of tomato, 1 anchovy per pepper, 4 slices of garlic, few sprigs of fresh basil, drizzle with extra virgin olive oil, salt and pepper.
3. Bake 1 hour at 350°, basting occasionally. Serve warm with toasted French bread.

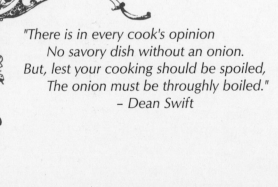

"There is in every cook's opinion
*   No savory dish without an onion.*
But, lest your cooking should be spoiled,
*   The onion must be throughly boiled."*
*   – Dean Swift*

Corn Oysters

Makes about 18

What to do with those leftover ears of corn?

2 cups fresh, cooked sweet corn, tightly
   packed
3 eggs, separated
$1/4$ cup plus 1 tablespoon flour
$1/2$ teaspoon baking powder
1 tablespoon sugar
$1^1/2$ tablespoons butter, melted
1 teaspoon salt
$1/4$ teaspoon pepper

1. Place corn in a large bowl. Add 3 egg yolks; stir until blended. Sift flour, baking powder and sugar. Add the dry ingredients to egg/corn mixture. Stir until blended. Add melted butter and season with salt and pepper. Blend together well.
2. Beat egg whites until stiff peaks form. Fold whites into egg/corn mixture. Drop by teaspoons onto hot, oiled griddle. Fry until nicely browned on both sides, turning once.

Le Bon Temps Rollé Pecans

Makes 4 cups

This combination surfaced one harried holiday and has been a Christmas tradition ever since.

1 pound shelled whole pecans
8 tablespoons butter (1 stick)
1 cup sugar
$1/2$ cup rum, dark is best

1. Spread pecans on a baking sheet which has been lightly greased or sprayed with nonstick vegetable spray. Be sure to use a pan with sides.
2. Melt butter in a heavy saucepan, add sugar and rum. Bring to a boil and cook for 2 minutes. Pour over pecans and shake to coat evenly. Slow roast in a 250° oven for 1 hour, stirring every 15 minutes to prevent from sticking. Remove from pan and cool. May be put in decorative jars or boxes for gift giving. (Keeps unrefrigerated.)

Louisiana Pecan Tasties

Makes 24

A prize winner for teas and receptions.

Pastry:
1/4 pound butter or margarine
1 3-ounce package cream cheese
1 cup all purpose flour
2 small muffin tins (12 muffins each tin)

Filling:
1 tablespoon butter or margarine, softened
1 egg, slightly beaten
3/4 cup light brown sugar
1 cup chopped pecans
1 teaspoon vanilla
1 teaspoon corn starch
1 pinch of salt
whipped cream (optional)

1. Preheat oven to 350°. Let butter and cream cheese soften, add flour and mix well. Divide in two and form 12 small balls with each large ball, using fingers. Spread dough on sides and bottom of tins leaving small edge.
2. Mix filling ingredients thoroughly and fill cups by teaspoonfuls. Do not overfill. Bake in preheated oven at 350° for 20 minutes. Let cool five minutes before removing from cups. Serve plain or with a dab of whipped cream.

"O dainty and delicious!
Food for the Gods."
– Croffut

Remarkable Old-Fashioned Rice Pudding

Serves 10

A Canterbury favorite - this defies all other proportions for rice pudding and makes a velvety pudding.

1 quart milk
4 tablespoons rice (right! only 4 tablespoons!)
1 cinnamon stick
pinch of salt

Combine all ingredients in the top half of a double boiler. cook for one hour over a medium simmer, stirring often.

Add:
3 eggs, well beaten
2/3 cup sugar
1 teaspoon vanilla

Mix together well and pour into a lightly buttered 2-quart casserole. Place casserole in a pan of boiling water, going halfway up the sides of the casserole. Bake in a 350° oven for 1/2 hour, stir, and continue to bake for 30 to 45 minutes until a knife inserted in the center comes out clean. Serve with a dollop of fresh whipped cream.

"Tis the dessert that graces all the feast,
'For an ill end disparages the rest."
– William King

242

Marty and Sharon's Deckhouse Pie
Serves 6

On board... quick and easy for the boat.

4 egg yolks
1 8-ounce can sweetened condensed milk
1/2 cup freshly squeezed lime juice (grate peel for garnish)
1 prepared graham cracker crumb crust

"Simplicity talks of pies."
— **Wilks**

In a medium bowl, combine egg yolks, condensed milk and lime juice, mixing well by hand. Pour into crust and refrigerate for at least 2 hours before serving, sprinkled with lime zest. No cooking is needed as the citric acid in the lime juice "cooks" the egg yolks without heat.

My wife, Sharon, has used this recipe for many years while on many different boats up and down the East Coast and the Gulf. It is so simple to make up on the spur of the moment with only 4 ingredients we always keep on hand.

Holding Ground Mud Cake
Serves 6 to 8

From sailing friends along the Connecticut shore.

1 1/2 cups flour
3 tablespoons cocoa
1 teaspoon baking soda
1/2 teaspoon salt
1 cup sugar
5 tablespoons oil
1 tablespoon vinegar
1 teaspoon vanilla
1 cup cold water

1. In an 8- or 9-inch square baking dish or cake pan, mix flour, cocoa, baking soda, sugar and salt.
2. "Artfully" pour in oil, vinegar and water, mix well. Bake in a 350° oven for 1/2 hour and cool before cutting. You can sprinkle confectioners sugar on top or make your own frosting but it tastes great without.

Herb Society Hummingbird Cake   Serves 12-20

A show stopper at any meeting.

3 cups all-purpose flour
$^1/_2$ teaspoons salt
1 teaspoon cinnamon
1 teaspoon baking soda
2 cups sugar
$1^1/_2$ cups vegetable oil
3 eggs, beaten
$1^1/_2$ teaspoons vanilla
1 8-ounce can crushed pineapple, including juice
2 cups chopped pecans, divided
2 cups chopped bananas
2 apples, peeled, cored and chopped
1 3.9-ounce can flaked coconut

Cream cheese frosting:
1 8-ounce package cream cheese
$^1/_2$ cup butter (8 tablespoons)
1 teaspoon vanilla
1 teaspoon milk
1 pound powdered sugar

1. Combine dry ingredients in a large bowl. Add eggs and oil, stir until dry ingredients are mixed. Do not use a mixer, this all must be mixed by hand. Slowly stir in vanilla, pineapple and juice, 1 cup of the pecans, apples and coconut. Add bananas and stir.

2. Spoon batter into 3 well greased and floured 9-inch cake pans or 1 9-by-13-inch pan. Bake at 350° for 25 to 30 minutes or when tester comes out clean. Cool 10 minutes before removing from 9-inch pans (if using 9x13, leave in pan). Cool thoroughly before frosting with cream cheese frosting. Sprinkle remaining pecans over cake. Freezes well.

Cream cheese and butter must be at room temperature. Beat together and add vanilla and milk. Add powdered sugar gradually. This will frost 9x13-inch cake.

"The daintiest last to make an end more sweet."
– William Shakespeare

INDEX

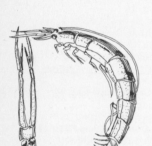

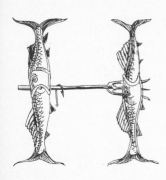

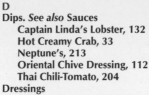

Order Blank

Mail to: Mystic Seaport Store,
75 Greenmanville Avenue, Mystic, CT 06355
or call 1.800.331.BOOK (2665)

Please send me:

_____ copies of A New England Table
@ $16.95 ea. _____

_____ copies of Seafood Secrets Volume I
@ $16.95 ea. _____

_____ copies of Seafood Secrets Volume II
@ $16.95 ea. _____

_____ copies of Global Feasts
@ $15.95 ea. _____

_____ copies of Moveable Feasts
@ $14.95 ea. _____

_____ copies of All Seasons Cookbook
@ $15.95 ea. _____

_____ copies of Christmas Memories Cookbook
@ $15.95 ea. _____

CT residents add 6% Sales Tax _____

Packaging and Shipping
($5.95 for 1 book, add $1.00 ea. additional book) _____

TOTAL _____

Please Send to:

Name _____

Address _____

City _____

State _____ Zip _____

___ Check ___ VISA ___ AMEX ___ MC

Exp. Date _____

Card No. _____

Signature _____

All prices subject to change without notice.

Order Blank

Mail to: Mystic Seaport Store,
75 Greenmanville Avenue, Mystic, CT 06355
or call 1.800.331.BOOK (2665)

Please send me:

_____ copies of A New England Table
@ $16.95 ea. _____

_____ copies of Seafood Secrets Volume I
@ $16.95 ea. _____

_____ copies of Seafood Secrets Volume II
@ $16.95 ea. _____

_____ copies of Global Feasts
@ $15.95 ea. _____

_____ copies of Moveable Feasts
@ $14.95 ea. _____

_____ copies of All Seasons Cookbook
@ $15.95 ea. _____

_____ copies of Christmas Memories Cookbook
@ $15.95 ea. _____

CT residents add 6% Sales Tax _____

Packaging and Shipping
($5.95 for 1 book, add $1.00 ea. additional book) _____

TOTAL _____

Please Send to:

Name _____

Address _____

City _____

State _____ Zip _____

___ Check ___ VISA ___ AMEX ___ MC

Exp. Date _____

Card No. _____

Signature _____

All prices subject to change without notice.

Mystic Seaport Cookbooks

Seafood Secrets Volume I
Martini Bait, Put On The Pot, Luxurious Lobster, Light the Fire, and Top it Off, are only a beginning to the tempting chapters in our original collection of over 400 seafood recipes. From simple to elegant, these imaginative recipes can enhance cooking and dining experiences both ashore and afloat! This delectable repertoire of family favorites is amusingly illustrated by Sally Caldwell Fisher. Spiral bound, 9 1/4 inches by 8 inches, 256 pages, $16.95.

Seafood Secrets Volume II
An encore to the original Seafood Secrets, this book contains over 400 recipes from the sea, as well as fabulous side dishes selected specifically as those that complement the tantalizing recipes in the book. We've even included Bare Bones, a chapter containing recipes just for those fat-conscious folks, who want to enjoy neptune's magic in a low-fat manner. Again, Sally Fisher's whimsical illustrations are throughout the book, making this book our most enjoyable one ever. Spiral bound, 9 1/4 inches by 8 inches, 264 pages, $16.95.

Christmas Memories Cookbook
Block Island Turkey and Captain Cooke's Plum Pudding are only a sampling of the recipes in this collection. Recreate imaginative variations on classic New England cooking. Great for year-round entertaining and original gift ideas. Ample pages for "recording your" favorite holiday menus and recipes. Spiral bound, 9 1/4 inches by 8 inches, 272 pages, $15.95.

Global Feast
This book will transport you around the world with its unique collection of 350 very special family heirloom recipes. Hundreds of anecdotes, histories, family photographs, and illustrations. Spiral bound, 9 1/4 inches by 8 inches, 256 pages $15.95.

The Mystic Seaport All Seasons Cookbook
Compiled from recipes in the private files of Mystic Seaport Museum members, this exciting cookbook offers traditional as well as new and unusual ideas for entertaining throughout the year. Illustrated by Sally Caldwell Fisher, the cookbook is filled with tips, culinary lore, and a treasure of recipes pertaining to each season. Spiral bound, 9 1/4 inches by 8 inches, 248 pages, $15.95.

Moveable Feasts
The book for everyone who has ever planned a concert in the park, a trek through the woods, a day on the boat, or any meal to go. This cookbook not only has hundreds of recipes for all kinds of excursions, but it also plans out a whole exciting menu from Pepper Soup to Pecan Tarts. Delightfully illustrated by Sally Caldwell Fisher. Spiral bound, 9 1/4 inches by 8 inches, 256 pages, $14.95.

A New England Table
The pride of recipe collecting seems to be a New England tradition...from old cookbooks with faded and worn bindings, scraps of paper carefully tucked away over the years, or recipe cards passed on from mother to daughter. A look back to when good cooking was a way of life, this collection of over 450 recipes from friends and members of the Mystic Seaport community is a treasury of good food and tradition. The enchanting artwork on the cover is done by Carol Dyer. Spiral bound, 9 1/4 by 8 inches, 264 pages, $16.95.